East Asian
Economic Regionalism

# East Asian Economic Regionalism

Edward J. Lincoln

COUNCIL ON FOREIGN RELATIONS
*New York, N.Y.*

BROOKINGS INSTITUTION PRESS
*Washington, D.C.*

*Library of Congress Cataloging-in-Publication data*
Lincoln, Edward J.
East Asian economic regionalism / Edward J. Lincoln.
   p.    cm.
Includes bibliographical references and index.
  ISBN 0-8157-5216-4 (cloth : alk. paper)
  ISBN 0-8157-5217-2 (pbk. : alk. paper)
1. East Asia—Economic integration.   2. East Asia—Foreign economic relations.
3. East Asia—Commercial policy.   4. Regionalism—East Asia.   5. Asia Pacific
Economic Cooperation (Organization)   I. Title.
  HC460.5.L5635 2004
  337.1'5—dc22                                        2004000195

9 8 7 6 5 4 3 2 1

The paper used in this publication meets minimum requirements of the
American National Standard for Information Sciences—Permanence of Paper for
Printed Library Materials: ANSI Z39.48-1992.

Typeset in Adobe Garamond

Composition by R. Lynn Rivenbark
Macon, Georgia

Printed by R. R. Donnelley
Harrisonburg, Virginia

# Contents

Acknowledgments    vii

1 Introduction    1

2 Characteristics of the East Asian Region    15

3 Trade Links    42

4 Investment Links    72

5 Broad Regional Institutions    114

6 The East Asian Alternatives    140

7 More Exclusive Trade Alternatives    159

8 East Asian Monetary Cooperation    194

9 Regional Leadership    231

10 Conclusion and
U.S. Policy Recommendations    250

Notes    269

Index    285

# *Acknowledgments*

The author is grateful to C. Fred Bergsten, Hugh Patrick, Elizabeth Economy, and two anonymous readers for helpful comments on the draft manuscript. Excellent research support was provided by Angela Stavropoulos. At the Brookings Institution Press, Janet Walker guided the publication process, Eileen Hughes edited the manuscript, Inge Lockwood proofread the pages, and Enid Zafran compiled the index.

# 1

## Introduction

Something was stirring across East Asia in the opening years of the twenty-first century. A region that had been notable for its lack of internal economic links over the previous fifty years was talking actively about regional cooperation. Given the consolidation of the European Union, the formation of the North American Free Trade Area, and the rapid proliferation of bilateral free trade areas around the world, the talk was not surprising. Nevertheless, East Asia's relative lack of past action raises many questions about its emerging regionalism. Why has the region suddenly shifted from taking a global approach to economic issues to discussing a regional bloc? How fast and how far will the new regionalism progress? Will the region become a version of the European Union, or something far less? What is the probable impact on American economic and strategic interests—are the likely developments something that the U.S. government should encourage or discourage? This book takes up these questions.

Some advocates envision an East Asian equivalent of the EU—a region linked both by preferential trade and investment and by a common currency. The same vision underlies worries in the United States that if it is realized, East Asia may drift away from its strong trans-Pacific economic ties. Some may find this vision so unrealistic as to represent a straw man; nevertheless, the talk in East Asia makes it a straw man worth analyzing.

So far, nothing akin to the economic consolidation of Europe or North America has occurred in East Asia. However, regional institutions do exist, and others under discussion or negotiation could evolve in a manner that either aids or obstructs American interests in the Asia-Pacific region. The core issue is whether East Asia will drift toward a more exclusive economic regionalism that specifically shuts out the United States or continue to embrace broader regional and global institutions and their more liberal rules for economic interaction. Recent developments suggest that the region is indeed moving, albeit slowly and cautiously, toward a more exclusive regionalism that could have negative consequences for the United States. Certainly much of the rhetoric concerning East Asian regionalism has sounded a strong anti-Western or anti-American theme. Nonetheless, a principal conclusion of this book is that such moves are relatively weak and slow.

This book takes a skeptical view of regional groupings in general. Formal blocs involve distortions of trade and investment that generally are undesirable. Furthermore, a tight regionalism like that of the European Union can also involve an ethnic or racially inspired hubris that can complicate international relations more broadly. That might be especially true in East Asia, where there has been a tendency to emphasize "Asian values" and reject "Western" economic, political, or social principles. With notions of cultural superiority that are at least as explicit as those ingrained in the European Union, East Asian regionalism carries the potential for promoting an unhelpful divisiveness and tension in the region's economic and political relations with the rest of the world.

In addition, manufacturing technology, as well as the information technology that underlies much of the service sector, has been moving steadily toward larger economies of scale, which lead to global competition. Firms also are developing the personnel and technical capability to engage in global direct investment. As much as some interest groups in society may deplore globalism, economic activity should continue to move in that direction. To divide the world up into a variety of groupings, each with different rules of access, can only impede progress; an East Asian economic bloc therefore would not be desirable.

A fascinating disconnect has emerged between the growing American embrace of globalism as an economic and business concept and the rising Asian resentment of what some Asians view as American or European interference in their economies. Whereas twenty years ago, purchase of American companies or real estate by foreign investors generated media coverage, today most Americans appear to have abandoned a nation-centered view of the economy. While there is a "globaphobia" problem in the United States, the predominant world view among business people and policymakers has become much more open.[1] This openness includes less reliance on legal means to block foreign businesses from the U.S. market and a stronger global strategic view among corporate managers. But in Asia, concern over American influence or dominance continues to be a factor behind the interest in regional economic cooperation.

Resentment of the United States is not new, and it may be simply one of the costs of being the world's largest economy and having globally active firms. However, in East Asia resentment of the United States and the West more generally received a boost from the 1997 Asian financial crisis. From an Asian perspective, the crisis was precipitated by Western speculators. Some point out that the U.S. government initially downplayed the crisis in Thailand and Indonesia, in contrast to its swift engagement in some other crises, such as that in Mexico. Once engaged, the U.S. government worked with the International Monetary Fund (IMF) for solutions, but the IMF imposed conditions for its loans that many felt were unfair or wrong. Of course, criticism of the IMF has not been confined to Asians; however, they have argued that the IMF has tried to "force" Western or American capitalism on Asia. Some voices in the region have argued that therefore the East Asian nations need to band together to protect themselves from the ravages of Western speculators and the unfair demands of the U.S. government and the IMF. Feelings of frustration and angry words, however, do not always find expression in action. This book looks at what has been happening with trade and investment links and with the development of regional institutions. The fundamental conclusion is that far less movement toward a regional bloc is occurring than the rhetoric would suggest.

A conundrum faces the developing countries of Asia and those elsewhere. They, or at least the noncommunist nations in the region, liked the framework imposed by the cold war. During that era, most developing countries maintained stiff import and investment barriers that were tolerated by the United States, which wanted to humor its friends in the struggle against communism. Those barriers enabled these nations to develop on their own, reversing several centuries of foreign domination of their economies through colonialism, and because of that they were politically popular. On the other hand, protectionism resulted in weak or flawed legal and institutional systems for pursuing modern economic development and often promoted inefficient or corrupt business practices. For a time, these nations managed to maintain high rates of economic growth and industrialization anyway. But the 1997 financial crisis was a potent lesson in the problems that eventually befall flawed economic systems. So now these countries must deal with the contradiction between their nationalistic urge to keep foreigners (especially Americans and other Westerners) out of their core economies and the need to open up in recognition of the fact that their institutions and behavior must accommodate international trade and investment if they hope to underwrite more robust economic growth and industrialization. Even Japan faces this dilemma. The emergence of economic regionalism in East Asia is, in part, an attempt by these countries to find a middle path by creating a preferential opening up among themselves, thereby still keeping the West at some distance.

How great that distance should or will be remains debatable. A decade ago, Lester Thurow wrote of a coming competition between three large economic blocs—Europe, North America, and Asia.[2] That prediction has not come true. Nothing resembling an economic bloc has yet to emerge in Asia, but discussion in that direction has progressed over the past decade. Some now see it as a real possibility. Writing in 2001, C. Fred Bergsten stated that "East Asia, for the first time in history, is creating its own economic bloc, which could include preferential trade arrangements and currency cooperation in the form of an Asian monetary fund (AMF)."[3] The reality thus far appears to be less dramatic.

A number of Asian nations are involved in negotiations or proposals for regional or bilateral free trade agreements (FTAs). The Association of Southeast Asian Nations (ASEAN) is in the process of forming an ASEAN free trade area; China has entered negotiations for an ASEAN-China FTA; and Japan has signed a bilateral FTA with Singapore. Other ideas—including a proposal for a broader free trade area among ASEAN, China, South Korea, and Japan—have been floated informally. The change in Japan's trade policy, which until the late 1990s had been firmly rooted in globalism—that is, centered on the General Agreement on Tariffs and Trade (GATT) and the World Trade Organization (WTO) rather than on regionalism—has been dramatic, at least in terms of rhetoric. Analysis of these discussions and agreements, however, reveals that Asian nations face considerable difficulty in opening up, even among themselves.

On the currency front, the principal accomplishment has been a series of swap agreements among pairs of central banks that enable one bank to borrow foreign exchange reserves from another in order to intervene in exchange markets to defend its national currency. Some governments and individuals in the region have proposed tightening regional links in various ways: adopting some form of regional currency, pegging individual currencies to the yen, or at least adopting stronger regional cooperation strategies to protect their currencies from fluctuations in global currency markets. In the past, most countries in the region had pegged their currencies to the dollar. That strategy was flawed, as it is for any country that tries to peg its currency to that of another nation while liberalizing international capital flows but rejecting the stiff requirements to subordinate its macroeconomic policies to its currency policy. Strategies that involve pegging to the yen instead of the dollar entail the same problem. Indeed, any strategy short of freely floating currencies is vulnerable whenever international investors detect a disparity between the fixed or quasi-fixed exchange rate and the economic fundamentals of the economy.

Informal talk of a regional Asian monetary fund continues, as well as proposals for stronger coordination of regional exchange rates. The institutional setting for these discussions has been ASEAN+3 (the three being China, Japan, and South Korea), set up in 1997. To date, however, this group has not moved very far beyond the central bank swap agreements it endorsed in 1999, which are largely inconsequential economically. The larger reality is that a number of countries in the region that had pegged or heavily managed exchange rates now have floating rates. Swap agreements make sense only in the context of pegged rates, and even then their value is debatable. What has occurred in the region appears to be a largely symbolic move to demonstrate regional cooperation while pursuing a more practical shift to floating rates.

Neither the moves toward regional free trade nor the discussion of currency cooperation is likely to produce anything akin to the European Union or even to the North American Free Trade Agreement (NAFTA). This book argues that a variety of constraints will continue to impede the tightening of economic regionalism in East Asia over the next five to ten years. What happens more than ten years in the future is more uncertain and depends on future economic and political factors. Within the next decade, however, it is unlikely that strong policy steps will be taken toward an East Asian version of the European Union.

Furthermore, narrow economic regionalism is not in the interest of these nations. The region has strong trade and investment ties with the United States and Europe, ties that would be attenuated should the region turn inward. To the extent that the region wants a useful dialogue on trade and investment issues, the appropriate institutional setting for that discussion remains the Asia-Pacific Economic Cooperation forum (APEC), a grouping that includes the United States and other non-Asian participants. APEC is a somewhat unwieldy organization that will not yield dramatic progress on lowering trade and investment barriers, but it serves the interests of the region better than a narrower approach.

Nevertheless, the rising drumbeat of discussions around a narrow East Asian regionalism has raised alarm in Washington over the past decade. Discouraging Asian regionalism, however, presents a real dilemma for American international economic policy, which continues to grapple with the alternatives of globalism and regionalism. Current U.S. policy favors a mix of globalism, regionalism, and bilateralism on the presumption that movement toward lower trade and investment barriers is desirable in any of those contexts. Whatever approach is likely to yield more rapid progress, in this view, is worthwhile pursuing. The Bush administration, for example, is simultaneously pursuing the Doha round of global WTO negotiations, a regional free trade area of the Americas, and various bilateral free trade agreements. It is difficult for the U.S. government, having adopted a favorable view of regionalism over the past two decades, to discourage similar moves by other groups of nations.

Given this book's conclusion that significant obstacles to Asian regionalism remain, the dilemma for American policy is largely moot. The U.S. government need not adopt a strongly negative public stance toward the various discussions ongoing in Asia since they are unlikely to proceed very far. Instead, the U.S. government should focus on the following:

—*The WTO/IMF.* The WTO should remain the primary multilateral trade organization, putting primary emphasis on concluding the Doha round of negotiations. This helps keep American, European, and Asian regionalism at bay while producing nondistorting global progress toward more open trade and investment. A similar argument applies to the primacy of the IMF on the financial front. To the extent that the IMF has institutional flaws, the U.S. government should work to fix them so that the IMF retains legitimacy as the sole multilateral mechanism for addressing financial crises.

—*APEC.* If the U.S. government wants to discourage narrow East Asian economic regionalism, the most appropriate way to do so is to reinvigorate APEC, which currently is regarded as ineffective and a waste of time in Washington. APEC has the obvious advantage of including the United States as a member, as well as other nations (principally Australia, New Zealand, and Taiwan) that are routinely but inappropriately left out of the narrower discussions currently occurring in Asia. The imprecise goals adopted in 1994 to implement free trade and investment throughout APEC by 2010 for the developed members and by 2020 for developing members are unrealistic. However, APEC can pursue more modest steps that would help reinvigorate the process.

## Organization

The starting point for any discussion of East Asian economic regionalism is a factual analysis of what is actually happening to trade and investment flows within the region and between Asia and the rest of the world. Such analysis, which is critical to any consideration of institutions, occupies the first part of this book.

Chapter 2 takes up the basic characteristics of the region. Asia, of course, is a diffuse geographical concept; it can be so broad as to include every country from the Middle East across the continent to Japan and others off the eastern shore of the continent. For the purposes of this book, East Asia is defined as the ASEAN nations plus Taiwan, Hong Kong, Macau, China, South Korea, and Japan. The various islands in the South Pacific might also be included, but their economies are tiny and are excluded here for reasons of convenience and clarity in analysis. The East Asian nations (or "economies" since neither Hong Kong nor Taiwan have formal status as nations) are much more diverse on a number of dimensions than the members of the European Union or NAFTA. The nations included range in population from the largest in the world to some of the smallest. Economic size varies enormously, with Japan alone representing some 70 percent of regional GDP at market exchange rates. Affluence also varies, from a very wealthy Japan to very poor developing countries. Some nations are highly open to both trade and investment; others are relatively closed. These nations also vary widely on noneconomic variables. History, culture, and religion vary much more widely among these nations than in Europe or North America. The baseline economic and social characteristics of this region therefore militate against the sort of economic integration that has characterized Europe and North America.

Chapter 3 considers trade flows. The basic reality here is that the trade links between the region and the United States (and to a somewhat lesser degree, Europe) will continue to be important. The widespread perception that intraregional trade is increasing relative to the share of trade between the region and the rest of the world is largely an artifact of the emergence of China. As China has become integrated into the global trading system over the past two decades, all nations have shown a rising share of trade (both exports and imports) with China. For other Asian nations, this takes on the appearance of rising intraregional trade. Stripped of this phenomenon, the trend toward intraregional trade has been mild.

Offsetting the increase in ties with China has been the decrease in ties with Japan. The relative decline in Japan's importance as a trading partner for Asian countries—as well as for the United States and Europe—has been a significant story over the past decade. Economic stagnation, which affected imports, and a stronger yen, relocation of some production to overseas subsidiaries, and a competitive stumbling in some leading export industries all have contributed to this outcome. In the 1980s, Japan appeared to be on track to become the hub of a regional trade network, but that vision has never materialized.

The mild increase in intraregional links has come largely at the expense of the region's *relative* links with other parts of the developing world rather than with the United States. The United States alone, for example, continues to absorb close to 30 percent of Japan's exports and just over 20 percent of the exports of the rest of the region—levels little changed since twenty years ago. These facts suggest that the image of coalescing trade ties among Asian nations is largely untrue, undermining the rationale for an institutional arrangement to ratify the trend. In addition, if the Asian nations do want a regional dialogue, given their strong trade relationship with the United States, it would be better to include the United States.

Chapter 4 takes up investment flows—defined broadly to include loans, portfolio investments, direct investment, and foreign aid. On a net basis, most countries in the region do not depend on inflows of capital from abroad, in contrast to common perception. Those that were dependent on net capital inflows in the first half of the 1990s reversed their position in the wake of the 1997 financial crisis. Nevertheless, various forms of gross capital inflow are sizable and important:

—*Bank lending.* The region has become less dependent on itself as Japanese banks have withdrawn from regional lending and American and European banks, despite the 1997 financial crisis, have remained engaged. Japanese loans to the region have dropped by almost 70 percent. Loans from other countries also fell but not as much, and while they eventually began to recover, those from Japan have not.

—*Foreign aid.* Japan has been the predominant source of funds to the rest of the region, but even on this dimension, change is under way. Japanese aid has stagnated since the mid-1990s and now is beginning to fall. Back in the 1980s, Japan's aid seemed designed to curry favor and gain economic advantages with other Asian nations, but today any such expectations appear to have been unrealized.

—*Direct investment.* Data are difficult to aggregate since each nation uses different criteria for measuring direct investment, but they indicate that intraregional connections are important, especially in the form of investments by Japanese firms. So, too, however, are investments from the United States and Europe.

A decade ago Japan appeared to be on the way to achieving dominance in all of these areas—bank lending, foreign aid, and direct investment. The story since the mid-1990s, however, has been one of a diminishing Japanese role that further lessens the rationale for a narrow East Asian economic regionalism. Put in the bluntest terms, why would other Asian nations choose to tie themselves more closely to a Japanese economy that has played a shrinking role as a source of capital and whose role, in relative terms, is likely to continue to shrink?

Chapter 5 takes up the history of existing broad institutional arrangements, among which APEC is now predominant. The creation of APEC capped a long process complicated by the cold war and its sharp division of the region into communist and noncommunist blocs. The journey began with the Asian Development Bank and the Pacific Basin Economic Council (PBEC), a discussion group of business leaders. The direct progression began with an academic discussion group known as the Pacific Trade and Development Conference (PAFTAD), formed originally to study ideas for a broad Asia-Pacific, government-level organization. That led to a nongovernmental organization, the Pacific Economic Cooperation Council (PECC) and finally to APEC in 1989.

Begun as a ministerial meeting with no overarching goals other than fostering a vague notion of "cooperation," APEC added a leaders' meeting in 1993 and adopted a long-term goal of free trade and investment throughout the region in 1994. That goal was expressed in the Bogor Declaration, which set 2010 as the date for the developed members of APEC to achieve open trade and investment and 2020 for the developing members. The Bogor Declaration speaks of "open regionalism." This phrase is often assumed to mean that market liberalization measures should be implemented on a most-favored-nation (MFN) basis rather than restricted to other APEC members, but it has never been defined by APEC. Without a definition of "open regionalism"and with a weak implementation process, APEC has made only marginal progress toward this goal over the past decade. In addition, however, APEC has pursued a variety of trade facilitation measures, trying to lower some of the other costs of doing business. All the Asian economies considered in this book belong to APEC, including both China and Taiwan, which have been excluded from many other regional forums. But enthusiasm for APEC, with its limited progress toward lower trade barriers and only minor accomplishments on trade facilitation, has waned in Washington and around the Asian region.

Chapter 6 considers the more narrow East Asian groupings of nations. The first among them, though it includes only a subset of East Asian countries, was the Association of Southeast Asian Nations, dating back to 1967. ASEAN's main purpose was largely political, not economic. Nevertheless, in 1992 ASEAN adopted the objective of establishing free trade among its members through the ASEAN Free Trade Area (AFTA), although the group remains incompletely implemented. In the late 1980s the Japanese appeared to be building a "soft" regionalism based on foreign aid, direct investment, and trade, but the effort included no formal regional institution. In the early 1990s, Prime Minister Mahathir Mohamad of Malaysia proposed creating an organization that was to be called the East Asian Economic Caucus (EAEC), but the proposal was dropped following American objections. In the wake of the 1997 financial crisis, however, the EAEC finally emerged in principle, dubbed ASEAN+3. ASEAN+3, which involves meetings of leaders, ministers, and some subcabinet officials, is now the main forum for East Asian dialogue. Whether the ASEAN+3 group will be a major force in regional economic integration remains to be seen. Its only policy initiative of any significance has been the central bank swap arrangements already mentioned.

Chapter 7 takes up the narrower trade arrangements that have come under consideration as interest in APEC has weakened. The AFTA group, as noted earlier, is still in the implementation stage. Meanwhile, Singapore has been quite active in forming free trade agreements with individual trade partners (including the United States and Japan), China is negotiating one with ASEAN, and Japan is negotiating one with Mexico while considering the possibility of negotiations with ASEAN or others in the region.

Perhaps the most interesting development has been the shift in the position of the Japanese government. Officially committed to a global approach until the late 1990s, Japan has now enthusiastically endorsed the rhetoric of bilateral and regional free trade areas. Its recent agreement with Singapore, however, is quite weak in a number of respects, especially in its exclusion of agriculture products due to intense opposition from Japanese farmers and the agriculture ministry. That exclusion has undermined the drive by proponents in the Japanese government to extend the bilateral free trade area to include other nations that have more substantial agricultural interests. The Japanese government has entered negotiations with Mexico and finally announced that it would begin negotiations with Korea, Thailand, and Malaysia as this book was going to press.

The inability to truly let go of domestic protection for the sake of closer relations with a limited set of nearby neighbors has plagued other agreements in the region as well, notably the ASEAN free trade area—where, to put it charitably, the definition of "free" has been quite flexible. In addition, the pattern of negotiations and agreements shows no exclusive focus on regional partners. Singapore has reached out to the United States and Australia. Thailand is negotiating with the United States, and Japan with Mexico. Overall, developments in regional and bilateral free trade show few signs of leading toward an East Asian regional bloc.

Chapter 8 turns to regional monetary cooperation. At the time of the Asian financial crisis in 1997, the Japanese government had advocated an Asian monetary fund to act as a regional parallel to the International Monetary Fund. That idea was quickly scuttled by opposition from the United States and others. In its wake, however, the Japanese government provided some added financial support to the countries most affected by the crisis. More important, finance ministers from around the region met as part of the ASEAN+3 dialogue, endorsing an expanded set of swap arrangements between their respective central banks to help individual countries engage in exchange market intervention to defend their currencies. In reality, this agreement has been largely moot since the region has begun to move to floating exchange rates, obviating both large, sudden exchange rate shocks of the sort that occurred in 1997—when fixed rates became untenable—and the need to defend against such large shocks. Loose talk of greater cooperation continues, including eventual formation of an AMF or even a common currency. Nevertheless, there is little evidence that any serious movement in that direction will occur, at least within the next decade.

Chapter 9 explores the broad question of regional leadership. If East Asia were to coalesce into a tighter regional bloc, the process would have to be led by one of the region's giants—Japan or China. For different reasons, neither country appears to be a convincing leader. Japan is hampered by its shrinking economic role in the region as well as its crumbling reputation for domestic economic success and astute economic policies. Japan also is hampered by continuing protectionism. Its somewhat demeaning attitude toward its neighbors also has been a problem, including its inability to sound sufficiently contrite about Japanese atrocities committed during the Second World War. Finally, Japan is hampered by its close ties to the United States. For all the rhetoric in favor of regionalism expressed by Japanese officials, they know they are tied closely to the United States, both economically and militarily.

China also has problems as a leader. China remains a socialist nation attempting to transform its economy to a market-based system, and that transformation remains incomplete. Meanwhile, the Chinese government still manages to arouse concern around the region with its foreign policies, of which one of the most important is its stance toward Taiwan. From an economic standpoint, Taiwan is an important member of the region, but institutionally it will continue to be excluded from any regional dialogue in which the Chinese have a strong voice, such as the ASEAN+3 dialogue. For those reasons, China, too, appears to be an unlikely leader of an East Asian economic bloc. With neither Japan nor China able to project a convincing image of leadership, evolution of a cohesive East Asian regionalism is much less likely.

The final chapter, chapter 10, tackles the question of American economic policy toward the region and the evolution of new institutional arrangements. The starting point for American policy is to maintain the primacy of a global approach through the WTO and IMF. Aside from the straight economic arguments concerning the desirability of a global approach in both trade and finance, this stance undercuts the East Asian regional impulse.

At the WTO, the key issue is to move forward with the Doha round of negotiations. Global negotiations absorb the negotiating energy of government officials at the expense of regional negotiations, and if trade barriers fall globally, it lessens the impact of any regional preference schemes. At the IMF, the issue is mainly one of reform. Nothing will ever eliminate resentment of the IMF; no nation likes to be given strong, unpleasant conditions for reform in exchange for a financial bailout. But the IMF policymaking process has been strongly criticized by many observers—including Americans. Reform at the IMF would help dampen the talk of an Asian monetary fund or other regional schemes to lessen the impact of IMF conditions, leaving any regional institutional arrangements with a supplementary role.

The strong conclusion of this book is that participation in APEC should continue to form the core of U.S. economic policy toward Asia at the regional level. The economic developments discussed in the early chapters indicate that a broader arrangement in which the nations of Asia continue to have an institutional involvement with the United States argues in favor of APEC. The same, by the way, applies to the inclusion in APEC of Australia and New Zealand—two countries with strong economic ties with their Asian neighbors that are left out of all the alternatives. And, of course, APEC includes Taiwan, which also is not included in the alternatives. In narrower terms of national interest, obviously institutional arrangements that exclude the United States could yield outcomes that put American firms at a disadvantage. Meanwhile, there is no reason for the U.S. government to adopt a highly critical stance toward the cooperative developments in the region. Most of these are either relatively harmless (such as the bilateral swap arrangements among central banks) or unlikely to proceed very far (such as Japan's new strategy of forging bilateral free trade areas). The rhetoric accompanying such initiatives may sound alarming, but most of them have little content.

All of this discussion has broader strategic implications as well. The rejection of the West that is implicit in much of the discussion of regionalism in East Asia has a divisive impact on diplomatic relations. At the very least, Asian efforts to limit the ability of American firms to do business in the region would undermine U.S. support for playing a regional security role. This eventuality, however, seems remote, for all of the reasons suggesting that the reality of Asian economic regionalism will be far less than the rhetoric. In addition, regional dialogue—whether in APEC or the narrower alternatives—produces discussions that help to quell tensions on noneconomic issues. Japan, for example, has perennial difficulties with its "history" problem, but mutual economic interests and dialogue keep the problem from spinning out of control and act as a brake on both Japanese behavior and Asian reactions to it. While APEC continues to stand out as the most desirable institutional format, from a strategic as well as economic standpoint, there is no reason to discourage East Asian governments from talking and acting among themselves.

# 2

## Characteristics of the
## East Asian Region

B ecause nations can be expected to have closer economic ties with their nearby neighbors than with the rest of the world, the geographic proximity of the East Asian countries might be enough, from a purely economic standpoint, to drive the economic integration of the region. However, geographic proximity by itself is not enough to support a regional economic bias. The neighboring nations need to have some commonality in terms of economic factors (sheer size, affluence, economic system, and openness to trade and investment), historical experience, culture, or religion. This chapter considers those aspects of the East Asian region, asking whether commonalities exist there that could facilitate economic regionalism. The basic answer is no; on a variety of economic and social dimensions—including population, economic size, economic affluence, and openness to trade as well as culture, history, and religion—this region is very diverse. Its diversity is wider than that prevailing in either Europe or North America and therefore is an important factor in explaining its relative lack of regional economic integration. Over the next half-century, these nations may overcome their diversity and work toward greater cohesion, but diversity certainly makes the process more difficult and suggests that it is likely to be slow.

The conclusion of this chapter—that the region's wide diversity inhibits economic regionalism—is at odds with some recent writing on the subject. The new view is that the historical diversity of the region has been diminishing, reduced by common historical experiences in the twentieth century (such as the regionwide impact of the Korean and Vietnam wars), some common cultural threads, a distinctive form of capitalism, and the wave of Japanese investment around the region over the past two decades.[1] In searching for explanations of why East Asian nations have come together for a dialogue of any sort, it is easy to be carried away by enthusiasm for Asian communality. For example, Yoichi Funabashi, a Japanese journalist, opined a decade ago that "an Asian consciousness and identity" were emerging.[2] Such pronouncements notwithstanding, this chapter argues that diversity remains a fact in several important dimensions. Subsequent chapters will argue that the extent to which Japan has knitted the region together through trade, investment, and foreign aid has been overestimated and is now diminishing. This book does, however, agree that the 1997 Asian financial crisis contributed to a sense around the region of "Asia versus the West." But when East Asian nations gather to discuss the trade or financial issues in which they think they have a common interest, discussion and regional policy formation are hindered by the wide differences discussed in this chapter.

This book uses the term "East Asia" to mean a specific set of nations in East and Southeast Asia. It includes, roughly from north to south, Japan, South Korea, China, Taiwan, Hong Kong, Macao, the Philippines, Thailand, Malaysia, Myanmar, Singapore, Vietnam, Laos, Cambodia, Indonesia, Brunei, and Papua New Guinea. This definition leaves out the small island nations in the South Pacific, mainly because they are so small that economic data either are unavailable or would not alter the conclusions of this analysis. It also leaves out Central Asia and South Asia on the grounds that the economic ties between East Asia and these parts of what is commonly considered to be Asia are very tenuous. Australia and New Zealand could be considered part of the East Asian region, but it is more useful to include them in the broader Asia-Pacific region since the Asian nations considered here generally exclude these two—although for reasons considered later, their exclusion is unfortunate.

Figure 2-1. *Asian Population Distribution*

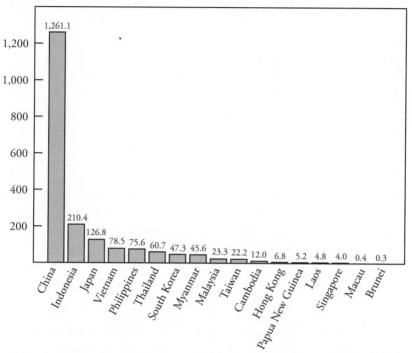

Millions

Source: World Bank, *World Development Indicators* (www.worldbank.org [December 10, 2001]). Taiwan data are from "Taiwan: People 2000" (www.photius.com/wfb2000/countries/taiwan/ taiwan_people.html [July 12, 2002]).

## Population

Consider first the region's diversity on the dimension of population. Figure 2-1 shows the population of the countries of East and Southeast Asia. A huge 64 percent of the region's entire population, 1.3 billion people, is located in China, followed by Indonesia, with 210 million people, and Japan, with 127 million. From there population size trails off rapidly, down to a collection of tiny countries and city-states with less than 10 million people. China's huge population immediately becomes an intimidating factor in regional cooperation, as most nations are apprehensive about being dominated by China. For example, China's labor force is so large that other nations in the region express concern about losing jobs to China as it continues to open up to the outside world.

With China and Japan being the two obvious leaders of any move toward regionalism, it is worth keeping in mind that while China's population will continue to grow slowly for some time to come, Japan's population is on the verge of a long-term decline. Knowing that their country is about to shrink in terms of population makes the Japanese even more apprehensive about their potential regional role relative to that of China.

One possible remedy for Japan's shrinking population and work force is to permit larger numbers of temporary foreign workers and even permanent immigrants to reside in the country. While some foreign workers in the past fifteen years have come from ethnic Japanese communities in Latin America and from Iran and elsewhere, the logical source of foreign workers and immigrants is from nearby Asian nations. However, accepting large numbers of foreigners as long-term residents in Japan continues to be a huge political and social issue for a society that for the past century has been used to viewing itself as both a nation and an ethnic group. Closer institutional ties with the region might provide easier access for workers and immigrants, but such access is not on the Japanese policy agenda. Instead, the fear of being swamped by inflows of foreigners acts as a brake on Japanese enthusiasm for its regional neighbors.

The population distribution in Asia is very different from that in Europe. As shown in figure 2-2, population among the five largest European countries is much more even, with each of the five having from 10 to 22 percent of the total population. To be sure, both regions have a fringe of countries that each have 5 percent or less of the total population. But the comparison does indicate a strong difference. Whereas small European nations may feel that the community is led by competition or coordination among a subset of large nations relatively equal in terms of population, Asia tends to see China as the population giant that it is. Achieving greater coordination or cooperation consequently becomes more difficult because other nations are uneasy about getting too close to the giant in their midst.

Population disparity in NAFTA looks more like that in Asia, with 69 percent of the population represented by the United States, 24 percent by Mexico, and only 7 percent by Canada. This disparity implies that large size differences do not necessarily block formation of free trade areas. Certainly concerns about domination by the United States are common in both Canada and Mexico. However, other reasons for forging closer economic links outweighed whatever trepidation the Canadians and Mexi-

Figure 2-2. *Percent of Total Regional Population, Countries in East Asia, the EU, and NAFTA, 2000*

Percent

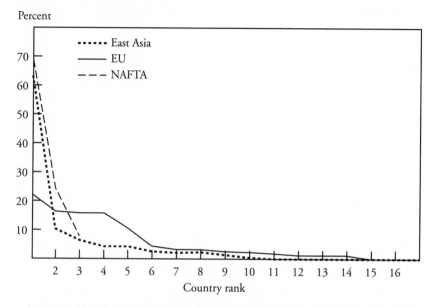

Source: World Bank, *World Development Indicators* (www.worldbank.org [December 10, 2001]). Taiwan data are from "Taiwan: People 2000" (www.photius.com/wfb2000/countries/taiwan/taiwan_people.html [July 12, 2002]).

cans felt about becoming more closely tied to their large neighbor—mainly that their existing trade and investment were overwhelmingly tied to the United States, to an extent that is not evident in Asian nations' ties to one another.

Having by far the largest population in Asia does mean that China is the regional leader or has a stronger voice in regional discussions, however. The issue here is the smaller Asian nations' fear of being overwhelmed economically by China's large population. Whether it is expressed as Japanese anxiety about Chinese workers entering Japan or the worry of small Southeast Asian nations about the migration of their foreign-owned factories to China, the concern around the region about the sheer size of China's population is real, and it gives added impetus to the ASEAN Free Trade Area (AFTA). The (imperfectly) unified ASEAN market has a population of 590 million, still much smaller than that of China but sufficiently large to attract foreign investors.

The concerns evident in East Asia do not apply to NAFTA. Mexico, for example, is not concerned about an influx of immigrants from the United States, and while Americans have expressed concerns over the "giant sucking sound" made by jobs shifting to Mexico, Mexico's much smaller population has limited the extent of their concerns. If Mexico were the size of China, one wonders whether NAFTA would have come into existence.

Population disparity is so obvious that it is easy to forget or dismiss. Most analysis of what is happening in the region focuses on speeches, meetings of leaders or officials, and policy developments. When the leaders of ASEAN+3 meet, for example, China and Singapore bring roughly the same number of representatives to the meeting. Nevertheless, it is important to remember that Singapore's leader represents only 4 million people, while China's represents 1.3 billion. The leaders are most certainly aware of their respective positions.

## Economic Size

Figure 2-3 shows the huge variation in economic size among Asian nations, measured in U.S. dollars at market exchange rates. In sheer economic size, Japan dwarfs the region. At market exchange rates in 2000, Japan, with its $4.7 trillion economy, represented 66 percent of regional GDP. China, despite its large population, is only one-quarter the economic size of Japan and represents only 16 percent of regional GDP. Even the third-largest economy in the region, South Korea, represents only 10 percent of Japan's economy and only 6 percent of regional GDP. Each of the other nations in the region represents well under 3 percent of total regional GDP. From this perspective, it is easy to understand why nations in the region are reluctant to engage closely with Japan. If, in some crude sense, economic size conveys leadership power in the region, then Japan easily dominates. As argued later, however, it is not at all clear that economic size has conveyed power to Japan since it has not exercised strong leadership in the region. Nevertheless, that does not mean that other nations in the region are unaware of the possibility or that they welcome it.

This huge disparity in economic size becomes a reason to favor either a more narrow grouping of developing nations in the regions—without Japan—or a broader grouping that includes the United States, such as APEC. Without Japan, nations can band together to collectively bargain with large, industrialized nations for their common interests. Bringing the economically small nations of Southeast Asia together to face their large

Figure 2-3. *GDP in 2000 at Market Exchange Rates,*
*Selected Asian Countries*[a]

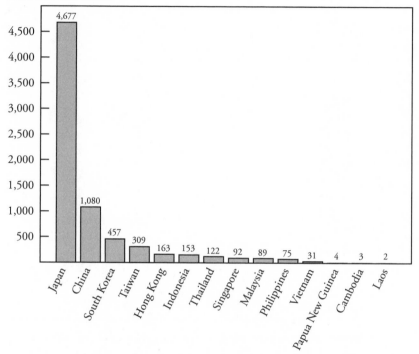

Billions of U.S. dollars

Source: World Bank, *2001 World Development Indicators,* CD-ROM, Win STARS version 4.2.
Taiwan data for exchange rate in 2000 are calculated from "The Economy: Macroeconomic Indicators"
(www.gio.gov.tw/taiwan-website/5-gp/yearbook/chpt10-1.htm [July 12, 2002]) and from Ministry of
Economic Affairs, Government of Taiwan, "Economic Indicators," table A-1, "GNP and Expenditures
on GDP" (www.moea.gov.tw/~meco/stat/four/english/a1.htm [August 16, 2002]).

a. This figure excludes Brunei and Myanmar because of lack of data.

economic partners—the United States and Japan—for their mutual benefit provides an additional bargaining rationale for AFTA. With both Japan
and the United States in a regional group, as they are in APEC, the smaller
states can hope to play one off against the other.

Economists argue that using market exchange rates to compare nations
is inappropriate because these rates do not allow for comparison of purchasing power across countries. Economists therefore prefer using purchasing power parity exchange rates—rates that equalize the price of a basket of

Figure 2-4.  *GDP in 2000 at Purchasing Power Parity,*
*Selected Asian Countries*

Billions of U.S. dollars

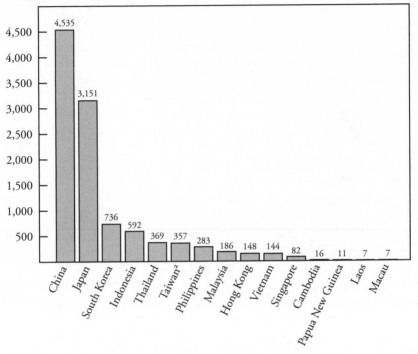

Source: World Bank, *2001 World Development Indicators,* CD-ROM, Win STARS version 4.2.
Taiwan data are from "Taiwan: Economy 2000" (www.photius.com/wfb2000/countries/taiwan/
taiwan_economy.html [July 12, 2002]).
   a. Data are for 1999.

goods and services across nations. Figure 2-4 compares Asian economies
using the World Bank's purchasing power parity exchange rates. In this
comparison, Japan's dominance disappears. Indeed, China (now representing 44 percent of regional GDP) appears to have a larger GDP than Japan
(with 30 percent). Japan's economic size is deflated because at market
exchange rates in 2000, prices for many goods and services in Japan were
very high relative to prices in other nations. China's economy is inflated
because the prices of many goods and services were very low relative to those
in other nations at nominal exchange rates.

The purchasing power parity comparison of economic size may not be very comforting, even though Japan's dominance appears diminished. According to these data, China and Japan together represent 72 percent of regional GDP. The next-largest economy still represents only 7 percent of regional GDP, roughly the same as the market exchange rate measure, with the rest of the region trailing off to insignificance. Perhaps, as in Europe, the smaller countries in the region believe that having two regional giants provides opportunities to play one off against the other. On the other hand, the notion that China is overwhelmingly largest in terms of both population and economy would be unsettling.

However, there are two reasons to discount the story told by these data. First, few economists believe that any reasonable adjustment would yield a Chinese economy larger than Japan's—a problem stemming from doubts concerning the accuracy of the Chinese GDP data, which probably are inflated, and from disagreements over what constitutes an appropriate exchange rate for making an adjustment. Second, when nations interact through trade and investment, it is not their theoretical purchasing power parity that matters but their actual market-determined purchasing power compared with that of their neighbors. When Japanese firms want to invest in China, they are driven by the cheapness of labor at the actual exchange rate, not by what it would be if purchasing power parity rates prevailed. When the Chinese export products, it is the low price of their products at actual exchange rates that gives them an advantage in global competition. In evaluating equality or disparity, therefore, market exchange rates provide a clearer picture of the region: Japan truly dominates.

This picture of economic size is changing over time. China is certainly perceived to be a much larger economy within the region than it was twenty years ago when it first opened up to trade and investment. If its relatively rapid economic growth continues (especially relative to Japan's growth), then in another decade China might be regarded as both a population and economic giant, even though it still will not have Japan's level of affluence or technical prowess.

Now consider Asia relative to Europe or NAFTA. Figure 2-5 compares economic size in 2000 for Asia, the EU, and NAFTA based on market exchange rates. All three areas have large differences among their members in terms of economic size. However, the EU has four large members— Germany, France, the United Kingdom, and Italy—that make up a core of relatively equal-sized economies. While some of the smaller members, such

Figure 2-5. *Share of Total Regional GDP at Nominal Exchange Rates, Countries in East Asia, the EU, and NAFTA*

Percent

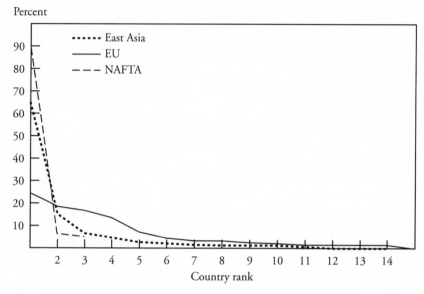

Country rank

Source: World Bank, *2001 World Development Indicators,* CD-ROM, Win STARS version 4.2. Taiwan data for exchange rate in 2000 are calculated from "The Economy: Macroeconomic Indicators" (www.gio.gov.tw/taiwan-website/5-gp/ yearbook/chpt10-1.htm [July 12, 2002]), and from Ministry of Economic Affairs, Government of Taiwan, "Economic Indicators," table A-1, "GNP and Expenditures on GDP" (www.moea.gov.tw/-meco/stat/ four/english/a1.htm [August 16, 2002]).

as Ireland and Luxembourg, may worry that their economic interests will be ignored by the bigger nations, at least they have four large nations to manipulate. In Asia, unlike in Europe, even the second- and third-largest economies (China and South Korea) are much smaller than the largest (only 25 and 10 percent the size of Japan, respectively). Consider also that all three, disparate as they may be, are geographically close in Northeast Asia and that all of the small economies are concentrated in Southeast Asia. This introduces a geographical divide that surely adds to the impression that the nations lack common interests.

In the case of NAFTA, the data indicate a size disparity that is somewhat similar to that in Asia. In fact, the United States represents almost 90 percent of combined NAFTA GDP. However, as noted earlier in regard to population, Canada and Mexico are so closely linked to the United States through trade and investment that they had reasons to embrace their over-whelming economic partner more closely despite apprehensions about the disparity in economic size. Asian countries do not have tight economic ties with Japan, nor do they appear to want to be so closely embraced. What Asian country could really act as a brake on Japan, with its enormous economic size? In a closer economic relationship, Japan could dominate them. And given the Japanese vision of permanent inequality between Japan and its less-developed neighbors (as exemplified in the popular Japanese notion of the "flying geese" pattern of Asian economies, with Japan as the lead goose), one can understand the other nations' reluctance.

## Economic Affluence

Sheer economic size is not the only measure sharply dividing this region; economic affluence also varies enormously. The region includes both affluent industrialized nations and some of the poorest nations on earth, especially now that several additional Southeast Asian states—Cambodia, Laos, Vietnam, and Myanmar—have become members of ASEAN. These data are presented in figure 2-6, showing per capita GDP in 2000 at market exchange rates. Japan, of course, is the most affluent nation, with a per capita GDP of $36,894. Several of the smaller states in the region also have achieved relatively high levels of affluence, including Hong Kong and Singapore. However, those at the other end of the spectrum are very poor. China has a per capita GDP of only $856, and the amount for both Laos and Cambodia is less than $400.

This huge disparity in affluence creates large divisions in economic interest on a wide variety of issues. Japan, for example, wants to protect its inefficient agricultural sector, while poor nations are eager to export agricultural products. As discussed in chapter 7, this particular issue is a major factor inhibiting Japan's ability to forge free trade agreements with its Asian neighbors.

An equally important issue in the region is the combination of low incomes and a huge population in China. Given China's per capita GDP of less than $1,000 and population of more than 1 billion, other Asian nations fear that if the region opened up within itself to trade and investment, manufacturing jobs would migrate to China on a grand scale. If Ross Perot could get at least a minority of Americans worried about the "giant sucking sound" of Mexico taking jobs away from American workers following its inclusion in NAFTA, imagine the imagery in Asia. This is

Figure 2-6.  *GDP per Capita, 2000, at Market Exchange Rates,*
*Selected East Asian Countries*

U.S. dollars

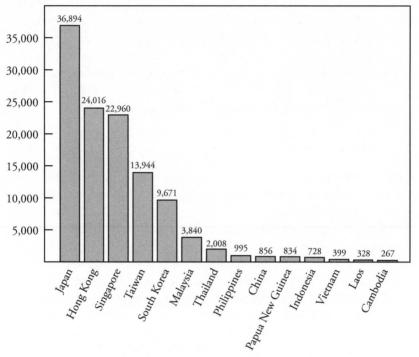

Source: World Bank, *2001 World Development Indicators*, CD-ROM, Win STARS version 4.2.
Taiwan data for exchange rate in 2000 are calculated from "The Economy: Macroeconomic Indicators"
(www.gio.gov.tw/taiwan-website/5-gp/yearbook/chpt10-1.htm [July 12, 2002]), and from Ministry of
Economic Affairs, Government of Taiwan, "Economic Indicators," table A-1, "GNP and Expenditures
on GDP" (www.moea.gov.tw/~meco/stat/ four/english/a1.htm [August 16, 2002]).

especially true of rich Japan, where decades of protectionism have left too
many workers still employed in relatively labor-intensive jobs that would
be at risk. Of course, from an economic standpoint, most of these fears are
nonsense. Whatever problems arose would be transitional. If China can
provide an enormous pool of low-cost labor, then it should attract investment in tradable manufactured goods industries and Japan should restructure its economy toward higher value-added industries.

Recently, expressions of concern also have come from some of the ASEAN countries, which fear that China's accession to the WTO will cause them to lose jobs to China as firms—especially foreign-owned firms—relocate to take advantage of lower wages. That fear may be exaggerated. As figure 2-6 indicates, per capita GDP in 2000 in most ASEAN countries was not that much higher than in China. Because of the 1997 currency collapse, for example, per capita GDP in Indonesia in 2000 at market exchange rates was actually lower than in China and the level in the Philippines was only slightly higher. Thailand and Malaysia may have more concern, since their per capita GDP is double to triple that of China. Singapore, the most affluent of the ASEAN nations, actually has little reason for concern—as an affluent but tiny city state, it has already adjusted to being surrounded by countries with low wages and much higher populations. More important, if wages were the only determinant of investment in manufacturing, then foreign direct investment would be migrating to Cambodia, Laos, and Vietnam, but it is not. The point is that wages are only one factor in determining direct investment. Thailand and Malaysia may well have advantages over China—a more developed rule of law (even if still flawed), greater political stability (or at least more predictable administrative rule at the local level), and perhaps better infrastructure for expatriate managers. And the very poorest nations—Vietnam, Laos, and Cambodia—are at a much earlier point in the process of creating the stability and infrastructure for modern industry. Nevertheless, the concern that China will suck foreign direct investment away from the ASEAN countries is widespread and has led to calls for more rapid progress at eliminating intra-ASEAN trade barriers through AFTA as a means of enhancing the attractiveness of ASEAN as a location for foreign firms.

The disparity in per capita income in East Asia is much greater than in either the EU or NAFTA, as shown in figure 2-7A. While all three areas have one very affluent country (Japan, Luxembourg, and the United States), most members of the EU have a per capita income in the range of $20,000 to $25,000. Even the poorest EU member, Portugal, has a per capital income of $10,000, so that the ratio of the richest to the poorest country is 4.1 to 1. In NAFTA, with Mexico's per capita income of only $5,000, the range is greater, and the ratio of incomes in the United States and Mexico is 6.0 to 1—hence Ross Perot's concern over the loss of jobs to Mexico. But in the case of Asia, the extremely low income levels in many of the nations means that the ratio of richest to poorest is a huge 138 to 1.

Figure 2-7A.  *GDP per Capita, 2000, at Market Exchange Rates, Countries in the EU, NAFTA, and East Asia*

U.S. dollars

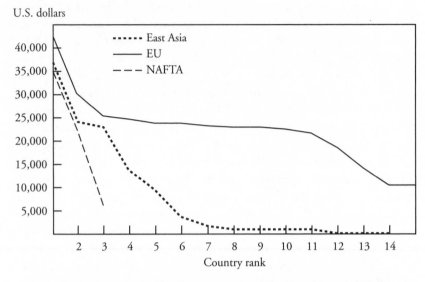

Country rank

Source: World Bank, *2001 World Development Indicators*, CD-ROM, Win STARS version 4.2. Taiwan data for exchange rate in 2000 are calculated from "The Economy: Macroeconomic Indicators" (www.gio.gov.tw/taiwan-website/5-gp/yearbook/chpt10-1.htm [July 12, 2002]), and from Ministry of Economic Affairs, Government of Taiwan, "Economic Indicators," table A-1, "GNP and Expenditures on GDP" (www.moea.gov.tw/~meco/stat/ four/english/a1.htm [August 16, 2002]).

Even after discounting the poorest as being only marginal members of any regional grouping, the ratio between Japan and Indonesia is 51 to 1.

As with overall economic size, per capita GDP at market exchange rates can give a misleading picture of real income disparities. Figure 2-7B shows GDP per capita using the World Bank's purchasing power parity adjustments. Japan's per capita GDP is lower because prices are high in Japan at market exchange rates, while those of developing countries like China are higher because prices are low at market exchange rates. There is a ninefold disparity between Japan, still the most affluent economy, and Indonesia. A similar adjustment for NAFTA members reduces the U.S.–Mexico income ratio to 3.9 to 1, also somewhat narrower than the ratio at market rates. Thus the income disparities in East Asia are still large, and larger than elsewhere. By either measure, per capita income in China is low relative to that in Japan or in the middle-income East Asian economies, although the disparity is somewhat less when adjusted for prices. How-

Figure 2-7B.  *GDP per Capita, 2000, at Purchasing Power Parity Exchange Rates, Selected Asian Countries*

U.S. dollars

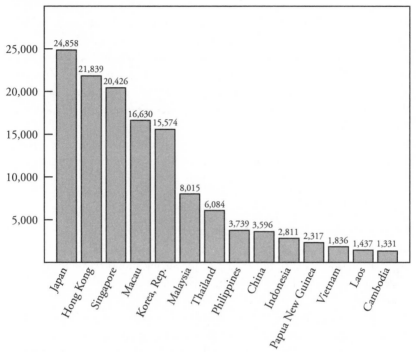

Source: World Bank, *2001 World Development Indicators,* CD-ROM, Win STARS version 4.2. Taiwan data for exchange rate in 2000 are calculated from "The Economy: Macroeconomic Indicators" (www.gio.gov.tw/taiwan-website/5-gp/yearbook/chpt10-1.htm [July 12, 2002]), and from Ministry of Economic Affairs, Government of Taiwan, "Economic Indicators," table A-1, "GNP and Expenditures on GDP" (www.moea.gov.tw/~meco/stat/ four/english/a1.htm [August 16, 2002]).

ever, as with overall size of GDP, the question is which measure matters most. When foreign firms build factories in China, it is the actual level of wages at current exchange rates and not a higher purchasing power parity comparison that matters. Overall, the conclusion stands that East Asia is characterized by very wide income disparities between rich and poor economies.

One can argue that in the case of the European Union, regionalism was helped by the rough equality in income levels among the bulk of its members. To be sure, equality may create problems as well, as each nation tries to protect a similar set of industries. Nevertheless, they have much in common and may find it easier to view themselves as having similar economic aspirations and problems. In NAFTA, as already noted, the inclusion of Mexico has created tension. The U.S. government was slow in implementing parts of the agreement, especially on trucking, because of fears among American workers that cheap Mexican wages would have a debilitating effect on U.S. jobs. But if Americans had some difficulty in coming to terms with Mexico, what about Japan coming to terms with the poor members of the Asian region? Whereas Mexico's population is only one-third that of the United States, China's population is ten times larger than Japan's. Other poor Asian nations are not as large, but the differences between them and Japan on some economic issues are so wide that it is difficult to imagine how a cohesive whole could be formed at the present.

## Openness to Trade

For some Asian nations, exports and imports are a very large share of GDP, but that is by no means true for all. People have a tendency to think of Japan as an open economy because of the strong brand-name recognition of certain successful Japanese exports. But Japan, it turns out, is the least open of all Asian countries—by a wide margin. The term "open" is used here only to refer to the ratio of exports or imports to GDP. Economies that trade a lot relative to their size are "open economies."

Figure 2-8 shows the ranking of Asian nations by total trade (exports plus imports) as a share of GDP in 2000. As one would expect, the list is topped by Singapore and Hong Kong—small city-states that engage in re-exports, resulting in a total volume of trade that is almost triple the size of their GDP. Malaysia also is an active trader, with a ratio of just over 200 percent. Even China, a geographically large continental country (such countries tend to have lower ratios of trade to GDP than small island or coastal states) that was a largely closed economy thirty years ago, now has a trade ratio of more than 40 percent. In the rest of the region—with one exception—the ratio ranges roughly from 60 percent to 100 percent. Then there is the exception: Japan, at less than 20 percent.

This measure of openness is not necessarily related to trade barriers. Because large countries have a more complete manufacturing sector than small ones, they tend to have a lower ratio of trade to GDP; it would be irrational, for example, for Singapore to manufacture automobiles for its small population. Inaccuracies in the measure of GDP as well as the use of

Figure 2-8. *Total Trade (Exports plus Imports) as a Share of GDP in 2000, Selected Asian Countries*

Percent

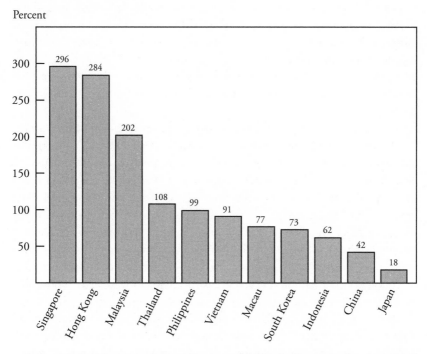

Source: Calculated from data on exports, imports, and GDP in local currencies from International Monetary Fund, *International Financial Statistics*, on CD-ROM. Taiwan data are from Ministry of Economic Affairs, Government of Taiwan, "Economic Indicators," table B-2, "Export by Key Trading Partners" (www.moea.gov.tw/~meco/stat/four/english/b2.htm), table B-3, "Import by Key Trading Partners" (www.moea.gov.tw/~meco/stat/four/english/b3.htm), and table A-1, "GNP and Expenditures on GDP" (www.moea.gov.tw/~meco/stat/four/english/a1.htm [August 16, 2002]).

market exchange rates rather than purchasing power parity rates may exaggerate the ratio of trade to GDP for some of these economies, especially China. The transshipment of goods through Hong Kong and Singapore creates a distorted view of the involvement of their manufacturing sectors in international trade. Nevertheless, figure 2-8 provides at least a rough picture of an underlying reality: some East Asian economies are much more engaged in international trade than others, and Japan is distinguished by its relatively low level of engagement.

One can imagine a desire for closer economic association among a group of nations that are heavily involved in trade, since a high share of

imports and exports to GDP suggests acceptance of international competition and nimbleness in responding to changing competitive conditions.
A group of nations that are not very open to trade also might find closer
association easier, since the relative lack of trade by their chosen partners
suggests that domestic industries would face relatively little need to adjust.
But the problem confronting Asian nations is this: why they should want
to open up to Japan, whose record of low involvement in trade combines
with a reputation for informal trade barriers that are difficult to negotiate
away?

This issue is thought of more clearly as an import issue rather than a
total trade issue. Figure 2-9 shows the same ranking of Asian countries by
the share of imports in GDP. The share of imports in GDP for Japan is
only 8 percent. The next-lowest share is more than double that—19 percent, for China. The rest range from just over 20 percent to well over
100 percent. While Japan's low import ratio may have many explanations,
trade barriers have been one important element. As documented by many
economists over the years, the low level of imports in Japan is not related
to tariffs or quotas but to an array of nontariff barriers.[3] Asian nations such
as Indonesia that export raw materials to Japan do well, as do those that
host Japanese manufacturing firms that produce goods for export to the
Japanese back home. But the overall low level of imports in Japan is surely
a discouraging statistic for any Asian nation contemplating opening itself
up to a closer economic relationship with Japan. If reductions in simple
trade barriers, like tariffs, that can be handled in a treaty do not yield
improved access and sale of imported products, then a free trade area with
Japan will provide few real benefits.

Incorporating more than just the ratio of trade to GDP, a recent study
by A. T. Kearney looked at the question of openness and receptivity to
international economic activity by combining data on openness to trade in
goods and services (using the ratio of domestic to international prices as
well as the usual ratio of trade to GDP), cross-border financial transactions, personal contact, and ease of Internet access. The results, published
as an index, list Singapore, Malaysia, and the United States in the top
twenty (the rest are European countries and Israel), but not Japan.[4] This
study reinforces the point that Japan is an unlikely leader for Asian economic regionalism. With its record of low globalization up until now, why
would other Asian nations want to tie themselves more closely to Japan?
And if Japan's low rate of globalization represents an illiberal attitude
toward foreign economic engagement, then any regional bloc in which

Figure 2-9. *Imports as a Share of GDP in 2000, Selected Asian Countries*

Percent

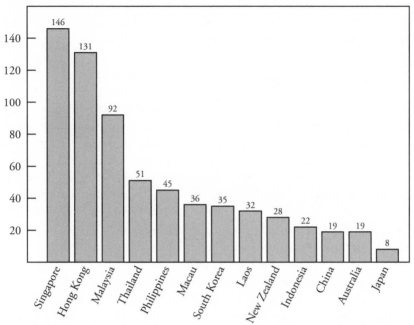

Source: Calculated from data on exports, imports, and GDP in local currencies from International Monetary Fund, *International Financial Statistics*, on CD-ROM. Taiwan data are from Ministry of Economic Affairs, Government of Taiwan, "Economic Indicators," table B-2, "Export by Key Trading Partners" (www.moea.gov.tw/~meco/stat/four/english/b2.htm), table B-3, "Import by Key Trading Partners" (www.moea.gov.tw/~meco/stat/four/english/b3.htm), and table A-1, "GNP and Expenditures on GDP" (www.moea.gov.tw/~meco/stat/four/english/a1.htm [August 16, 2002]).

Japan acted as a leader (due to its economic preponderance, discussed earlier) would be likely to take an illiberal approach to its group engagement with the rest of the world.

Japan is not the only economy in East Asia to have trade barriers. Indeed, the ASEAN members have had considerable difficulty in negotiating away trade barriers among themselves. But the fact remains that even with trade barriers, other Asian economies have experienced higher levels of import dependence. Regardless of what the full range of explanations for these differences might be, one conclusion is that in a world where all are sinners, Japan has sinned most successfully in obstructing imports. In addition, other governments believe that Japan, as an affluent industrial nation with a sizable trade surplus, should be more liberal on imports. The perception among Japan's East Asian neighbors that Japan is more protectionist than other nations, combined with the expectation that it should be more liberal and that more liberal policies should be manifested by higher levels of imports, adds to their wariness.

## Openness to Investment

As the A. T. Kearney index implies, openness involves more than just trade. Data on direct investment are less robust than trade data since each nation has a different approach to measuring investment, but figure 2-10 presents one attempt to provide data on the inward flow of direct investment around the world. Foreign direct investment as a share of gross domestic capital formation is quite high among Asian nations, topped by Hong Kong at 60 percent. The one negative note is Indonesia, where foreign investors were actually pulling out in 1999. Before the 1997 financial crisis, foreign direct investment in Indonesia had been running between 7 and 10 percent of gross domestic capital formation.

Along with the unusual withdrawal of investment from Indonesia, the other striking feature of these data is the very low inflow of foreign capital into Japan. In 1999 the inflow of direct investment, at 1.1 percent of gross domestic capital formation, was actually considerably higher than in previous years. Although the Japanese perceived it as a flood of foreign investment (made highly visible by the purchase of bankrupt Long-Term Credit Bank by a group of American investors and the partial purchase of Nissan by Renault), in reality Japan continued to absorb very little investment. Only Myanmar—a largely isolated military dictatorship affected by both its lack of substantial domestic economic reform and U.S. sanctions—had an inflow of direct capital as low as Japan's. Even South Korea, a country that has had strict capital investment rules in the past, the share of foreign direct investment in domestic capital formation in 1999 was almost ten times higher than that in Japan.

This picture parallels the trade picture. The nation that one would expect to be a leader by example—Japan—has an environment that is largely inhospitable to foreign direct investment. Since all government controls on direct investment were removed two decades ago in Japan, the explanation for the low inflow of capital does not lie in the kind of official rules and regulations that can be negotiated away in an agreement with other nations, although over the past decade the U.S. government has negotiated some of

Figure 2-10. *Inflow of Direct Investment as a Share of Gross Fixed Capital Formation, 1999, Selected Asian Countries*

Percent

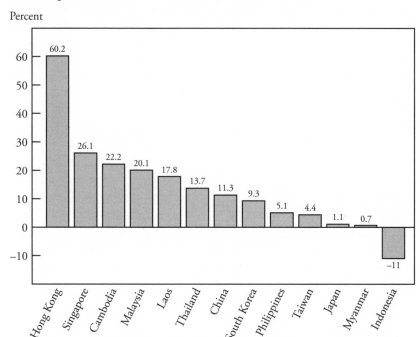

Source: United Nations Conference on Trade and Development, *World Investment Report 2001: Promoting Linkages*, annex B, Statistical Annex (New York: United Nations, 2001), pp. 312–24.

the various obscure rules that might affect investment. For some of Japan's Asian neighbors, this inhospitable climate matters little since they do not invest much abroad and are far more interested in attracting investment. But for some—Hong Kong, Taiwan, South Korea, and Singapore, for example—the difficulty of investing in Japan does matter, particularly in delivering goods and services that call for proximity to the customer.

Around the rest of the region, higher levels of inward direct investment have prevailed despite a legacy of various controls and performance requirements. However, the investment environment in these countries has improved steadily over the past two decades, and governments have actively pursued foreign investment as part of their development strategies. A striking contrast exists between the real increase in the inflow of capital that these nations have attracted as a result of liberalization and the lack of much change in Japan despite liberalization. This lack of direct investment inflows in Japan adds to the illiberal picture presented by the trade data. Do other nations desire a closer relationship with a nation that has been relatively closed or unattractive as a location for investment? To some extent, the answer may be "yes." The Japanese are active investors in the rest of the world, and these nations want to attract more of that investment. Nevertheless, the lack of investment in Japan stands out as another dimension of the nation's basic lack of openness.

## Noneconomic Dimensions of Diversity

The wide disparity among Asian nations is by no means confined to economic dimensions; religion, history, and patterns of social behavior also vary widely. These differences do not necessarily block economic integration, since cooperation for mutual economic benefit has been nearly universal around the world. And as noted earlier in this chapter, some of these noneconomic factors may be diminishing in importance. Nevertheless, the lack of commonality leads to different perceptions of national interest and complicates the task of communicating across the negotiating table.

### Religion

While Europe is tied together by a common thread of Christianity, Asia is home to a number of very different traditions. Buddhism predominates in parts of Southeast Asia, but there are large Muslim communities in Malaysia, Indonesia, and parts of the Philippines. Although Buddhism passed through China, it never became a major religion there, where Confucianism is more common. The predominant religion in the Philippines is Christianity, setting it very much apart from all of its Asian neighbors, with the qualified exception of South Korea, where a sizable Christian minority has emerged. Japan has very few Christians and virtually no Muslims. Instead, Buddhism and Shintoism prevail—and, with the predominance of Shinto weddings and Buddhist funerals, they enjoy an even share of people's lives in a society that sees religion largely as a convenience for conducting such ceremonies in the journey of life rather than as a guide for daily behavior. To the extent that politicians and government officials are affected by their various religious backgrounds, they bring to regional discussions and negotiations very different world views. The Japanese, for example, have no idea what religious values motivate Catholic Philippine leaders or Muslim prime minister Mahathir Mohamad of Malaysia.

## History

The European countries have had at least 2,000 years of intimate economic, social, and political interaction with one another; Europe even was largely unified for a time under the Roman Empire. North America is built on a common heritage of European colonialism dating back to the sixteenth century. To be sure, the experiences of different American nations vary, but a European colonial heritage provides some commonality. Furthermore, the three North American nations have interacted intensively throughout their modern history. In Canada, as manufacturing replaced the fur trade, which was the basis of the country's early existence, factories were located on the border with the United States, and cross-border trade and investment has prevailed for a hundred years. Mexico also has had extensive trade with the United States across a common border, and the country has attracted U.S. investment for decades.

The East Asian countries included in this study, in contrast, have never been very close. China has certainly been a major influence over parts of the region at various times over the past 2,000 years. But the most important fact of East Asia's modern history was the division of the region by Western colonial powers, starting in the sixteenth century. Because the region was cut up, trade and other connections between various segments of the region diminished. Meanwhile, the Japanese avoided the early thrust of Western imperialism by largely isolating themselves from Asia and the world for two and a half centuries, from the early 1600s until the mid-nineteenth century. To be sure, the Japanese (like the Germans in Europe) briefly consolidated all the countries considered here in an empire during the Second World War. But Japan's empire had such a short and unpleasant history that it did little to foster a sense of regional cohesion. Japan and South Korea, for example, were unable to conclude a treaty of friendship and commerce until 1965. Indeed, Japan's brief history of empire continues to hinder regionalism because of the alleged failure of Japan to apologize to its Asian neighbors for atrocities committed during the colonial period and the war. Postwar animosity toward Japan and the artificial nature of forced colonial trade patterns meant that former colonies tended to move away from their close ties to Japan. In the case of Taiwan, for example, the share of exports headed to Japan dropped from a range of 50 to 60 percent of total exports in the early 1950s to less than 20 percent by the 1970s, while those to the United States rose from 5 percent in the early 1950s to 40 percent by the 1970s.[5]

Because the countries that had been colonized by the West came out of that experience only after the end of World War II, they have only a very recent history of trying to rebuild regional interaction. This implies that the process of regional economic integration has proceeded on a much weaker historical base than was the case in postwar Europe or in North America. Eventually the region will overcome the legacy of its past, driven by experiences gained through trade and investment plus the personal negotiating experiences of government officials around the region. But this process takes time, and these countries may encounter many bumps along the way.

### Social and Economic Behavior

East Asia also is characterized by wide variations in social and economic behavior. One need not be a sociologist to recognize the obvious differences in behavior among, for example, the Japanese, Koreans, and Chinese—and these are three societies that are geographically close and share at least a few common historical roots. The issue of "Asian values" was used in the 1990s to motivate regional economic cooperation, but the reality is that the region shows a high degree of variation in social behavior. The directness of Koreans and Chinese in social interaction stands in great contrast to the indirectness of the Japanese.

Similarly, economic behavior varies widely. Some economies are thoroughly rooted in market-based capitalism, while others are struggling to move away from decades of socialist economic planning. Even among the capitalist economies, the extent of government involvement in the operation of the economy varies widely. Economic disparity has not prevented some from claiming that a special Asian economic development model exists, as with "Asian values"; however, little commonality is evident.

These aspects of regional diversity are important to keep in mind because claims to the contrary have been used to justify regional economic cooperation. In essence, what has happened is that a goal (cooperation) has been searching for a rationale (Asian values and the Japanese development model). While the quest has been an interesting sociological phenomenon, its claims have little basis in reality.

## Conclusion

East Asia is highly disparate on many dimensions, and the region defies any attempt to identify the kind of commonalties that characterize Europe or North America. China is the population behemoth in the region, having a larger share of the region's population than any European country has of Europe's. Japan, on the other hand, is the overwhelming economic behemoth, in terms of both sheer economic size and affluence. The disparity in size makes economic integration more difficult—either because others in the region fear a "giant sucking sound" as cheap Chinese labor attracts manufacturing investment away from everyone else or because they fear Japan's economic domination by virtue of its economic size and wealth.

Meanwhile, the same economic giant is off the bottom of the scale in terms of its openness to imports and investment. If Japan were to emerge as the region's leader, its leadership probably would be of a decidedly illiberal sort. The fact that Japan's low levels of absorption of both imports and inward direct investment have persisted despite the dismantling of most official barriers should be even more worrisome to the rest of the region. If the reduction of Japan's barriers through several rounds of GATT/WTO negotiations over the past four decades has not produced much of an increase in either imports or investment, why should anyone believe that a preferential economic bloc with the rest of Asia would make a difference? The hope that it would give the rest of Asia some advantage in access to Japanese markets is illusory.

As is evident with NAFTA, disparity in population, affluence, and economic size need not prevent development of regional institutional links. In some ways, disparities in size may be helpful. Larger countries incur relatively small domestic adjustment costs in making trade and investment deals with small, low-wage partners. Meanwhile, those small partners may perceive very large gains in having preferential access to the market of a large, developed neighbor. Canada and Mexico are often nervous about American cultural domination, but they had much to gain economically from NAFTA. On the other hand, countries that do not trade much with each other (such as the United States and Jordan) may find it easy to create a preferential trade agreement because the adjustment costs on both sides are very low.

These reasons why size disparity should not inhibit—and might even enhance—formation of a preferential trade bloc do not characterize East Asia. First, the population giant is a poor country, not an affluent one as in NAFTA. This heightens fears of high adjustment costs if regional integration accelerates relocation of manufacturing and jobs to China. Second, gains for smaller partners depend on whether preferential access to their large partner has a real impact on their economies. That may have been true for Canada and Mexico in NAFTA, but not in East Asia, where concerns persist regarding the difficulty of addressing informal trade barriers in Japan. These differences with NAFTA call for greater wariness about the positive payoffs from regional integration.

Somewhat offsetting these concerns may be some expectations concerning investment. For ASEAN countries, the fear has been that foreign direct investment already is shifting to China. In that context, an ASEAN-China free trade area might encourage foreign firms to remain in ASEAN since they would have preferential access to Chinese markets from that base. Similarly, preferential deals with Japan might attract more investment from Japanese firms, which would see some advantage in exporting their products back home. These possible gains imply that the disparities in size do not entirely preclude discussion of free trade areas with China or Japan. Nevertheless, the region's economic disparity gives rise to wariness and caution.

Reinforcing the economic disparity of the region is a broader disunity in terms of religion, history, and social norms. The Europeans share a common religious and historical heritage even though they speak different languages. Canada and the United States share a common language and much the same historical background, while Mexico has been extensively engaged economically with the United States throughout the past century. The East Asian countries, on the other hand, have deeply divided historical and religious backgrounds. These differences form an important part of the explanation for why they have not pulled together as a more cohesive economic bloc in the past half-century. Optimists like to view the region as being similar to Western Europe in the early post–World War II period. But even that analogy is misleading, given the legacy of weak economic connections over the past several centuries, the lack of a common religious heritage to provide a sense of "togetherness," and the wide variation in culture and social behavior patterns.

Perhaps such differences could be overcome under the leadership of visionaries like those who shaped European cooperation in the early postwar years. But that kind of leadership has not appeared in Asia, which also helps explain the rather tenuous moves toward economic regionalism. To be sure, a number of regional leaders, including Prime Minister Mahathir, have used a strong rhetoric of regional cooperation, but his rhetoric has served mostly to proclaim an "Asian Way" as a means of building regional consciousness. As illustrated throughout this chapter, there appears to be no common Asian way. The rhetoric is largely hollow.

The one aspect of the "Asian Way" that matters most has been Japan's espousal of its domestic economic model, which the government claimed had been imitated by the rest of the region, thereby explaining Asian economic growth over the past several decades. This proposition, too, is very dubious. Japan's economic model has been distinctive—of that there is no doubt. But even in Japan the utility of the model has been under attack for a decade because of poor economic performance. And the assertion that the rest of the region imitated Japan is not correct, as the World Bank pointed out in a study entitled *The East Asian Miracle*.[6] But the notion of a non-Western model of capitalism that is more appropriate for Japan and Asia is one that continues to pervade much of Japanese rhetoric. Since the Japanese model has been an illiberal one, especially as it relates to imports and inward investment, advocating its use raises serious questions about the shape of any future East Asian economic bloc.

Overall the evidence of this chapter indicates wide disparities among the East Asian nations that help explain why the region has been so slow to develop the kind of economic regionalism that has emerged in Europe and North America over the past several decades. The differences in population, economic size, affluence, openness to trade, openness to inward direct investment, history, religion, and behavior have been simply so large that deep economic integration has been strongly impeded. Perhaps the most remarkable development is that East Asian nations have bridged their differences sufficiently to engage in some dialogue on economic issues.

The recent notion that a sense of common interests and purpose exists in East Asia has also rested on the presumption that trade and investment ties within the region have grown. Driven largely by Japan, these enhanced ties presumably have come at the expense of a relative decline of trade and investment with the West. If true, those developments would surely give East Asian nations something to discuss among themselves and perhaps promote through regional cooperation. However, the following two chapters show that this view is largely incorrect—the trend toward regional trade and investment is by no means as strong as commonly perceived.

Later chapters of this book will consider what has been occurring institutionally among the nations of this region, including bilateral and subregional free trade areas, plus discussions on financial cooperation. These are important new developments and imply that the region is moving to overcome some of its past divisions. But the wide economic and other disparities discussed in this chapter provide a critical backdrop to these regional initiatives. Any expectation that East Asia will evolve to form a close regional bloc like that of the European Union within the next five to ten years would be mistaken.

# 3

## Trade Links

Merchandise trade is a key part of the economic attraction and interaction among nations. Global trade has generally expanded in the past half-century, and as nations have become more open to imports, it has expanded faster than global economic growth. This chapter considers the question of whether East Asian nations' trade with one another has expanded faster than their global trade. While the simple answer is yes, the change has been rather moderate and generally has not come at the expense of the relative strength of trade links with the United States or Europe. The region has not turned away from the West toward itself in any meaningful sense.

After the end of the Second World War and the start of the cold war, the region was sharply divided between communist and noncommunist blocs. The noncommunist nations evolved a new, strong relationship with distant markets, especially the United States; purely regional trade and investment lagged behind. Meanwhile, South Korea and Taiwan, former colonies of Japan, moved away from the colonial-era dominance of Japan to pursue their own trade and investment arrangements.

A principal cause for the relative lack of intraregional trade in the first few decades after the end of the Second World War, at least among the noncommunist nations, was the lack of foreign direct investment by Japanese firms. These firms preferred to keep manufacturing at home and handle trade through a handful of large trading companies rather than invest in the markets where they sold their products. Since transactions between the home base and foreign branches of firms that have invested abroad are an important component of global trade, the lack of investment by Japanese firms in the countries in the region (and therefore the absence of exports by such firms back to Japan) helps to explain why intraregional trade was low.

However, this picture of the region should have changed dramatically in the past two decades, for two reasons. First, Japanese firms finally began to invest heavily abroad, beginning in earnest when the yen rose dramatically against the dollar in 1985. Unable to export from home at a profit, some firms relocated parts of their production capacity abroad. Some of that capacity has been relocated in Asia, but it is not the major location. Second, following the initial opening of China in the 1980s and the accelerated liberalization of access to its markets after the end of the cold war, trade links with China have opened for all the economies in the region. To a much lesser degree, the region's previously isolated small socialist or communist states—Vietnam, Laos, Cambodia, and Myanmar—also have opened up.

The integration of China into the global economy has been an important development for both the region and the world; nevertheless, it is a questionable indicator of East Asian regionalization. China has emerged on a global, not just regional, scale. While its emergence appears to have caused other Asian nations to trade increasingly within the region, the United States and Europe also are trading more with the region for the same reason. Meanwhile, the presumed importance of Japanese investments in weaving the region into a more unified whole is difficult to see. Trade between the rest of the region and Japan as a share of the region's total trade has not been rising. Japan's trade with the region has risen, though a large part of the shift is due to its trade with China. The region's trade with Japan, however, has actually been shrinking in relative terms; from the region's perspective Japan is a considerably less important trading partner today than a decade ago. A major part of the trade story involves offsetting trends in the relative roles of Japan and China in regional trade.

The remaining part of the story concerns what has happened to the rest of the region—East Asia minus Japan and China. Trade among these countries shows only a modest rise. Japanese firms certainly have invested across the region; some, such as Matsushita Corporation, have a regionwide production network, shipping components and finished products around much of Southeast Asia. But the trade data imply that such behavior has not been extensive enough to make a major difference in trade patterns.

The whole story, then, does not support the likelihood of formation of an East Asian economic bloc. When dissected, economic trends within East Asia are modest and contradictory. The continued importance of the United States supports the notion that it should be included in any regional dialogue; furthermore, Australia and New Zealand also have important linkages with East Asia. Overall, the data presented in this chapter provide a rationale for a broad Asia-Pacific dialogue rather than a more narrow East Asian one.

The analysis in the remainder of the chapter relies on trade data from the International Monetary Fund. An important caveat about these data is in order: Taiwan is not a member of the IMF; the electronic version of the IMF's trade data, therefore, does not include Taiwan. Oddly enough, the printed version of the same data does include Taiwan, at least as a separate destination for the exports of other countries and as a separate source of their imports. However, even the printed version provides no separate table for Taiwan itself showing its exports and imports by individual trading partner. Therefore the figures in this chapter include all the East Asian nations except Taiwan, though the trade of these nations with Taiwan is included. This annoying glitch in the data is part of a broader problem in data concerning East Asia. Neither the IMF nor the World Bank publishes any statistical data on Taiwan. This small but economically significant and centrally located economy is simply invisible.

Another data issue concerns China. The data for China are somewhat muddied by the transshipment of goods through Hong Kong and, to a lesser extent, Macau. Some of Hong Kong's trade is independent of China, consisting of exports from Hong Kong's factories or imports for use in Hong Kong. But some of its trade is transshipments of goods from China to the rest of the world or from the rest of the world to China. One way around this problem is to consolidate China, Hong Kong, and Macau, looking at their trade with the rest of the world and ignoring trade among them. The reversion of Hong Kong to Chinese control enhances the sensibility of this approach. In this chapter, therefore, trade with China is

Figure 3-1. *East Asia, Intraregional Trade as a Share of Total Trade*

Percent

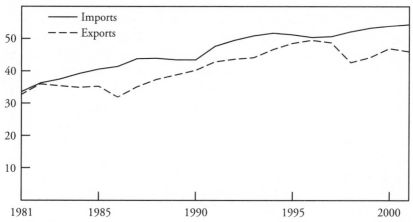

Source: Calculated from data in International Monetary Fund, *Direction of Trade Statistics*, 1988, 1993, and 2001.

calculated as trade with the People's Republic of China plus Hong Kong and Macau.

## Overall Statistical Evidence of an Emerging East Asian Bloc

The argument in favor of an emerging East Asian regional bloc comes from the summary data for trade in the region. Figure 3-1 shows the percentage of regional trade in total trade of the nations in the region. In 1981, 31 percent of the exports of these countries went to other nations in the region and 32 percent of their imports came from the region. Those percentages have slowly increased over time: by 2001, 41 percent of exports went to others in the region and 50 percent of imports came from others in the region. The share of exports had been higher, at 44 percent in 1996, but fell a bit in the wake of the 1997 financial crisis. The share of imports has grown somewhat more steadily, though the increase since 1994 has been slow.

These percentages are sufficiently large to argue that something very interesting is occurring: East Asian trade patterns are beginning to look like those of the members of the European Union. Perhaps this simple picture is sufficient to argue that intraregional trade is high enough to warrant some sort of institutional arrangement among these countries to ratify and encourage its further development. However, the overall picture is rather misleading.

Even the overall data paint a picture of regional proclivities that is less clear than one might imagine. Since many of these nations have been growing more quickly than the rest of the world, as have their exports to the world, their increasing relative size should be taken into consideration. Simply because these nations have had above-average economic growth and have developed successful export sectors, one would expect intraregional trade to have expanded more relative to trade with the rest of the world. For example, if a country exports equal amounts to countries A and B, and country A begins to grow more rapidly than country B, it is reasonable to assume that exports to A will increase faster than to B. Over time, exports to country A will become a larger share of total exports.

This simple statistical outcome can be measured. Assume that nations' imports are a fixed percentage of GDP. Take actual intraregional trade at some point in the past to represent the sum of all relevant factors—straight economic determinants of trade and any regional preference or bias. Then ask what has happened over time to the overall size of the region in global trade (an outcome of both their economic growth and development of internationally competitive export sectors relative to those in other parts of the world). Then ask whether actual regional trade today as a share of the region's global trade is larger or smaller than one would expect given the benchmark for regional trade at the earlier date.

Jeffrey Frankel explored this question a decade ago, arguing at that time that a de facto East Asian trade bloc was not forming. Indeed, looking at trade ties, he observed that Asian countries traded with one another *less* than one would expect given their rapid growth. To be sure, intraregional trade was rising, but the increase was more than accounted for by the rapid growth of their economies or their role in world trade.[1]

This simple approach is easily updated to 2001. Table 3-1 duplicates Frankel's calculations, updating them to cover the period from 1981 to 2001. Beginning with all of East Asia (that is, including Japan), in 1981 the region's total trade (exports plus imports) with itself was 33.3 percent of its global total trade. Meanwhile, the region's global total trade was 14.5 percent of the world's total trade. This yields a regional bias or preference factor in 1981 of 2.16 (that is, 33.3 divided by 14.5). If that benchmark for 1981 is applied to the share of the region in global trade in 2001 (19.8 percent), the result is a predicted value of 42.9 percent for the share of intraregional trade to the region's global total trade. However, the actual

Table 3-1. *East Asia, Regional Trade Preferences*

| | Total trade | | Exports | | Imports | |
|---|---|---|---|---|---|---|
| | *Region with Japan* | *Region without Japan* | *Region with Japan* | *Region without Japan* | *Region with Japan* | *Region without Japan* |
| (A) Intraregional trade as a share of region's total trade in 1981 | 33.3% | 16.9% | 30.79% | 18.8% | 31.8% | 15.2% |
| (B) Region's total trade as a share of global trade in 1981 | 14.5% | 7.0% | 14.8% | 6.9% | 14.1% | 7.0% |
| Regional bias factor in 1981 (A/B) | 2.16 | 2.17 | 2.08 | 2.72 | 2.25 | 2.17 |
| Region's total trade in 2001 as a share of global trade | 19.8% | 13.7% | 22.1% | 14.6% | 18..4% | 12.8% |
| Predicted Intraregional trade as a share of region's total trade in 2001 | 42.9% | 27.8% | 44.4% | 39.8% | 41.3% | 27.8% |
| Actual Intraregional trade as a share of region's total trade in 2001 | 45.3% | 31.1% | 41.4% | 28.5% | 49.7% | 34.0% |
| Difference in percentage points[a] | +2.4 | +3.3 | −3.0 | −11.3 | +8.4 | +6.2 |

Source: Calculated from data from International Monetary Fund, *Direction of Trade Statistics*, 1988, p. 114, and 2001, CD-ROM.

a. + indicates an increase in regional bias; − indicates a decrease.

percentage of intraregional to global total trade in 2001 was 45.3 percent, 2.4 percentage points higher than predicted. This implies that the region has demonstrated an actual expansion of intraregional trade that is slightly higher than one would expect from Frankel's findings. Leaving Japan out of the region does not alter the results very much. In this case, the predicted share of intraregional trade is 27.8 percent, while the actual share is 31.1 percent. Thus, with or without Japan, the region has shown a mild tendency to trade with itself more than one would expect due to the region's rapid growth in world trade.

The same exercise can be done for exports and imports separately. For East Asia as a whole, the result is an actual level of exports (41.4 percent) in 2001 that was 3.0 percentage points lower than predicted. The same calculation for the region minus Japan yields an even stronger outcome: the actual percentage of intraregional trade is 11.3 percentage points less than predicted. Thus the region is exporting considerably less to itself than would be expected.

On the import side, the data show something different, giving some support to the concept of an evolving region. Looking first at the region with Japan included, the predicted percentage of intraregional imports as a share of total imports by the region for 2001 is 41.3 percent, lower than the actual 49.7 percent—suggesting that on the import side a shift toward a regional bias did occur. If Japan is excluded from the definition of the region, then predicted intraregional trade for 2001 is 27.8 percent, which also is lower than the actual 34.0 percent.

What does all this mean? Frankel used his results to dismiss regionalism by saying nothing *unusual* had occurred in trade patterns—that is, that intraregional trade had increased but that the increase could be more than explained by the rapid growth of the region relative to that of the rest of the world. That picture has now changed, but not dramatically. Intraregional trade has expanded just a bit faster than one would have expected from the natural effect of the faster relative growth of the region. But that shift toward a more regional orientation applies only to imports. Therefore, the implications are ambiguous.

However, the fact remains that intraregional trade has increased. Whether the increase was caused by natural economic growth relative to that of the rest of the world or not, it might justify a closer institutional arrangement. If ordinary economic factors make trade and investment among a group of nations more important, then why not pursue a process of institution building that would enhance or accelerate the process? Of course, one could turn this argument on its head: if these nations already trade so much among themselves, without any special regional preference scheme, why bother? Do they really want to bias their trade patterns in a regional direction?

## Evolution of Trade by Region

The more detailed look at the evolution of trade patterns by country or region that follows provides a more nuanced assessment of what is happening in the region. While this investigation of trade patterns does not negate the picture of rising intraregional trade, the data undercut much of the image provided by the overall data.

## Japan

To identify patterns of regional trade and how they have evolved, it is useful to separate Japan from the rest of the region. Japan is such a large component of the regional economy and its economic behavior is different enough from that of the other countries that a number of useful questions emerge from the separation. For example, could changing Japanese trade patterns explain the Japanese government's surprising recent embrace of the ideology of regional and bilateral free trade areas?

Figure 3-2 shows the share of Japan's imports from various parts of the world from 1981 to 2001. The conventional belief that Japan has become more closely connected to Asia is partly true—but only partly. Imports from the rest of Asia have risen sharply as a share of total Japanese imports, especially since 1990. After fluctuating around 25 to 30 percent from 1980 to 1990, this share rose to 41 percent by 2001. However, most of the increase was due to rising imports from China, which rose from only 4 percent of total Japanese imports in 1981 to 17.0 percent by 2001—a huge 13 percentage point gain. Meanwhile, the share of imports from the rest of the Asian region excluding China shows very little change, fluctuating in the 20 to 25 percent range. In 2001 the level was only 5 percentage points higher than in 1981. Most of this increase occurred between 1981 and 1987.

Equally important, the role of the United States changed little until the period from 1999 to 2001. In 1981 imports from the United States were 18 percent of total imports; they increased to 23 percent by 1986 and remained at that plateau until 1998. Imports from the United States declined to 17 percent in 2001, but whether that represents a trend or just a temporary drop is unclear. The stagnation and recession in Japan may have had a larger impact on the capital goods that Japan imports from the United States (especially high-tech equipment) than on the textiles and consumer electronic products that it imports from developing countries. The larger picture therefore is one of relative stability in the share of imports from the United States. A similar story can be told about imports from the EU, which rose after 1985, jumping from 6 percent in 1981 to the 12 to 15 percent range in the 1990s. Although the EU share has eroded slowly since its high in 1989, it remained substantially higher in 2001 (12 percent) than in 1981.

Figure 3-2. *Japan, Imports by Region as a Share of Total Imports*

Percent

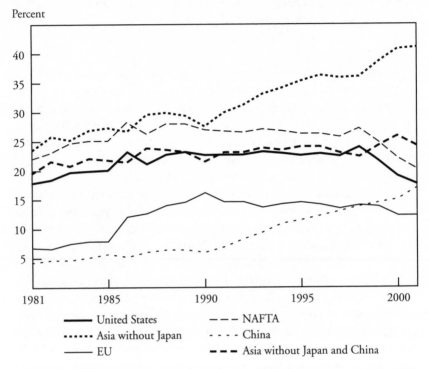

Source: International Monetary Fund, *Direction of Trade Statistics,* 1988, pp. 243–45; 1993, pp. 240–42; and 2001, CD-ROM.

One could argue that NAFTA might be a more appropriate focus than the United States alone. However, the two data series track closely, since Japan's trade with Canada and Mexico is much smaller than with the United States. Therefore, to reduce clutter in the figures, the data presented for the rest of the countries and subregions considered in this chapter leave out NAFTA. Other Asian nations are similar to Japan—they trade extensively with the United States but not very much with Canada or Mexico.

What do all of these import trends mean? One major fact to keep in mind is that these rising shares have been affected by the fall in the price of oil since the early 1980s. As a result, Japan's imports from the Middle East declined sharply, from almost 30 percent in 1981 to the 11 to 14 percent range in the 1990s. That drop caused the relative shares of all other regions to rise—a fact that creates a somewhat artificial appearance of rising regional imports from the rest of Asia. Meanwhile, the data suggest a shift toward greater reliance on imports from China, not the rest of Asia. Since much of this can be explained simply by the emergence of China on the global scene, it undermines the notion of a rising regional emphasis in Japan's import patterns. Finally, the apparent rise in imports from the region did not result from any turning away from the United States or Europe. The notion that Japan has turned from the West to Asia, therefore, is incorrect.

Now consider Japan's exports, shown in figure 3-3. Overall, Japan's exports to the rest of Asia rose sharply over the twenty-year period. They had been relatively stable at 23 to 25 percent in the first half of the 1980s but rose sharply in the next decade, reaching 43 percent by 1996; they then fell back to 39 percent in 2001. Unlike with the increase in imports, China played a small role in this increase. Exports to China were 7 percent of Japan's total exports in 1981; they fluctuated between that level and 10 percent for the rest of the 1980s and settled in at a new plateau of 11 to 13 percent in the 1990s. The increase in the share of exports to China has been very modest. In contrast, Japan's exports to the rest of Asia, excluding China, rose from 14 percent in 1981 to 30 percent by 1995 and subsided to 26 percent by 2001.

Why is the export pattern so different from that for imports? The probable answer is that the increase in Japanese exports to the region has been affected by direct investment by Japanese firms around the region. While investing, these firms rely heavily on equipment manufactured in Japan, and once in operation they absorb components imported from Japan. That explains why the share rose after 1985, when the value of the yen appreciated sharply—an exchange rate effect that curtailed the price competitiveness of Japanese exports.

However, just as with imports, the sharp rise in the role of Asia did not affect the relative role of the United States. In 1981, Japan's exports to the United States were 26 percent of its total exports; they rose to a temporary peak of 39 percent in 1986 because of the strength of the dollar against the yen and other major currencies, which gave Japanese exports a temporary but strong price advantage in American markets. Since 1992, that share has settled into the 28 to 30 percent range; in 2001 it was 30 percent, still higher than it was at the beginning of the 1980s. Also note that the United States remains *by far* the largest single-nation destination for Japanese

Figure 3-3. *Japan, Exports by Region as a Share of Total Exports*

Percent

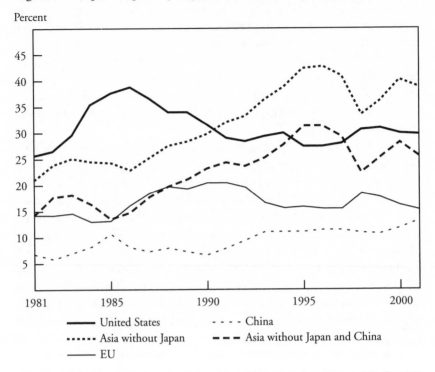

Source: International Monetary Fund, *Direction of Trade Statistics*, 1988, pp. 243–45; 1993 pp. 240–42; and 2001, CD-ROM.

exports. As with imports, the regional export share exceeds that of the United States only if exports to all of the countries in the region are added together.

This trend is identical but higher for NAFTA as a whole. In 2001, the share of Japanese exports to the NAFTA region was 33 percent. In both 1981 and 2001, 3 percent of Japan's exports went to Canada and Mexico; creation of NAFTA therefore does not appear to have played any role in increasing Japanese exports to Mexico or Canada—for example, to feed factories producing for the American market. As a destination for Japanese exports, NAFTA as a whole is still equal in size to East Asia, although East Asia was somewhat larger in the mid-1990s before the Asian financial crisis. Finally, the share of exports to Europe has fluctuated in the 15 to 20 percent range without any clear trend up or down.

What do these export data imply? All of the rising shares have been affected somewhat by the declining share of exports to the Middle East, though the decline was not as pronounced as it was for imports. (The share of exports to the Middle East dropped from 12 percent in 1981 to just under 3 percent in 2001.) The main conclusion is that Japan is most certainly not turning away from the United States or from Europe toward Asia. Certainly the share of Japanese exports to Asia has risen quite dramatically, in contrast to imports, although the unusual peak in the mid-1990s probably should be discounted. If the rapid increase in Japanese direct investment in the region was a cause for the increase in exports, the future may bring stability or, because direct investment has dropped, a relative decline in the share of exports to the region.

This picture of Japan's imports and exports contrasts strongly with the image commonly presented in Japan. For example, C. H. Kwan, an economist at the Nomura Research Institute, argues that "despite a tactical retreat during the Asian crisis, the Asianization of the Japanese economy is likely to continue."[2] The data in figures 3-2 and 3-3 do not support that conclusion, especially if Asianization means a relative shift from the United States and Europe to Asia, as Kwan implies in his writings. What has happened has been the rise of China as a source of Japanese imports and some increase in Japanese exports to the region, which now is likely to flatten or fall, at the expense of ties with the Middle East and other parts of the world rather than with the United States or Europe. The "Asianization" of Japanese trade patterns, therefore, is largely a figment of the imagination.

### The Rest of East Asia

Trade data for East Asia excluding Japan provide a different perspective. In broad terms, this subregion has not become much more closely tied to all of East Asia (that is, to itself plus Japan). In 1981, the subregion sent 42 percent of its exports to all of East Asia; by 2001 that share had risen only a tiny amount, to 43 percent. These data also show that the subregion is not moving closer to Japan in terms of trade flows and that both the United States and Europe remain important trade partners. The real story for the subregion has been the rapid rise of China.

Figure 3-4 provides data on the destinations of exports of East Asian countries excluding Japan. The first remarkable trend is the sustained

Figure 3-4. *Asia without Japan, Exports by Region as a Share of Total Exports*

Percent

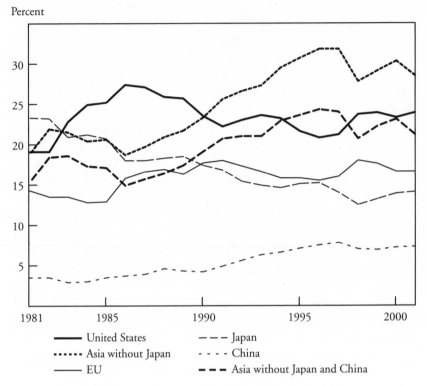

Source: Calculated from data in International Monetary Fund, *Direction of Trade Statistics*, 1988, 1993, and 2001.

decline in the share of East Asian exports to Japan, which has dropped slowly but rather steadily from 23 percent in the early 1980s to 14 percent by 2001. Meanwhile, exports to the United States have fluctuated, first expanding from 19 percent in 1981 to a peak of 27 percent in 1986 and then falling again, to 24 percent in 2001. Whereas in 1981 the share of exports to Japan actually exceeded the share to the United States by a small margin, the United States was by far (10 percentage points) the bigger destination for Asian countries by 2001. At least since the beginning of the 1990s, the share of exports to Europe fluctuated somewhat less, remaining around 16 percent, and even that was larger than the share to Japan by 2001. The notion that Asia is becoming more closely tied to Japan therefore is simply incorrect. At the margin, the region has turned away from Japan, leaving it a smaller export destination than either the United States or Europe.

Offsetting the decline in the share of exports to Japan has been a rise in the share to the subregion itself—to East Asian countries excluding Japan. This share, which was 19 percent in 1981, expanded to a peak of 32 percent in 1996 before declining to 29 percent in 2001. The downturn is an obvious consequence of the 1997 Asian financial crisis, after which these Asian nations expanded their exports to the United States while their exports to one another were constrained by the economic recession that followed the crisis.

These data suggest, therefore, that if any trend toward regionalism is occurring it is occurring among the countries of the subregion, excluding Japan. However, that view also is somewhat faulty. Figure 3-5 shows exports of Asian countries other than Japan or China. The data still show the sustained decline in Japan as an export destination—from absorbing a 26 percent share of exports in 1981 to only 13 percent in 2001. The share of exports to the United States first rose to 27 percent in 1987 before dropping to 19 percent in 2001, although, as in the broader picture of Asia, it was still 6 percentage points higher than the share to Japan in 2001. The share of intraregional trade shows an upward trend, from 16 percent in 1981 to 27 percent by 1996, after which it declined a bit, to 26 percent in 2001. In addition, the region experienced a rise in the share of exports to China. From only 5 percent in the early 1980s, China's share of exports had reached 12 percent by the end of the period.

Therefore, for East Asian countries other than Japan and China, export markets shifted away from Japan toward China. In 1981, Japan had been the largest export destination by a wide margin. But the steady decline in the share going to Japan plus the sustained rise in the share to greater China meant that Japan, China, and the EU all were roughly equal export markets by 2001. Meanwhile, the United States replaced Japan as the largest extraregional market, and the region shifted somewhat toward more trade with itself.

Now consider the import side of these trade relationships, beginning with the East Asia region excluding Japan but including China, shown in figure 3-6. On the import side, the data show the same slide in Japan's relative share. In 1981, Japan was the source of 25 percent of the region's total imports, but by 2001 its share had dropped to 18 percent. However, a somewhat similar though milder slide occurs in the share of imports from

Figure 3-5. *Asia without Japan and China, Exports by Region as a Share of Total Exports*

Percent

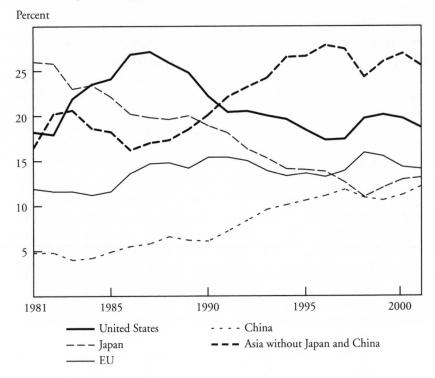

United States ——— 
Japan — — — 
EU ———
China - - - - 
Asia without Japan and China ▬ ▬ ▬

Source: Calculated from data in International Monetary Fund, *Direction of Trade Statistics*, 1988, 1993, and 2001.

the United States, which drifted down from 17 percent in 1981 to 13 percent in 2001. The share of imports from Europe remained relatively stable, in the range of 12 to 14 percent. Offsetting these trends was a strong, sustained increase in the share of imports from within the region itself, climbing from 15 percent in 1981 to 34 percent in 2001.

As with exports, the impact of China on these trends is easily visible by looking at Asia without Japan and China, shown in figure 3-7. For this East Asian subregion, between 22 and 26 percent of imports came from Japan until the mid-1990s; thereafter the share dropped, to 18 percent by 2001. The United States also dropped a bit as a source of imports, from 16 percent to 14 percent, with that drop occurring only since 1998. Note, however, that while both Japan and the United States declined as sources

Figure 3-6. *Asia without Japan, Imports by Region as a Share of Total Imports*

Percent

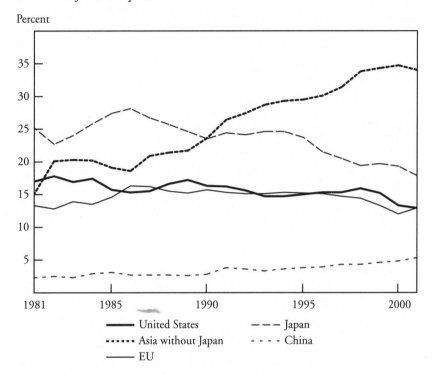

United States ——— 
Asia without Japan ••••••
EU ———
Japan – – –
China – - - -

Source: Calculated from data in International Monetary Fund, *Direction of Trade Statistics,* 1988, 1993, and 2001.

of imports, the disparity between the two also fell. In other words, while Japan remained a larger source of imports for Asian countries other than China than did the United States, Japan exceeded the United States by a smaller margin than earlier. As before, Europe represented a relatively stable source of imports; its share was slightly less than that of the United States—12 percent at the beginning of the period and 11 percent at the end. Intraregional imports, on the other hand, rose from 14 percent in 1981 to 26 percent by 2001. Finally, imports from greater China also rose, from 3 percent to 9 percent.

Although the export and import data display somewhat different trends, both suggest several important facts about the trade of this subregion of Asia. First, Japan has shrunk in relative importance as a trading partner for

Figure 3-7. *Asia without Japan and China, Imports by Region as a Share of Total Imports*

Percent

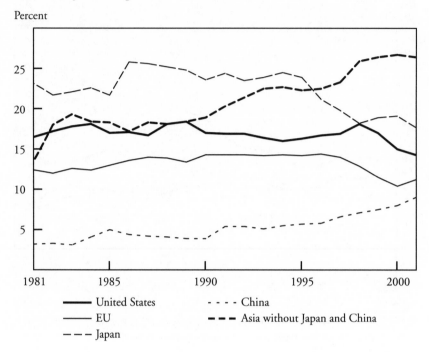

United States ————     China - - - -

EU ————          Asia without Japan and China — — —

Japan — — —

Source: Calculated from data in International Monetary Fund, *Direction of Trade Statistics*, 1988, 1993, and 2001.

other East Asian nations through a combination of exchange rate shifts that resulted in a dramatically stronger yen after 1985, causing imports from Japan to be less price competitive; lack of economic growth, which made Japan a less vibrant destination for Asian exports; and protectionism, which limited the growth of exports to Japan even after the yen rose dramatically in 1985, a rise that should have made Asian exports much more price competitive in the Japanese market.

Second, the United States has remained a large trading partner, having roughly the same importance in regional exports and imports that it had at the beginning of the 1980s. The EU, while generally a less important trading partner than the United States, also has had a relatively steady relationship with the region. These facts belie the notion of a region turning away from the West toward itself.

Third, much of the image of rising intraregional trade is an outcome of the rise of China. Although this is more pronounced on the export side than on the import side, trade within the subregion excluding both Japan or China has risen only modestly over time, while the importance of trade with China has risen quickly.

## China

As noted earlier, evaluation of China presents a problem because of the transshipment of goods through Hong Kong and Macau. Therefore, consistent with the discussion of the rest of the region, the following analysis deals with greater China—with the net trade of China, Hong Kong, and Macau with the rest of the world. The trade flows among these three are left out.

Figure 3-8 shows what has happened to the exports of these three economies. Their share of exports to Japan remained relatively constant, fluctuating around 15 percent. A similar steadiness characterized the share of exports to both the rest of East Asia (also around 15 percent) and the EU (around 20 percent). The share of exports to the United States, however, rose over time, beginning the period at 22 percent and ending at 32 percent.

These trends are seemingly at odds with the data presented earlier concerning the strong increase in imports from China for both Japan and the rest of East Asia. The difference in perspective comes from the explosive growth of total Chinese exports to the whole world. As noted by Nicholas Lardy, no other nation has ever expanded its role in global trade as rapidly as China.[3] In the twenty years of data shown in figure 3-8, China's global exports expanded from $21 billion to $317 billion, for an annual growth rate of 14.5 percent. That is, while China's exports to the rest of the region as a share of its total exports did not increase much, that share was part of such a rapidly rising amount of total exports that it represented a strongly rising share of total imports of other East Asian nations.

These export data do not sustain any notion of an increasing connection between greater China and East Asia. Exports to the whole region—including Japan—fluctuated around 30 percent, beginning at 28 percent in 1981 and ending at 30 percent in 2001. Exports to the United States and Europe began at 42 percent and ended at 52 percent. At the margin, greater China became increasingly linked to the distant markets of Western countries rather than those of its nearby Asian neighbors. This tendency would appear even more pronounced if the focus were reduced to the People's Republic of China alone. Hong Kong has long been integrated

Figure 3-8.  *Greater China, Exports by Region as a Share of Total Exports*

Percent

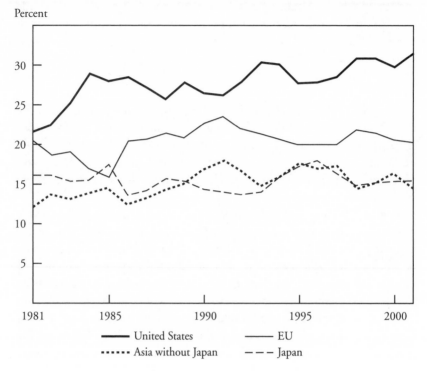

1981          1985          1990          1995          2000

United States ———          EU ———
•••••• Asia without Japan          – – – Japan

Source: International Monetary Fund, *Direction of Trade Statistics,* 1988, pp. 136–38; 1993, pp. 134–36; and 2001, CD-ROM.

into global markets. The People's Republic of China, however, sent more to the West and less to Asia over time (although one must keep in mind the uncertainty in the data due to transshipments through Hong Kong). This trend is a natural consequence of the rising investment by American and European firms in manufacturing capacity in China, as well as the relocation of Japanese production facilities for products for Western markets from Japan to China.

Figure 3-9 shows the sources of greater China's imports. These data show two dramatic developments—a major decline in Japan as a source of imports and a major increase in imports from the rest of East Asia. The share of imports from Japan peaked at 37 percent of total imports in 1985 and then slid almost continuously to only 18 percent by 2001, a drop of

Figure 3-9. *Greater China, Imports by Region as a Share of Total Imports*

Percent

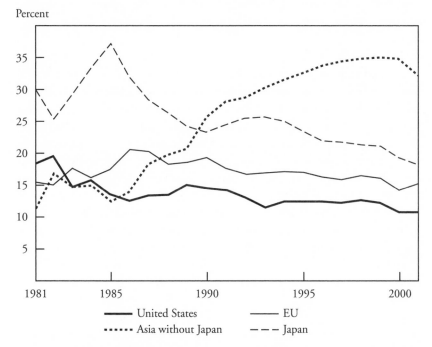

United States ——— EU

•••••• Asia without Japan — — — Japan

Source: International Monetary Fund, *Direction of Trade Statistics*, 1988, pp. 136–38; 1993, pp. 134–36; and 2001, CD-ROM.

just over 50 percent. The share of imports from the rest of East Asia, on the other hand, almost tripled, from 11 percent in 1981 to 32 percent by 2001. Meanwhile, the share of imports from the United States also declined, from 18 percent in 1981 to 11 percent in 2001. The share of imports from Europe began and ended the period at 15 percent, although they declined from a peak of 20 percent in 1986.

The import data provide a different picture of greater China's relationship with the rest of Asia. The region as a whole rose from supplying 41 percent of imports to 51 percent over this twenty-year period, while the United States and the EU declined from 34 percent to 26 percent.

Taken together, the data for greater China's exports and imports paint a mixed picture: the rising relative importance of the United States and Europe for exports and the rising relative importance of its Asian neighbors on the import side. Within that overall picture, however, Japan became less important, with a relatively constant share of Chinese exports but a sharply declining share of imports.

### The United States

Now consider regional trends from the perspective of the United States. Has rising intra-Asian regional trade meant that U.S. trade ties to the region have weakened? The following data draw exactly the opposite picture: U.S. trade ties with the region have experienced a modest rise in relative importance. The data indicate the emergence of stronger ties with China but a decline in relative ties with Japan. The decline in the position of Japan is rather remarkable, since Japan is the second-largest economy in the world, one that has affluent markets that absorb the sorts of products that American firms produce and that has made some progress in opening up to imports. However, Japan's very low growth in the 1990s, remaining import barriers, and direct investment abroad (relocating the manufacture of Japanese products destined for the United States) have resulted in this unusual drop in its relative position in both the U.S. export and import markets.

American exports to East Asia as a whole rose modestly from 18 percent of total American exports in 1981 to 24 percent by 2001. Figure 3-10 shows what has happened in greater geographic detail. The share of U.S. exports to Japan has been declining since 1990. Despite a stronger yen and some market opening, Japan absorbed only 8 percent of American exports by 2001, in contrast to the more than 12 percent it absorbed in 1990—when Japan's economy was smaller, its markets less open, and the dollar stronger. Offsetting the decline in the share of U.S. exports to Japan has been some rise in the share to China, though not much. The share of American exports to China rose gradually from just under 3 percent in 1981 to the 4 to 5 percent range in the 1990s. Therefore, the dramatic portion of the increase (as is the case with Japan's exports) went to Asian countries excluding Japan or China. That share increased from 6 percent in 1981 to 15 percent by 1995 and subsided to 12 percent by 2001. Meanwhile, the share of U.S. exports to the EU, which was around 25 percent in the 1980s, declined to the 21 to 22 percent range in the 1990s, perhaps reflecting some negative trade diversion as the EU further reduced internal barriers on European trade.

Affecting all the trends shown in figure 3-10 has been a shift in the share of American exports going to NAFTA—from 25 percent in 1981 to

Figure 3-10.  *United States, Exports by Region as a Share of Total Exports*

Percent

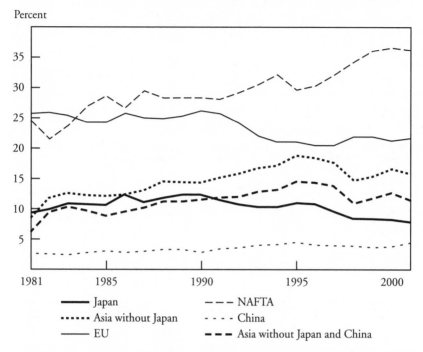

Japan
Asia without Japan
EU
NAFTA
China
Asia without Japan and China

Source: International Monetary Fund, *Direction of Trade Statistics*, 1988, pp. 406–08; 1993, pp. 403–05; and 2001, CD-ROM.

37 percent by 2001. This shift represents some trade diversion, both to sell to the Canadian and Mexican domestic markets and to service American factories, especially those newly attracted to Mexico, first by tariff advantages established for foreign-owned factories that export their output (the maquiladora system) and then by Mexico's inclusion in NAFTA. Given this strong regional shift, it is interesting that the share of exports to Asia has managed to rise modestly as well.

The picture of American imports largely parallels that of exports, though it is somewhat more pronounced. Asia as a whole was the source of 25 percent of American imports in 1981 and of considerably more, 34 percent, in 2001. Figure 3-11 provides the geographical detail. Remarkably, the general rise in the share of imports from this region occurred despite a substantial decline in the share of imports from Japan. After peaking at 22 percent in 1985, the share of imports from Japan fell quite steadily, to

Figure 3-11. *United States, Imports by Region as a Share of Total Imports*

Percent

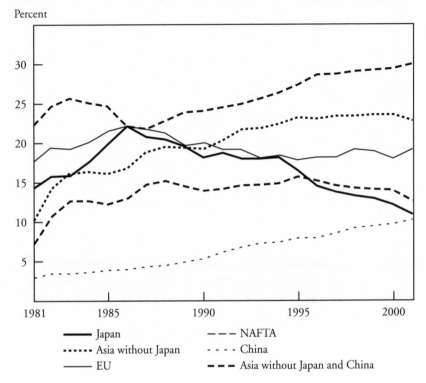

Japan

Asia without Japan

EU

NAFTA

China

Asia without Japan and China

Source: Calculated from data in International Monetary Fund, *Direction of Trade Statistics,* 1988, 1993, and 2001.

only 11 percent by 2001—a drop of 11 percentage points in fifteen years. Partially offsetting this decline has been a sharp rise in the share of imports coming from China, from only 3 percent in 1981 to almost 10 percent by 2001, when imports from China were almost as large as those from Japan. There also has been an increase in the share of imports from the rest of Asia, other than China and Japan. From only 7 percent in 1981, the share of imports from this subregion rose to a peak of 15 percent in 1995 before subsiding to 13 percent in 2001. Meanwhile, the EU's share of total imports to the United States, 18 to 20 percent, has been fairly steady over most of the period.

Again influencing all of these trends has been the role of NAFTA, although its impact has been more modest than in the case of U.S. exports. The share of imports coming from NAFTA rose from 22 percent in 1981 to 30 percent by 2001. However, the rise began before formation of either the U.S.-Canada Free Trade Area or its expansion into NAFTA.

These data on the U.S. trade relationship with Asia lead to two important conclusions. First, much of this description of the trends in the American relationship with East Asia (or at least that part of the region other than Japan) sounds very much like the description of trends in Japan's relationship with the region. China has risen quickly as a manufacturing base for the world, so that a much larger share of both American and Japanese imports have come from China. Similarly, the rapid growth and favorable climate for direct investment in the rest of Asia have led to those countries having a higher share of both American and Japanese imports and exports. Therefore the United States could make the same claim that Japan has made about having closer ties with the region.

Second, the increase in American links with non-Japan East Asia has been offset by a sharp drop in Japan's share of both American exports and imports. This is a truly remarkable development. In the 1980s, Japan appeared to be on the path to being the dominant U.S. trading partner, providing an ever-increasing share of American imports. Meanwhile, concerned over the relatively closed nature of many Japanese markets, the U.S. government embarked on a decade of sustained effort to lower those barriers, which ought to have led to an increase in the importance of Japan's large, affluent market to American exporters. However, exactly the opposite has occurred. The enormous appreciation of the yen in 1985 sharply cut the price competitiveness of Japanese exports to the United States, while some remaining trade barriers and, more important, the stagnation of the Japanese economy since the early 1990s meant that it did not become a magnet for American exports.

One possible explanation for the decline of Japan and rise of the rest of East Asia in U.S. trade could be the relocation of Japanese manufacturing from Japan to other East Asian countries after the yen appreciated in 1985. That is, Americans might still be importing Japanese products, but those products may be manufactured in Southeast Asia and China rather than Japan. There is undoubtedly some truth to this hypothesis. However, the investment data in the next chapter indicate that U.S. and European firms also are important investors in Southeast Asia and China. Therefore, while some American imports from this region are undoubtedly manufactured by Japanese firms, many are manufactured by American and European firms.

## Australia and New Zealand

So far the discussion of the Asian region has excluded Australia and New Zealand, which sit on the southern edge of the region. While they are small nations in terms of population, they are geographically close to the others, and their trade relationships ought to be considered. Inclusion here is all the more important because Australia has been a major voice in the past quarter-century in advocating a broad Asia-Pacific institution and was a prime mover in the establishment of APEC in 1989. Equally important, neither is included in the principal alternative to APEC—the ASEAN+3 group. However, including these two countries would not have altered any of the conclusions of the trade data analysis in the previous pages, while it would have complicated the figures with additional lines.

The export picture that emerges for Australia and New Zealand on the export side is somewhat similar to that for the United States. The share of exports to East Asia rose slowly from 43 percent to 51 percent over the 1981–2001 time period. Breaking this down as shown in figure 3-12 indicates that the share of exports to Japan fell over the course of the 1990s from the 23 to 25 percent range that prevailed in the 1980s to 18 percent by 2001. But as the share to Japan declined, the share to the rest of Asia rose quite strongly, from 18 percent in 1981 to 33 percent by 2001. Of that subset of countries, part of the increase went to China, whose share rose from 5 percent of total exports to 9 percent. Meanwhile, the share of exports to the United States remained rather constant at about 11 percent, while the share of exports to Europe sagged slowly: after reaching a peak of 18 percent in 1987, it declined to 12 percent by 2001.

A similar story emerges from the import data. The share of Australia/New Zealand imports from Asia rose strongly, from 31 percent in 1981 to 42 percent by 2001. Figure 3-13 shows the detail. Japan declined substantially as a source of imports; its share was 19 percent in 1981 but dropped to 13 percent by 2001. Offsetting the relative decline of Japan has been an increase for China and the rest of Asia. The share of imports from China rose from only 3 percent to 10 percent over the period, and the share from the rest of Asia increased from 8 percent to 20 percent. The share from the United States, on the other hand, was quite steady, fluctuating between 20 percent and 22 percent until 1998 and then falling some-

Figure 3-12. *Australia and New Zealand, Exports by Region as a Share of Total Exports*

Percent

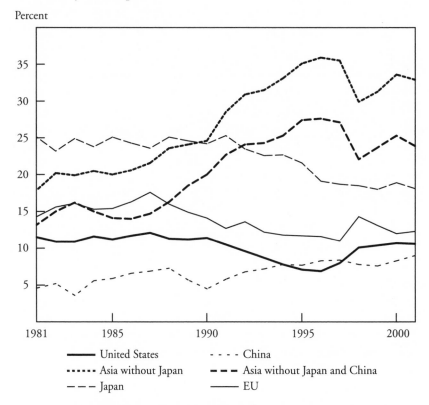

1981          1985          1990          1995          2000

————— United States        - - - - China
••••••• Asia without Japan    ▬ ▬ ▬ Asia without Japan and China
― ― ― Japan                 ————— EU

Source: International Monetary Fund, *Direction of Trade Statistics*, 1988, pp. 85–87, 298–300; 1993, pp. 85–87, 296–98; and 2001, CD-ROM.

what to 18 percent. The share of imports coming from Europe has been relatively steady, fluctuating mainly between 20 and 25 percent over the period.

The data for Australia and New Zealand indicate quite strongly why the Australian government has been such a strong advocate of a broad approach to regionalism. Historically, both of these countries were closely tied to Britain, but the economic connections that came with their colonial past have atrophied, especially after the imperial preference system of trade ended in the 1970s. Meanwhile, as the data above indicate, these countries have become more closely linked to East Asia. Initially they heavily favored

Figure 3-13. *Australia and New Zealand, Imports by Region as a Share of Total Imports*

Percent

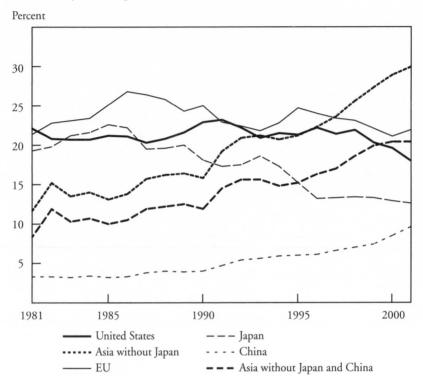

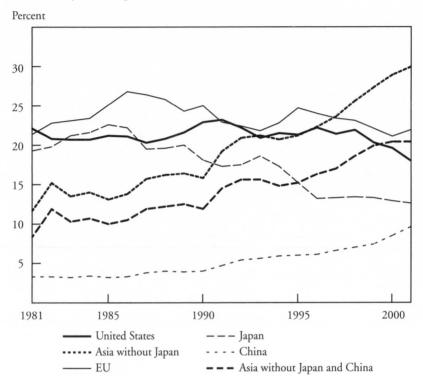

Source: International Monetary Fund, *Direction of Trade Statistics*, 1988, pp. 85–87, 298–300; 1993, pp. 85–87, 296–98; and 2001, CD-ROM.

Japan, which became a major purchaser of iron and coal from Australia and even invested in mines and railroads to move the ore to port. As the stagnation in Japan caused trade to diminish, however, trade with the rest of the region has risen. The relative strength of the trade ties between these two countries and their East Asian neighbors is actually as high as that of the intraregional ties among East Asian nations. Nevertheless, their ties with Asia did not come at the expense of trade with the United States or what remained of their European connections. From the standpoint of Australia and New Zealand, therefore, some sort of institutional arrangement that includes both the Asian countries and the United States makes sense, and that is what the Australians have advocated for a number of years.

## Conclusion

The trade data presented in this chapter imply that the case for a narrow East Asian economic regionalism is modest at best. To be sure, intraregional trade is up, as indicated by the overall trade data for the region as a whole. But that picture comes with very important caveats.

First, the region is most certainly not coalescing around Japan. The data for the rest of East Asia, China, the United States, and Australia/New Zealand uniformly indicate that trade with Japan, including both exports and imports, has fallen relative to trade with other countries. This decline in the relative importance of Japan as a trade partner was one of the major developments of the past decade, and it was largely unexpected. In the 1980s no one anticipated that Japan would fade so much as both a source of imports and a destination for exports. Perhaps other Asian nations feel that a closer institutional bond with Japan would offset this relative decline in trade flows, but given the fact that remaining Japanese trade barriers are not very amenable to resolution through regional or bilateral agreements, that is probably a forlorn hope. Furthermore, because the economic stagnation that has affected Japan shows few signs of ending, Japan is unlikely to become a vibrant growing market for exports of other nations in the near future. If that is true, then one wonders why the region would seek a closer institutional arrangement with the one member of the region with which their relative trade is shrinking.

Second, rising intraregional trade has not come at the expense of trade with the United States. The United States has remained the largest single national export destination for Japan, China, and the rest of the region. The United States remains Japan's largest single source of imports and is only slightly behind Japan as a source for the rest of East Asia. While the members of the European Union are generally somewhat smaller trade partners of the region, ties with the EU also have been generally steady over time. This means that the relative losers as trade partners of this region have been other parts of the world—the Middle East, Latin America, and Africa. This conclusion is at odds with the common perception that rising intraregional East Asian trade links have come at the expense of ties to the United States or Europe.

Third, much of what appears to be a stronger Asian regionalism reflects the emergence of China as an economic power. That emergence has affected nations all around the world, not just those in East Asia. Indeed, from the perspective of Chinese trade data, there is no remarkable trend toward engagement with the rest of the region; ties with Japan have weakened while those with other parts of East Asia have risen. With China's membership in the WTO, the tendency toward global Chinese engagement is likely to strengthen, reinforced by continued investment in manufacturing in China by firms from a number of industrial nations, to supply both the Chinese domestic market and the rest of the world. When China is left out of the analysis, the rising tendency for East Asian intraregional trade is much milder. Across the region, ties with Japan have weakened while those among the non-Japan, non-China East Asian subset have strengthened somewhat, but not a lot.

Fourth, from a U.S. perspective, East Asia has become somewhat more important as a trade partner over time. Despite some evidence of a shift in U.S. trade patterns toward Canada and Mexico because of NAFTA, the relative share of East Asia in American trade has risen moderately. Indeed, if a case can be made for a narrow East Asian regionalism, the same case can be made for including the United States within the region. To be sure, East Asian nations other than Japan have generally imported somewhat more from Japan than from the United States, but they export more to the United States than to Japan. If the region's sense of connection to Japan is strong enough to drive aspirations of establishing a more formal institutional arrangement, then why shouldn't its recognition of its reliance on the United States as an export market and import source drive similar aspirations? The answer is to pursue an institutional arrangement that includes both the United States and Japan, and that institution is APEC.

Fifth, the kind of trade links discussed in this chapter differ enormously from those that characterize North America. Some of the data on economic size and population in chapter 2 indicate that the wide disparities in size that might inhibit closer ties applied to both Asia and NAFTA. However, both Canada and Mexico are very closely tied to the United States through trade. In 2001, 87 percent of Canadian exports went to the United States, as did 83 percent of Mexican exports. High dependency on the U.S. market characterized these two countries even before NAFTA was created. In 1981, 64 percent of Canadian exports went to the United States, rising to 75 percent by 1985, just before the creation of the U.S.-Canada Free Trade Area that preceded NAFTA. For Mexico, 55 percent of exports went to the United States in 1981, rising to 81 percent in 1992, just before the creation of NAFTA. The same picture pertains to the imports of these countries. No nation in Asia has trade ties remotely resembling these—they have strong connections with both Japan *and* the United States, as well as ties among themselves and with Europe. Reflecting this reality, a periodic opinion poll found that 70 to 80 percent of Asians surveyed in 2001 picked the United States as the nation with which they wanted to promote closer trade relations. Japan ranked second and fell further behind over time).[4]

The trade data, therefore, do not support any notion that the Asian nations are forming a closer trade union among themselves based on an ongoing shift away from the United States or the West and toward each other. The data point toward the rationality of a dialogue among all the major trade partners around Asia Pacific, a grouping that logically includes both the United States and Australia/New Zealand. The one counter-argument to this conclusion is that the relative shift in trade away from Japan toward the rest of the region is simply a by-product of Japanese direct investment in manufacturing around the region. That is, while a smaller share of American imports comes from Japan directly, imports are still coming from Japanese-owned firms that have relocated to other parts of Asia. The next chapter, however, indicates that investment data do not support this simple conclusion either, as Japan has become a less significant source of investment around the region.

# 4

## *Investment Links*

The flow of money in the form of foreign aid, bank loans, bonds, investment in equity markets, and direct investment by foreign firms and individuals is the other key part of the economic interaction among nations. As with trade, the important question for East Asia is whether anything unusual has happened to investment flows that indicates an increase in intraregional links at the expense of ties to the rest of the world. Of the countries in East Asia, Japan has had the most potential for holding the region together because the Japanese became major investors in the outside world. In the late 1980s, Japan rose rapidly as a major foreign aid donor and as a source of both bank loans to and direct investment in the rest of East Asia. Its rise suggested a new Japanese focus on East Asia, but it largely reflected the broader picture, in which Japan was a rapidly rising global investor. Furthermore, from the standpoint of the rest of the region, the past several years have brought a decline in Japanese investment—both in absolute amount and relative to the investments of other countries.

The simple view of the decline in Japan's role in regional trade—that it merely reflected the relocation of Japanese-owned production to other Asian countries—is largely untrue. And, in general, economists see direct investment as complementing trade rather than substituting for it. To be sure, this chapter shows that Japanese direct investment in the region has been significant. However, the Japanese have not dominated direct investment around the region, and both the absolute and relative roles of Japanese firms in regional investment flows are now in decline. The other forms of capital flow largely repeat this pattern: money from Japan has been a significant factor over the past decade and a half, but the size of those flows has been decreasing for several years. Japan therefore is not (or at least is no longer) the hub of an Asian economic bloc that it formed around itself through investment flows.

There are a number of ways of looking at capital flows. One is to look at net financial resource flows, asking whether countries are net absorbers or providers of capital. Another is to look at gross flows. Statistical data exist for bank loans, portfolio investment (though only for Japan), foreign aid, and direct investment. This chapter considers all of these aspects of capital flow, but the analysis begins with an important caveat: data on capital flows are incomplete, and their quality varies from country to country. Some of the relevant questions cannot be answered, and in other cases the answers are less than conclusive.

## Net Financial Resource Flow

Current account balances provide a rough picture of the extent to which nations either absorb investment funds from abroad or are net investors abroad. The reason lies in the nature of double-entry accounting: to put it simply, what enters a nation must equal what leaves it; a nation's balance of payments is always zero. What deviates from zero are the various subsets within the balance of payments, such as the flows of goods, services, investment income, and capital investments. The current account consists of trade in goods and services, foreign aid grants, and repatriation of earnings on existing investments. If a nation has a current account surplus, then something else must be negative. That something else is capital flows— bank loans, purchase or sale of bonds, other forms of lending, portfolio equity investments, and direct investment (that is, equity investment yielding a controlling interest in a local company). In other words, if a nation has a current account surplus, the net surplus of foreign currency earned through trade and repatriated investment earnings is recycled in the form of net investments abroad. The opposite is true for nations with current account deficits. In this case, the net deficit in earnings on trade and repatriated income is offset by an inflow of currency in the form of net investment by foreigners.

Therefore, nations with current account deficits are fueling part of their domestic investment with foreign funds on a net basis, while those with current account surpluses are investing abroad. These net flows should not be confused with gross capital flows. A pair of nations with zero current account balances may well have large cross-border capital flows in both directions if their capital markets are open to foreign participation. Investors in each country may have a large investment stake in the other. But on a net basis, neither is dependent on foreign investment since its investment positions cancel each other out.

Just before the Asian financial crisis hit in 1997, a number of Asian countries had net current account deficits and therefore were net absorbers of capital from the rest of the world. As shown in figure 4-1, Indonesia, Malaysia, the Philippines, Cambodia, Thailand, Vietnam, and Laos all had current account deficits, ranging from 3.4 percent of GDP for Indonesia to 8.6 percent for Vietnam and 18 percent for Laos (possibly the result of inaccurate statistics for Laos). These nations had experienced current account deficits and net capital inflows through the whole first half of the 1990s that were generally a bit smaller as a share of GDP than was the case in 1996. However, even in the days of heady growth before 1997, not all nations in Asia were dependent on a net inflow of capital. Japan, China, Singapore, and Papua New Guinea all had surpluses, and that was true for most of this group for the whole first half of the 1990s (except for Papua New Guinea, which had fluctuated between deficits and surpluses).

Of course, the data presented in figure 4-1 are in the form of percentages of GDP. Since these nations vary so widely in size, the percentage data can obscure the size of the actual capital flows. In 1996, for example, Japan had a current account surplus of only 1.4 percent of GDP (a percentage that has varied between 1 and 4 percent of GDP since the early 1980s), but it represented $66 billion, and the amount has been as high as $130 billion in some years. Singapore, even though it had a much larger surplus as a share of GDP, 14 percent, had a current account surplus of only $13 billion. The surpluses of Taiwan ($11 billion), Papua New Guinea ($200 million), and China ($7 billion) also are all much lower than Japan's surplus.

Figure 4-1.  *Current Account Balances as Percentage of GDP,*
*Selected Asian Countries, 1996*

Percent

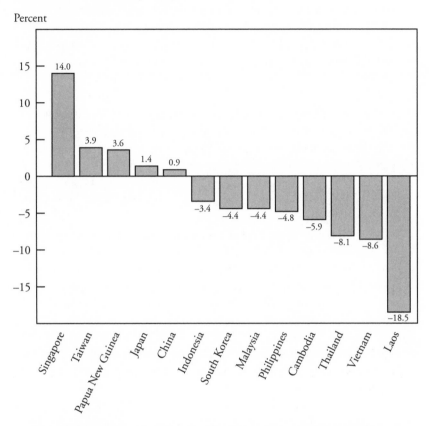

Source: International Monetary Fund, *International Financial Statistics*, 2001, CD-ROM.

China is a surprising case because it is a rapidly growing developing nation, and such nations often depend on a net inflow of foreign capital. But on a net basis, China is not absorbing foreign capital; in fact, it is a small net supplier of capital to the rest of the world, which comes mostly from the government's accumulation of foreign exchange reserves.

These data imply, therefore, that Japan is a potentially significant source of net capital flow to those economies in the region that have a current account deficit. The picture actually is somewhat more complicated. Even Asian countries that are net absorbers of capital overall may be absorbing net inflows of capital from some parts of the world while having a net out-flow of capital with other parts of the world. Most nations do not supply current account data on a bilateral or regional basis. However, the Japan-ese government does, although it did not include Asia as a region in the published data before 1988. For at least that far back, however, it is possi-ble to see Japan's current account balance with the rest of Asia. The only drawback is that the regional data provided by Japan include in the "Asia" category both the Pacific Islands and South Asian countries. With that caveat, Japan's current account balance with the world, Asia, and the United States for 1988 to 2001 is presented in figure 4-2.

What matters in analyzing the Japanese economy is the current account balance denominated in yen. However, since the point here is to look at the impact of Japan on the rest of Asia, figure 4-2 shows Japan's current account balances with the world, Asia, and the United States denominated in dollars. All three of these balances have fluctuated considerably. Japan's global current account surplus has gyrated between a low of $36 billion in 1990 (because of the negative effect on the current account balance of Japanese payments to the United States to help finance the Gulf War) and a high of $131 billion in 1993. The gyrations in the global current account over the course of the 1990s were due to movements in exchange rates (with downward pressure from an extremely strong yen in the 1994–96 period) and fluctuations in Japan's economic growth rate. Japan's surplus with Asia in the late 1980s had been in the range of $12 to $17 billion, but it rose during the first half of the 1990s to a peak of $76 billion in 1995. Thereafter, it declined sharply, sinking to only $16 billion in 2001— roughly the same value it had more than a decade earlier in the late 1980s. The surplus with the United States, in contrast, dipped in the mid-1990s but subsequently rose sharply, from $37 billion in 1996 to $91 billion by 2000 and $82 billion in 2001. Keep in mind that the regional balances shown in this figure occasionally exceed Japan's global current account bal-ance because Japan runs a deficit with some countries, such as the oil-exporting nations of the Middle East. However, the overall picture is one of a declining Japanese current account surplus with Asia since 1995, off-set by a rising surplus with the United States.

What do these data imply about capital flow? The net flow of capital is the mirror image of the current account balance, so Japan went through a period of sharply rising net capital flow to the rest of the Asian region from the beginning of the 1990s to 1995. But since that time, net capital flow to Asia has fallen by almost 80 percent, while the net flow to the United

Figure 4-2. *Japan's Regional Balance of Payments*[a]

Billions of U.S. dollars

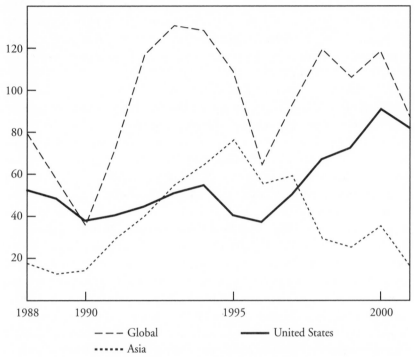

Source: Bank of Japan, *Balance of Payments Monthly,* April 1997, p. 91; April 2000, p. 91; April 1995, p. 81 (www.mof.go.jp/bop/1c004y16.htm; www.mof.go.jp/bop/c13all1.htm; www.mof.go.jp/bop/c12all1.htm; www.mof.go.jp/bop/1c004k16.htm [June 21, 2002]) and International Monetary Fund, *International Financial Statistics,* 2001, CD-ROM.

a. Since 1994, Japanese balance-of-payments data have been published only in yen; prior to that they were published only in U.S. dollars. For this figure, the more recent yen-denominated data have been converted to dollars using the IMF's average annual dollar-yen exchange rate.

States has risen. To some extent—namely, $16 billion in 2001—Japan still acted as a net supplier of capital to Asia. But that amount was only one-fifth of the net flow to the United States and one-fifth of the flow to Asia in the mid-1990s. This sharp shift has been brought about by a combination of factors: the Asian financial crisis, economic stagnation and financial problems within Japan, and rapid economic growth in the United States, which pulled in more imports on the goods side of the current account and more capital inflows to fuel investment. Therefore, in terms of where the

Japanese send their capital, the past several years have drawn Japan closer to the United States and weakened the relative importance of its flows to Asia—hardly the picture of a nation heading toward closer embrace of its Asian neighbors. This is especially true because the importance of these nominal dollar flows also is smaller relative to the size of the Asian economies, which have grown considerably since the start of the 1990s despite the interruption of the 1997 financial crisis.

It is easy to understand why the predominant view back in the mid-1990s was that Asia was increasingly in Japan's embrace, with this rising net flow of capital complementing strengthening trade ties. But that trend proved to be relatively short-lived. The obvious question now is whether the decline in Japan's current account surpluses and net capital flow to Asia also will prove to be a temporary phenomenon. The answer is that this diminished capital flow is likely to continue, at least in the short run. Domestic economic problems in Japan continued unabated in the early years of the new century. Economic stagnation and the use of expansionary fiscal policy to remedy the situation altered the domestic balance between savings and investment in a way that has diminished Japan's global current account surplus. Slowness in resolving the huge nonperforming loan problem at Japanese banks implied that the banks' ability to mediate a flow of loans from Japan to the region would continue to be impaired for at least several more years. Finally, some further ease of access to Japanese markets and exchange rate factors led to the relocation of some manufacturing production to lower-cost Asian nations, with some of the output exported back to Japan. While this final factor hardly amounts to the "hollowing out" feared by the Japanese media, one impact has been to lower the regional current account surplus.

If the Japanese economy resolves the problems it faces in the next several years, its current account surplus could rise as a share of GDP. The high and rising level of government debt as a share of GDP implies that government deficits will be constrained in the future. If, as many economists expect, the private sector continues to save more than it invests at home, a falling government deficit means that a rising current surplus (and net investment abroad) must offset the domestic savings surplus. In this context, though, it is not clear whether these net investment funds would flow heavily to East Asia or to the United States and Europe. To the extent that net capital flows are seeking a safe haven, the United States may be the primary destination. Having been burned in the 1997 crisis, Japanese investors may be hesitant to return in force to East Asia. Meanwhile, Japanese banks may remain so weak that they will not return to their earlier role in lending to East Asia, while the institutions that replace them in mediating the flow of capital out of Japan, such as American investment banks, may have less of a focus on East Asia than the banks did. All of this is speculative, but there is at least no powerful reason to assume that a large net capital flow to East Asia will resume in the next five to ten years.

Meanwhile, a longer-term factor already is beginning to set in: demographic change in Japan in the form of a rapidly expanding elderly population and shrinking working-age population. This trend, which will be a major economic factor in Japan for at least the next two decades and probably much longer, will also work to diminish Japan's global and regional current account balances and net capital outflow. To put it simply, this demographic change will lower savings and have a negative impact on the government fiscal balance as the government copes with sharply higher costs for social security and national health care benefits. These are macroeconomic developments that tend to diminish the net outflow of capital to the rest of the world as domestically produced savings are absorbed at home rather than abroad. For all these reasons, Japan is unlikely to re-emerge as a huge net supplier of capital resources to the rest of Asia.

This picture of diminished Japanese capital flows to the rest of Asia is confirmed indirectly by the shift in the overall current account balances of Asian nations that has occurred since the Asian financial crisis of 1997. Figure 4-3 shows current account balances as a share of GDP in 2000.

All of these countries except Cambodia and Laos moved to a current account surplus, and even the Cambodian and Laotian deficits were much smaller than in 1996. This shift from deficit to surplus may be a temporary response to the 1997 crisis, necessitated by the need of deficit nations to reduce their international debt. In the longer run, if these nations are to return to higher economic growth rates, they again may need foreign capital on a net basis. Nevertheless, it is important to recognize that they are not currently dependent on inflows of capital from abroad on a net basis.

## Gross Capital Flows

Even though East Asia is not dependent on foreign capital on a net basis, various forms of gross capital flow can be important. Foreign bank loans, portfolio investments, direct investment, and aid all can help finance activities that domestic investment perhaps would not, or they may enable

Figure 4-3. *Current Account Balances as a Share of GDP,*
*Selected Asian Countries, 2000*

Percent

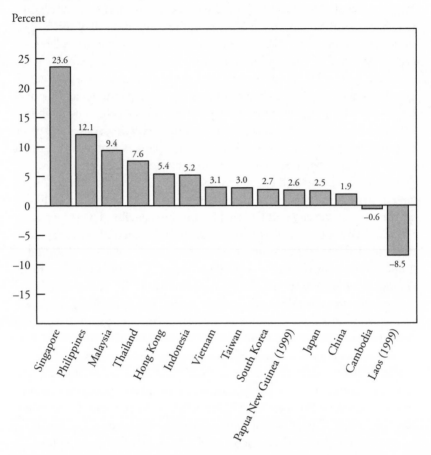

Source: International Monetary Fund, *International Financial Statistics,* 2001, CD-ROM.

use of foreign technologies that otherwise would remain out of reach.
Each of these flows is considered next.

### Bank Lending

Cross-border bank lending has been a significant source of gross capital
inflow to Asian nations, particularly as they loosened or removed restrictions on cross-border transactions in the late 1980s and early 1990s. Japanese banks, which exploded on the global lending scene in the early 1980s,

were an important source of the increase in lending to Asian countries. However, the role of Japanese bank lending has diminished substantially since the Asian financial crisis.

Data on cross-border bank lending come from the Bank for International Settlements (BIS), a multilateral organization based in Geneva. The BIS has published data on loans by region of recipient and nationality of lender only since June 1994. Data for cross-border lending to individual countries have been aggregated here to produce a total for the East Asian countries considered in this book. The BIS, in its subtotal for a broader Asia-Pacific region, excludes Hong Kong and Singapore, labeling them "money centers" rather than regional loan recipients. The argument for excluding them is that banks in Hong Kong and Singapore are major international lenders themselves. Therefore, loans from Japan or the United States to Hong Kong or Singapore might be to banks that, in turn, make loans to other Asian countries. That possibility would introduce double counting in the international flow of loans to the region, by including both loans to Hong Kong and loans from Hong Kong to others in the region. Therefore, figures 4-4A and 4-4B show international loans to the region excluding Hong Kong and Singapore and separate data for loans to these two.

The data in figure 4-4A show that total outstanding international loans to East Asian countries rose sharply from just under $200 billion in June 1994 to a peak of $361 billion in the middle of 1997, when the Asian financial crisis broke. Afterward, loans fell by just over one-third, to $224 by the middle of 2001, but they stabilized after June 2001. In September 2002, they totaled $226 billion. The data in figure 4-4B show much the same outcome for international lending to Hong Kong and Singapore. The peak, $473 billion, came earlier, in June 1995, and the decline was much steeper, leveling out at $185 billion by September 2002, in a 60 percent drop from the peak.

Japanese banks had a significant part in both the steep climb and reduction in lending. At the end of June 1994, Japanese banks had a total of $76 billion in outstanding loans to East Asian countries, and that amount rose to a peak of $119 billion at the end of June 1997—a 57 percent increase in just three years. However, as the Asian financial crisis broke and Japanese banks faced increasing problems back home, lending plummeted. From the June 1997 peak, Japanese loans to the region had fallen to only $39 billion by September 2002—a 68 percent drop. Japanese lending to Hong Kong and Singapore underwent an even more drastic change. After

Figure 4-4A.  *Loans to Asia minus Hong Kong and Singapore*

Billions of U.S. dollars

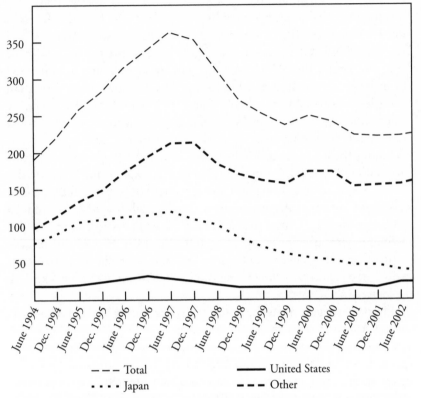

Source:  Bank for International Settlements, *The Maturity, Sectoral and Nationality Distribution of International Bank Lending* (Basel, Switzerland), various years;  *BIS Consolidated International Banking Statistics for End-1997*, various years; and *BIS Quarterly Review*, various years.

peaking at $274 billion in June 1995, lending declined almost continuously, to only $29 billion by September 2002—an 89 percent drop.

To be sure, the Japanese were not the only ones caught up in a frenzy of lending to the region. Loans from banks in Europe, Hong Kong, and Singapore showed an enormous 118 percent jump from 1994 to their peak in December 1997. By June 2001, these banks had cut their loans by 28 percent; the remaining loans then stabilized at $161 billion. The lending of all other banks to Hong Kong and Singapore also fell from a peak in June

Figure 4-4B. *Loans to Hong Kong and Singapore*

Billions of U.S. dollars

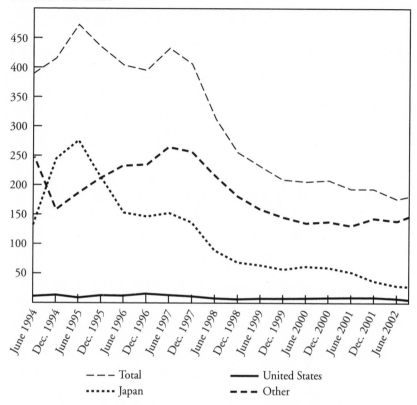

--- Total                          —— United States
······ Japan                       --- Other

Source: Bank for International Settlements, *The Maturity, Sectoral and Nationality Distribution of International Bank Lending* (Basel, Switzerland), various years; *BIS Consolidated International Banking Statistics for End-1997*, various years; and *BIS Quarterly Review*, various years.

1997, but they had stabilized by late 1999 at around $150 billion, 45 percent below the peak.

American banks, on the other hand, had never been large lenders to the region. Their loans increased from $17 billion in June 1994 to $32 billion in December 1996 before dropping back to $17 billion in December 2000; they subsequently rose again, to $26 billion by September 2002. American lending to Hong Kong did not rise rapidly in the mid-1990s (it was up only 28 percent from June 1994 to a peak in June 1996), though it fell slowly by 48 percent afterward, to $8 billion as of September 2002. In comparison with other banks' lending, then, lending by American banks amounted to less and was not as volatile.

The drop in Japanese bank lending came with a general Japanese withdrawal from global lending markets. According to data on Japan's balance of payments, total outstanding loans abroad by Japanese private sector banks dropped from a peak of ¥84 trillion in 1997 (or $694 billion at the average 121 yen-per-dollar exchange rate of 1997) to only ¥50 trillion (or $411 billion at the average 122 yen-per-dollar exchange rate of 2001).[1] That represents a 36 percent drop in dollar terms—very substantial, though much less than the percentage drop in lending to Asia. The diminished role of Japanese banks in global lending has been one of the major developments in international finance since the mid-1990s, but clearly something besides this overall drop affected Japanese lending to East Asia.

From the perspective of East Asia, the drop in Japanese bank lending has three important implications. First, Japan is simply far less important as a source of international loans. Japanese banks held 40 percent of all outstanding international loans to East Asian countries in 1994, but their share had dropped to only 17 percent by September 2002. The more cautious American banks have remained fairly steady at 6 to 9 percent of total lending to the region, and all other banks now hold 70 percent of the total. Much the same is true for Hong Kong and Singapore, though the change is more dramatic. At the end of 1994, Japanese banks briefly held a very large 59 percent of all international loans to these two regional money centers, but their share dropped to only 16 percent by September 2002. Thus all across East Asia, Japanese bank lending, which once appeared to dominate, has shrunk in absolute and relative terms to a rather minor level.

Second, Asian nations face a near-term future in which Japanese banks may well continue to cut their lending, making them even less of a factor than in the past. As the region continues to recover from the 1997 financial crisis and to move toward floating exchange rates and better rules for governing their financial sectors, foreign lenders other than the Japanese will extend more credit. But with the continuing domestic troubles of the Japanese banks, they will not be in a position to participate in this business.

Third, the relative and absolute decline in Japanese lending, plus the likely future trends, diminishes Japan in the eyes of other Asian nations as a close regional partner. Of all the lenders to the region, the Japanese have been most fickle, rushing in and then rushing out of the market. This decreases any momentum toward Asian economic regionalism and undercuts the image of Japan as a leader in the process. Other Asian nations may see little point in deepening their economic attachment to an unreliable nation whose banking sector has been so weakened by misbehavior in the past that its lending to Asia has dropped significantly, in both relative and absolute terms, and might sink further as the situation at home unravels.

## Portfolio Investments

Bank loans are only one form of financial flow. Data on forms of investment other than direct investment—portfolio equity investments, bonds, money market instruments, derivatives, and so forth—are difficult to find. The only perspective on these flows comes from the regional Japanese balance-of-payments data. Of course, these categories of investment depend on the existence of well-developed financial markets, which are not present in all Asian economies. Nevertheless, some—including Hong Kong and Singapore and increasingly Taiwan and South Korea—do have markets that are sufficiently well developed to afford foreign investors opportunities to engage in a variety of portfolio investments.

Table 4-1 presents statistics on Japanese international portfolio assets. Despite the existence of capital markets in parts of East Asia, Japanese portfolio investments at the end of 2001 were concentrated overwhelmingly in Europe and the United States. Of the total ¥170 trillion ($1.4 trillion at 2001 exchange rates) in overseas portfolio assets held by Japanese investors, 40 percent was invested in Europe, 38 percent in the United States, and only 1.7 percent (less than ¥3 trillion, or $26 billion) in Asia. Central and South America attracted more than seven times as much Japanese portfolio investment as Asia.

This pattern is true even for portfolio equity investments, the type most likely to be moderately well developed in other Asian countries. Of ¥30 trillion ($246 billion) in portfolio equity investments around the world, just over ¥1 trillion ($9 billion) was in Asia, or 4 percent of the total. Asian bonds and other debt securities make up an even smaller 1.3 percent of Japanese holdings of foreign debt securities.

Ideally, one would like to know the distribution of foreign ownership of Asian equity and debt securities by nationality, but these data are not available. The Japanese data, however, provide at least a weak indication that portfolio investments do not form a strong connection between Japan and the rest of the region. Japanese investors are heavily engaged with the West, not Asia. To be sure, much of that investment stems simply from the great depth and sophistication of American and European financial markets,

Table 4-1. *Japanese Holdings of International Portfolio Assets,*
*Year-end 2001*
Billions of yen

| | | | Debt Securities | | | |
|---|---|---|---|---|---|---|
| | Total | Equity Securities | Bonds and Notes | Money Market Instruments | Total | Financial Derivatives |
| Total | 169,990 | 29,965 | 132,443 | 7,582 | 140,025 | 395 |
| Asia | 2,870 | 1,089 | 1,739 | 42 | 1,781 | 4 |
| China | 220 | 104 | 116 | 0 | 116 | 0 |
| Taiwan | 63 | 52 | 11 | 0 | 11 | 0 |
| South Korea | 769 | 50 | 716 | 3 | 719 | 0 |
| Hong Kong | 806 | 639 | 165 | 2 | 167 | 1 |
| Singapore | 281 | 122 | 122 | 37 | 159 | 2 |
| Thailand | 137 | 38 | 99 | 0 | 99 | 0 |
| Indonesia | 21 | 7 | 14 | 0 | 14 | 0 |
| Malaysia | 335 | 45 | 290 | 0 | 290 | 0 |
| Philippines | 206 | 28 | 178 | 0 | 178 | 0 |
| India | 26 | 4 | 22 | 0 | 22 | 0 |
| North America | 67,496 | 16,644 | 48,273 | 2,579 | 50,852 | 92 |
| U.S.A. | 64,608 | 16,279 | 45,757 | 2,573 | 48,330 | 85 |
| Canada | 2,888 | 365 | 2,516 | 6 | 2,522 | 8 |
| Central and South America | 21,333 | 1,609 | 18,662 | 1,063 | 19,724 | 0 |
| Oceania | 2,854 | 420 | 2,078 | 356 | 2,434 | 3 |
| Australia | 2,528 | 396 | 1,855 | 277 | 2,132 | 2 |
| New Zealand | 326 | 24 | 223 | 79 | 302 | 0 |
| Western Europe | 67,548 | 10,130 | 53,948 | 3,470 | 57,418 | 296 |
| Eastern Europe | 179 | 5 | 174 | 0 | 174 | 0 |
| Russia | 17 | 1 | 15 | 0 | 15 | 0 |
| Middle East | 79 | 9 | 70 | 0 | 70 | 0 |
| Africa | 254 | 12 | 242 | 0 | 242 | 0 |
| International Organization | 5,754 | 0 | 5,745 | 9 | 5,754 | 0 |

Source: Bank of Japan, table labeled Regional Direct Investment Position and Regional Portfolio Investment Position (End of 2001) (www.boj.or.jp/en/stat/stat_f.htm [April 10, 2003]).

which creates a ready supply of relatively low-risk financial instruments. But whatever the reason, portfolio investment does not tie Japan to the rest of the region.

## Foreign Aid

An additional important form of capital flow can be foreign aid. Formally called official development assistance (ODA), it consists of the grants and concessional loans received by developing countries from the governments of developed countries or from the World Bank and regional multilateral development banks. Not all Asian countries receive aid. South Korea, Hong Kong, Taiwan, and Singapore graduated from the ranks of poor developing countries a number of years ago and no longer receive any foreign aid. But others do; in 1999, eleven countries in the East Asian region considered in this study were net recipients of foreign aid.

Japan has been a major donor of aid to the region. A decade ago, with the rapid increase in Japanese aid to the region, its overwhelming size relative to the aid of other donors by the early 1990s, and its reputation for being very closely aligned with Japanese commercial interests, it appeared that foreign aid was a key component of an Asian regionalism that was emerging under Japan's leadership. Although Japan remains a large donor of aid to those nations in the region that receive foreign aid, the image of a decade ago has faded.

Consider first Japan's overall role as a foreign aid donor. Since at least the beginning of the 1990s until 2001, Japan was the largest foreign aid donor among all the developed nations, but its role may now be changing (it slipped behind the United States in 2001). As shown in figure 4-5, Japan's ODA budget has stagnated since 1991. After peaking at close to ¥1.8 trillion ($18.8 billion at then-current exchange rates) in 1995, the budget dropped back to ¥1.2 trillion by 2003 ($10 billion), below the level of 1989. In fact, the rather wide fluctuation in the yen-denominated ODA budget during the 1990s is somewhat surprising given the rhetorical commitment to foreign aid that the Japanese government maintained through the decade. But the stagnation and decline in foreign aid since the mid-1990s represents an important shift rather than just a cyclical downturn. For the first time since Japan's foreign aid program began in the 1960s, it has come under fire at home for much the same reason that American foreign aid faces domestic criticism—principally the issue of the government

Figure 4-5. *Japan's Official Development Assistance Budget*

Billions of yen

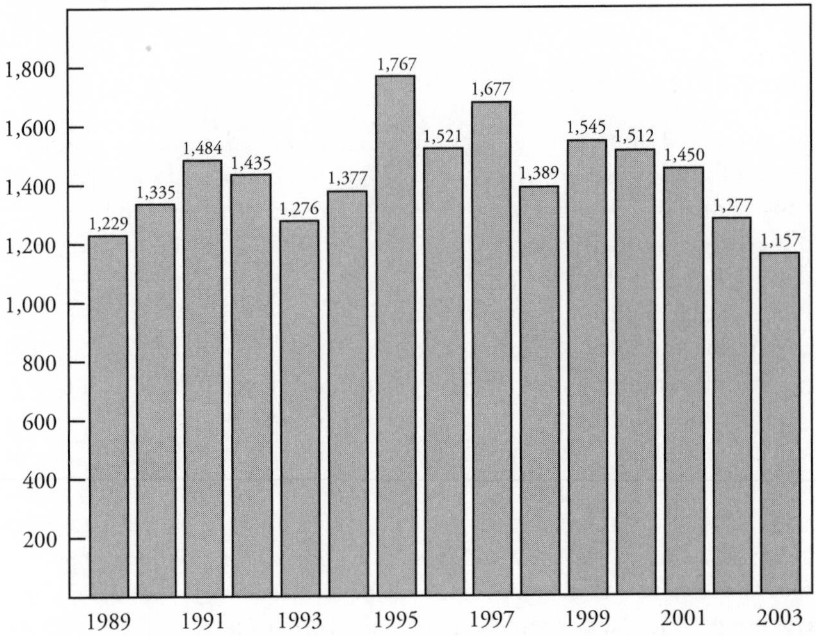

Source: Ministry of Foreign Affairs, *Japan's ODA Annual Report*, various years (www.mofa.go.jp/policy/oda [October 23, 2003]).

giving money to other countries when there are pressing domestic problems that lack funding. All of this follows two decades in which Japan's foreign aid expanded rapidly.

In such an unfavorable fiscal environment, it was likely that foreign aid to the Asian countries considered in this book would begin to fall. At least with China, such cuts already were becoming explicit. In late 2001, the government issued a report reassessing the state of foreign aid for China, taking a much less generous stance than in the past. At one point it notes, "Japan is China's largest donor country, and its presence in assistance to China is *extremely large*" [emphasis added].[2] The report then goes on to note the increasing skepticism at home about the advisability of giving so much aid to a neighbor with rapidly increasing economic and military power—a neighbor that competes in global markets with Japanese firms.

This report presaged a decision in early 2002 to cut ODA to China in the fiscal 2002 budget by a whopping 25 percent, a move that had editorial support in the Japanese media.[3] This unusual move even had support from the head of Keidanren (an association of large corporations), reflecting a shift in Japanese corporate leaders' thinking from wanting to give aid in order to build local infrastructure helpful to their factories in China to fearing that aid was helping their Chinese competitors.[4]

With the stagnation and recent decline in Japanese foreign aid, this form of financial interaction with developing Asia and the rest of the developing world was at least put on hold. Of course, placed in context, Japan's performance roughly mirrors that of all aid donors. According to the Organisation for Economic Co-operation and Development (OECD), total net flow of foreign aid peaked in 1992 at $61 billion and was somewhat lower, at $54 billion, in 2000. Aid from the United States also dropped, from $11 billion in 1990 to $10 billion in 2000. Japan actually looked somewhat better: its aid was still rising in the early 1990s, and its dollar-denominated aid rose from $9 billion in 1990 to $13 billion in 2000, though the amount bounced around due to exchange rate shifts.[5] But in any case, Japan has followed the international trend, with a lag of a few years; this now shows more clearly in the annual yen-denominated budget for aid.

Since its inception in the 1960s, Japan's foreign aid program has focused strongly on Asia. In 1980, 70 percent of Japan's bilateral aid (direct aid to individual countries) was allocated to Asian nations. Although that share subsided to 51 percent by 1990, it still represented half of Japan's total bilateral aid.[6] The most recent available data on overall bilateral aid allocation show 57 percent going to Asia in 2001.[7] Statistics for the Japan Bank for International Cooperation (JBIC) confirm Japan's heavy commitment to Asia. JBIC is a recent combination of Japan's export-import bank (making "hard" or near market-rate loans for trade finance) and the foreign aid lending agency (making "soft" or subsidized loans to developing countries, with foreign aid grants under the separate control of the Ministry of Foreign Affairs). Of the total outstanding foreign aid loans at the end of March 2001, 57 percent were to the Asian countries considered in this study. Even 45 percent of the hard loans went to Asia, a remarkable fact since these loans can be used to finance trade and investment with developed nations such as the United States as well. China alone represents 14 percent of Japan's foreign aid loans.[8] All these data confirm that Japan's strong preference for granting foreign aid to Asia remains unabated.

With its heavy concentration on Asia, Japan has long stood out among the donors of aid to Asian countries. In 1985, Japan supplied 26 percent of the total net ODA of the twelve countries in the region then receiving aid, and that share gradually rose, reaching 38 percent in 1999. These data imply that Japan is by far the largest single source of foreign aid to these countries. The United States, in contrast, was the source of only 2.2 percent of ODA receipts in 1999, and multilateral lending institutions (the World Bank and the Asian Development Bank) were the source of 45 percent.[9] Figure 4-6 shows Japan's share of ODA receipts by individual Asian countries in 1999. On a net basis, Malaysia was actually paying back loans from multilateral lending institutions, so that the positive net receipt of funds from Japan came to 205 percent of its total receipts (shown as 100 percent in figure 4-6; all of Malaysia's net ODA receipts were from Japan). That anomaly aside, figure 4-6 shows that a number of Asian countries have been exceptionally dependent on Japan for ODA. China, a very large recipient of ODA (with a net receipt of $3.9 billion in 1999), was somewhat less dependent on Japan; even so, Japan supplied almost one-third of its total aid. Only in Cambodia and Papua New Guinea was Japan's share of ODA less than 20 percent.

Since Japanese foreign aid tends to come with visible—or invisible—strings attached to Japanese economic interests, foreign aid has long been considered a means for Japan to increase its economic ties to the region.[10] However, it is questionable what all that aid bought Japan, even after several decades of dominating the foreign aid scene. Perhaps all that happened was that the Japanese government ended up too enmeshed in the corrupt crony politics of some recipient countries, especially Indonesia, Malaysia, and Thailand. One wonders, for example, why the Japanese government was so much slower than any other advanced nation to move away from supporting President Suharto of Indonesia when his government was collapsing in 1998. Or consider the fact that one objective of Japanese foreign aid has been to provide the infrastructure (roads, harbor facilities, and utilities) needed by Japanese firms investing in these countries, which might have given Japanese firms an advantage over their competitors in investing around the region. Nevertheless, Japan does not stand out as much as it might be expected to as a regional investor.

### Foreign Direct Investment

For many of the countries in Asia, gross inward foreign direct investment is a relatively important source of annual domestic investment.

Figure 4-6. *Share of Net Official Development Assistance from Japan, Selected Asian Countries, 1999*

Percent

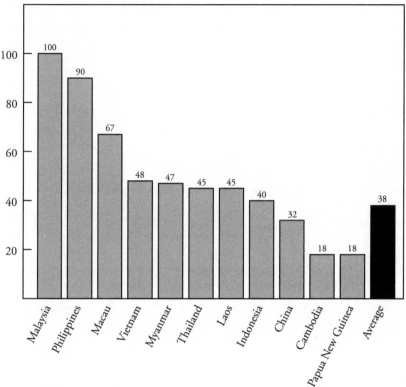

Source: Organisation for Economic Co-operation and Development, *Geographical Distribution of Financial Flows to Aid Recipients, 1995–1999.*

Table 4-2 shows foreign investment as a share of total private sector fixed capital formation for those Asian countries for which data are available. Although the accuracy of foreign investment data collected by some countries may be questionable, these data show that foreign direct investment provides more than 10 percent of total fixed capital investment in China and considerably more than that in some other countries. Even in Indonesia foreign direct investment appears to be important, as the withdrawal of investments—in reaction to the 1997 currency collapse, severe recession,

Table 4-2.  *Inward Direct Investment as a Share of Gross Fixed Capital Formation*
Percent

| Country | 1989 to 1994 Average | 1995 | 1996 | 1997 | 1998 | 1999 |
|---|---|---|---|---|---|---|
| World | 4.1 | 5.3 | 5.9 | 7.5 | 10.9 | 16.3 |
| United States | 4.8 | 5.3 | 7.0 | 7.9 | 11.3 | 17.9 |
| European Union | 5.4 | 6.7 | 6.5 | 8.3 | 15.6 | 27.7 |
| Japan | | | | | | 1.1 |
| Cambodia | 17.1 | 23.5 | 36.1 | 34.7 | 28.0 | 22.2 |
| China | 7.9 | 14.7 | 14.3 | 14.6 | 12.9 | 11.3 |
| Hong Kong | 14.8 | 14.6 | 21.7 | 19.8 | 29.9 | 60.2 |
| Indonesia | 4.0 | 7.6 | 9.2 | 7.7 | –1.6 | –11.0 |
| South Korea | 0.8 | 1.0 | 1.2 | 1.7 | 5.7 | 9.3 |
| Laos | 19.4 | 20.7 | 29.4 | 19.2 | 14.6 | 17.8 |
| Malaysia | 19.4 | 15.0 | 17.0 | 14.7 | 13.9 | 20.1 |
| Myanmar | 2.8 | 1.9 | 1.6 | 1.6 | 1.0 | 0.7 |
| Philippines | 7.5 | 8.9 | 7.8 | 6.2 | 12.7 | 5.1 |
| Singapore | 30.3 | 31.2 | 29.7 | 35.3 | 20.6 | 26.1 |
| Taiwan | 2.9 | 2.4 | 3.0 | 3.4 | | 4.4 |
| Thailand | 5.0 | 2.9 | 3.0 | 7.2 | 26.7 | 13.7 |

Source: United Nations Conference on Trade and Development, *World Investment Report 2001: Promoting Linkages*, annex B, *Satistical Annex* (New York: United Nations, 2001), pp. 312–24.

civil unrest, the fall of Suharto, and continuing political uncertainty and violence—was almost 11 percent of the size of total capital formation in 1999. The one Asian country with very little inward investment as a share of domestic capital formation is Japan. The 1.1 percent shown in table 4-2 is actually considerably higher than in earlier years, since the yen amount of inward direct investment had expanded enormously from the mid-1990s.

While the earlier balance of payments data indicate that these countries were generally not net absorbers of foreign capital, the gross flow of inward direct investment can still be important because it brings with it technology and management know-how, which benefits the domestic economy. Therefore, it is worth asking where these investments come from. To answer this question, it is necessary to look at countries individually.

JAPAN. The question here is whether Japanese firms have shifted their overseas investments toward East Asia and away from the United States or Europe. The rest of Asia certainly is a natural location for Japanese investment, or at least for investments motivated by a desire for lower labor costs. Other East Asian countries are relatively close geographically, they are not many time zones apart, and they generally have a relatively well-educated labor force. Therefore, as Japanese firms became more interested in finding locations with lower labor costs after the mid-1980s (when the yen rose dramatically against the dollar, making the export of many products from Japan unprofitable), a major surge in investment in Asia would have been quite logical.

Before one looks at the Japanese data, an important caveat is in order. Japanese direct investment data by country do not report disinvestment. That is, if a firm shuts down an overseas subsidiary, its withdrawal of investment is not counted. Therefore, Japanese data tend to overestimate actual investment flows. There is no way of knowing whether disinvestment and new investments follow the same pattern of geographical distribution.

With that caveat, Japanese data indicate that, quite contrary to the hypothesis of a rising concentration of investment in Asia, only a relatively small portion of Japanese direct investment has gone to the rest of Asia. As of fiscal year 1979, 27 percent of cumulative Japanese direct investment had gone to Asian countries, although the dollar amount was quite small. But in the 1980s, as Japanese direct investment surged, the share to Asia actually dropped, averaging only 11 percent from fiscal year 1985 to 1989.[11] Figure 4-7 shows relative shares of Japanese foreign direct investment by region for fiscal years 1989 to 2001 (with Japanese fiscal years beginning in April of the indicated year and ending in March of the next calendar year). By the mid-1990s, it appeared as though Japan was turning back toward Asia, with the share of new overseas direct investment in Asian countries rising to almost 24 percent of Japan's global investment for fiscal years 1994 through 1996. That surge, however, appears to have been temporary. By the late 1990s, the share of investment in Asia was back down to the 10 to 11 percent level, although it jumped back to 20 percent in fiscal year 2001. Whether the 2001 figure marks a renewed shift toward Asia is unclear. However, figure 4-8 shows that the increase was due more to a sudden drop in the yen amount of investment in the United States in the wake of the collapse of the information technology bubble. That suggests that the drop in the share of investment going to the United States and the

*Figure 4-7.  Share of Japan's Foreign Direct Investment, by Region*

Percent

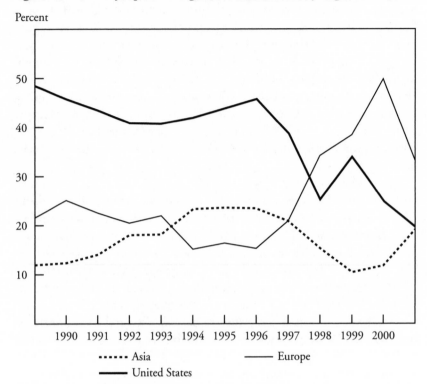

Source: Ministry of Finance, Japan, "Outward Direct Investment: Country and Region" (www. mof.go.jp/english/fdi/reference01.xls [June 29, 2002]).

increase in the share to Asia might be a temporary effect that will subside when the U.S. economy recovers.

Overwhelmingly, Japanese direct investment is not occurring in developing countries at all, but in the developed world. While the shares of investment in the United States and Europe have varied, the two together accounted for 60 to 75 percent of direct investment over the course of the 1990s, with the single exception of fiscal year 2001, when their share was 55 percent; however, that is likely to be an aberration rather than a new trend. Exactly why investment in Europe rose so sharply since the second half of the 1990s while the U.S. share fell is unclear, but the larger picture shows a continuing high percentage of investment occurring in developed countries. The modest downshift in the combined share in fiscal year 2001

Figure 4-8. *Japan's Foreign Direct Investment, by Region*

Trillions of yen

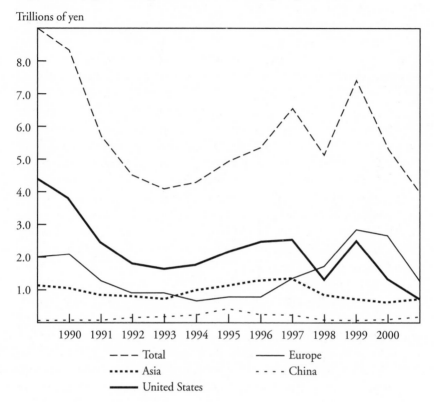

Source: Ministry of Finance, Japan, "Outward Direct Investment: Country and Region" (www.mof.go.jp/english/fdi/reference01.xls [June 29, 2002]).

was likely caused by temporary factors, such as the reduced profitability of some of the Japanese leading firms that had been active in acquiring European and American firms. The idea that one gets from the extensive talk in the Japanese media about the "hollowing out" of Japan's manufacturing sector and investment in Asia (with China figuring prominently is these images over the past several years) is that a much higher share of investment must be headed in that direction. But so far Japanese investment remains firmly embedded in other developed countries, not its Asian neighbors. Low labor cost is by no means the only reason for investing overseas; often proximity to customers, the ability to circumvent import barriers, and other factors predominate.

It also is worth looking at the actual amount of Japanese foreign direct investment, shown in figure 4-8. Starting in the mid-1980s, Japanese outward direct investment began to rise rapidly, but when the domestic asset price bubble burst at the beginning of the 1990s and the economy entered a decade of stagnation, Japanese firms initially sharply curtailed their overseas investments, a significant portion of which had been the same sort of speculative real estate deals that had gotten them into trouble at home. But after the mid-1990s, investment rose again, driven by the strong yen that prevailed in 1993–95. After 1997 the pattern became somewhat uneven, with some indication that the upturn in investment has been blunted by continuing economic problems at home, which have decreased corporate profits and investment in general.

Investments in Asia show a more definite trend. Asia was less affected by the downturn in investment in the early 1990s, and investment rose to a peak of ¥1.4 trillion in fiscal year 1997 ($12 billion at then-current exchange rates). But thereafter, the amount of direct investment flowing from Japan to Asia dropped by almost half, to only ¥773 billion by fiscal 2001 ($6.4 billion), a 47 percent drop in dollar terms. In China, investment dropped from a peak of ¥432 billion ($4.6 billion) in 1997 to only ¥180 billion in fiscal year 2001 ($1.5 billion)—a very large 58 percent decline in yen terms and an even larger 68 percent drop in dollar terms. This is a very important fact because it so completely contradicts the Japanese media hype about investment in China. Since about 2001, the Japanese media have perpetuated the notion that Japanese firms are flocking to China to locate their factories. To be sure, fiscal year 2001 investment in China was up from a temporary low of only ¥80 billion in fiscal 1999, but the ¥180 billion in fiscal 2001 was still low relative to earlier Japanese investment in China and as a share of total Japanese foreign direct investment.

Direct investment involves much more than just manufacturing, which has been the focus of the talk of "hollowing out," so it is worth looking separately at what has happened to manufacturing investment, shown in figure 4-9. Japanese global overseas manufacturing investment has bounced around since 1989, affected by exchange rates, particular large acquisitions in certain years, and the profitability of the investing firms. After a burst of manufacturing investment abroad in the late 1980s, the onset of economic stagnation and the consequent reduction in profits (from which companies finance investment) caused investment to subside in the early 1990s. Then the surge in the value of the yen in 1993–95 led to renewed investment

Figure 4-9. *Japan's Foreign Direct Investment in Manufacturing, by Region*

Trillions of yen

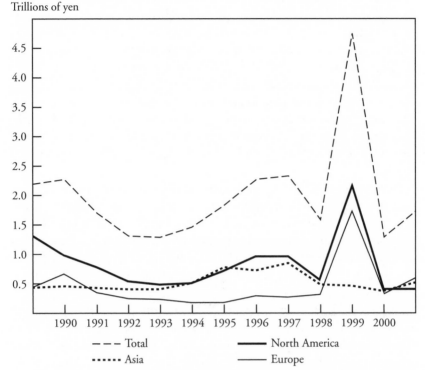

Source: Ministry of Finance, Japan, "Outward Direct Investment: Country and Region" (www. mof.go.jp/english/fdi/reference02.xls [June 29, 2002]).

overseas. Subsequently poor financial conditions at home have led to a decline in investment, except in 1999, which appears to have been characterized by several unusually large acquisitions in Europe and the United States.

The manufacturing investment data for Asia parallel the overall investment data. After peaking in 1997, the annual flow dropped by 44 percent in yen terms—almost in half. This reaffirms the disconnect between Japanese concerns over "hollowing out" and the reality of investment flows. Equally important, Asia is by no means the predominant location for Japanese manufacturing investment. In almost every year, either Europe or North America absorbed more Japanese investment in manufacturing than

Asia did. Even as the hollowing out talk was increasing in 2001, Asia absorbed only 29 percent of total Japanese foreign investment in manufacturing, with Europe taking 34 percent and North America 25 percent.

The data in figure 4-9 lead to two important points. First, economic malaise has affected the ability or desire of Japanese firms to invest abroad, including in its Asian neighbors. The very strong value of the yen in the mid-1990s obviously encouraged more firms to invest overseas, although at the same time that the amount and share of investment going to Asia were increasing, so too was investment in North America. After the mid-1990s, though, the financial problems of Japanese firms and the retreat of the yen from its historic high dampened overall investment, including investment in Asia.

Second, the notion of Japanese manufacturing hollowing out as firms fly to Asia is largely nonsense, since Asia as a whole does not absorb the major share of Japanese overseas investment. Even with manufacturing investment, the bulk of investment has gone to North America and Europe. For the period from 1996 through 2001, an average of 25 percent of Japan's foreign direct investment in manufacturing went to Asia, while 40 percent went to North America and 26 percent to Europe. Thus, even in manufacturing, Japanese firms have many reasons other than cheap labor to move abroad, and those reasons result in much more investment going to developed countries (66 percent) than developing ones. If Japanese want to worry about "hollowing out," they should worry about the loss of high-value-added manufacturing jobs to other developed countries rather than the loss of low-value-added jobs to neighboring Asian countries. What matters for this analysis is the fact that even in the area of manufacturing investment, Japan is hardly moving away from the West and attaching itself more closely to Asia. To be sure, the share of manufacturing investment absorbed by Asia is large, but it is not rising, and the connections with North America and Europe remain equally strong. If the rationale for creating closer ties with Asia is to cement increasing investment, it appears dubious from the standpoint of Japanese investment behavior.

Because Japan is a large, high-wage, technologically advanced industrial nation, it is natural to think primarily in terms of Japanese investment in other countries. Nevertheless, in considering how Japan is connected to the outside world, investment in Japan—both the amount and the source— also matters. The low level of investment in Japan was characteristic of the country for the second half of the twentieth century, even though the amount grew explosively at the end of the 1990s. In addition, very little of

Figure 4-10. *Direct Investment in Japan, by Source*

Trillions of yen

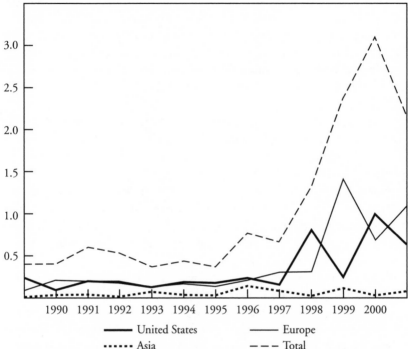

Source: Ministry of Finance, Japan, "Inward Direct Investment: Country and Region" (www. mof.go.jp/english/e1c008.htm [June 28, 2001]).

this investment has come from the rest of Asia. Figure 4-10 presents data on the inflow of investment from Asia, the United States, and Europe.

Throughout the 1990s, investment in Japan was dominated by the United States and Europe, with the balance between them fluctuating from year to year, depending for the most part on single large investments. From fiscal year 1989 to 1995, total inward investment was quite low, averaging about ¥384 billion (only $2.8 billion at then-current exchange rates). In 1989, the United States and Europe together represented 80 percent of new investment in Japan and Asian countries only 4 percent. After 1995, total investment exploded, reaching a peak of ¥3.1 trillion ($29 billion) in fiscal 2000. At the lower ¥2.2 trillion ($18 billion) of fiscal 2001, the

United States and Europe still represented 80 percent and Asia only 3 percent. In fact, the shares of the United States and Europe were probably higher, since investments by foreign companies already in Japan financed by local funds are counted as a separate category and are not broken out by country of corporate control. American and European firms would be the primary source of such investments. In only two years, 1996 and 1999, do investments from Asian countries show an uptick, reflecting sudden jumps in investments from Singapore, which probably reflect single acquisitions in each year.

These data on inward investment suggest several important points. First, Japan has not been strongly connected to the outside world by the presence of foreign-owned firms in its domestic economy. Given that the high level of inward investment in 1999 amounted to only 1.1 percent of domestic capital formation, as shown in table 4-2, the inflow of earlier years was truly trivial. Inward investment would have to continue at an even higher level than in the recent past for the stock of foreign investments in Japan to begin to approach the levels that prevail today in other industrial countries or around the rest of Asia.

Second, Asian firms have been an insignificant portion of total foreign investment in Japan. This matters for trade. Economists view investment as a complement to trade—local investments facilitate the sale of firms' goods and services in the local market, including both those that the firms produce locally and those that are imported. While chapter 3 indicated that Asian exports to Japan have risen, the lack of investment in Japan by Asian firms implies that these exports are carried out largely by Japanese firms. The nationality of the firm carrying out the trade matters; exporting firms generally prefer to maintain control of their products, selling in the foreign market through their own local subsidiaries rather than relinquishing control at the border. The fact that Asian firms are not handling the marketing and sale of their products in Japan limits their ability to penetrate the market, since the Japanese firms doing the marketing and sales often are less vigorous in marketing or more susceptible to anti-import cartel pressures from their Japanese competitors. In addition, from a Japanese perspective, Asia is almost invisible as an investment presence in Japan. Direct investment in Japan therefore provides no indication of a growing regional orientation.

Third, the connection that the Japanese see is with the United States and Europe rather than Asia. That was true throughout the 1990s and earlier. Even though the amounts of annual inflow remain small relative to

GDP, enough highly visible investments have occurred to make American and European firms a known presence in Japan. Shinsei Bank, owned wholly by Ripplewood Holdings of New York; Japan Leasing, the largest industrial leasing firm, owned wholly by GE Capital; and Nissan Motor Company, 38 percent owned by Renault, are some examples. Through such investments, the Japanese have come to have a greater sense of connection to the industrialized nations of the West.

CHINA. In the case of China, investment connections with Japan do not stand out. However, regional connections made through Hong Kong are very strong. Some of the inflow of investment from Hong Kong undoubtedly represents money from Taiwan or elsewhere, though there is no particular reason to believe that much of it is from Japan, the United States, or other developed nations. In fact, investment from Hong Kong reputedly includes a considerable amount from China itself being laundered through Hong Kong to obtain the favorable tax treatments available to foreign investors. Figure 4-11 shows the trends from 1986 to 1999 in the inflow of foreign direct investment by national origin.

In the 1980s, the share of investment from Japan was 10 percent of the total or just above that amount; in the 1990s, it was generally a bit below 10 percent. Therefore Japanese firms in general have been no greater investors in China than American firms. In fact, investment from Japan, the United States, and the EU and official investment from Taiwan all have been relatively close. While the argument can be made that China does have a strong regional connection because of Hong Kong's extraordinarily high share of the total inflow of investment, that conclusion must be tempered by the recognition of the political reintegration of Hong Kong into China. But the more important conclusion is that Japanese investment does not stand out relative to that from the United States or Europe.

These data suggest two important conclusions. First, from China's perspective, foreign investment is not something that ties the nation to the rest of Asia in any meaningful sense, aside from Hong Kong. China certainly has not experienced any surge in Japanese investment sufficient to justify a closer institutional arrangement with Japan. Second, the investment data suggest that the common perception that shifting trade patterns reflect the relocation of Japanese factories to China is largely erroneous. To be sure, some of the increasing American imports from China are produced by Japanese-owned firms. But if Chinese exports reflect at all the relative national shares of foreign direct investment in the country, then many of these products come from American- or European-owned firms.

Figure 4-11. *Share of Direct Investment in China, by Source*

Percent

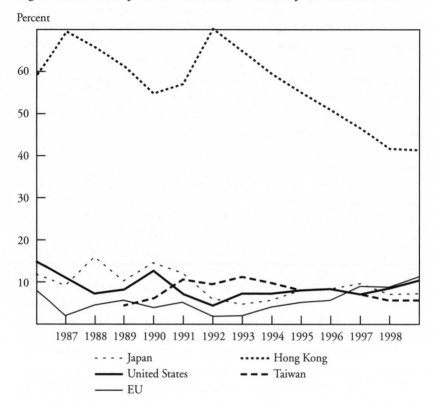

- - - - Japan          •••••• Hong Kong
——— United States    — — Taiwan
——— EU

Source: Ministry of Foreign Trade and Economic Cooperation, People's Republic of China (www.moftec.gov.cn/moftec_cn/tjsj/wztj/2000_9-22-13.html [January 30, 2002]).

SOUTH KOREA.  South Korea is Japan's closest geographical neighbor. Despite the fact that it is now a middle-income nation in which wages are far higher than those in China, wages are lower than those in Japan. The wage gap plus geographical proximity could have led to an investment relationship much like that between the United States and Canada or Mexico. That, however, does not appear to be the case, as shown in figure 4-12. The absolute value of direct investment in South Korea, published by the Korean government in dollars rather than won, has skyrocketed in recent years—from only $803 million in 1990 to $15.7 billion by 2000. Figure 4-12 presents relative shares of the total for each year rather than the dollar amounts.

Figure 4-12. *Share of Direct Investment in South Korea, by Source*

Percent

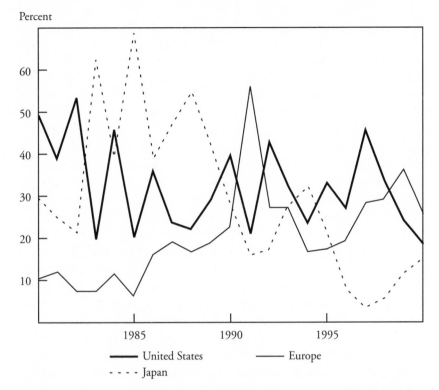

Source: Korea National Statistical Office, *Major Statistics of Korean Economy: 2001*, pp. 298–99.

The shares of major investors in South Korea have fluctuated wildly since 1980. In the 1980s, Japan was the major source of the small inflow of direct investment for a number of years; its share peaked at 70 percent in 1985. But as the total amount of investment rose through the 1990s, the share from Japan decreased. If these data are summarized by decade, the main shift is a drop in the 1990s in Japan's share of the total. In the 1980s, the total dollar value of investments was $5.5 billion, of which Japan represented a dominant 48 percent, the United States 26 percent, and Europe only 15 percent. But in the 1990s, the total inflow of investment was $58 billion (more than a tenfold increase), of which Japanese investment was a very small 12 percent. U.S. investment constituted 28 percent and European investment, 30 percent.

While South Korea was liberalizing its rules for inward investment and economic distress put a number of South Korean companies on the block for purchase, the Japanese did increase their investment in their next-door neighbor—and with explosive growth in the dollar value of the flows, even a shrinking share meant a larger dollar amount of investment. The actual value of Japanese investment in South Korea rose from $2.6 billion over the 1980s to $7.0 billion in the 1990s. However, Japanese firms certainly did not participate in the investment opportunities that were opening up as much as their American or European competitors did. Despite the increased rhetoric about greater regional focus, Japanese firms actually showed less of an increase in investment in their closest neighbor than did firms from other developed countries. From an investment standpoint, South Korea's links with the region have diminished while its links with the United States and Europe have increased.

ASEAN.  Most of the countries that make up ASEAN are too small to make it worthwhile to present individual data for each one. Figure 4-13 summarizes the inflow of direct investment to ASEAN from 1995 through 1999 (without showing the individual years). However, these data should be taken with a grain of salt. Since data collection methods differ among ASEAN countries, the data are not fully comparable across countries. Nevertheless, these countries have attempted to deal with disinvestment (the inflows from some source countries in some years are negative).

Over this five-year period, the largest source of investment was Europe (almost 26 percent), followed by Japan (19 percent), and the United States (18 percent). While Japan certainly was an important investor, it clearly did not dominate investment in ASEAN. Slightly behind the United States was ASEAN itself, with investments from one ASEAN member country in another totaling just under 16 percent, followed by the Northeast Asian middle-income countries (Hong Kong, Taiwan, and South Korea), whose investments totaled 13 percent. Of the investments by ASEAN countries themselves, note that Singapore, which supplied only 3.5 percent of total investment, is not the predominant source. As it is the financial hub of Southeast Asia, that is somewhat surprising.

These data indicate that the ASEAN countries are about equally dependent on East Asia and the West as a source of direct investment. Of the countries or regions shown in the figure, the ASEAN nations received 46 percent of their inward direct investment from developed nations outside the region (including Australia/New Zealand, Europe, and the United States) and 47 percent from within the region (Japan and ASEAN and

Figure 4-13. *Share of Direct Investment in ASEAN, by Source, 1995–99*

Percent

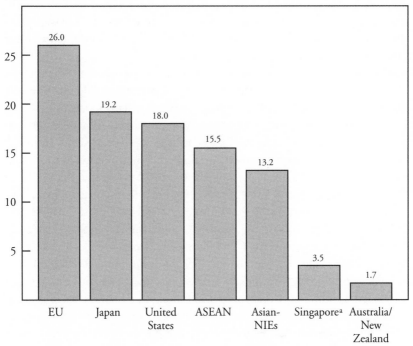

Source: ASEAN Secretariat, *ASEAN Statistical Yearbook*, p. 135, table VI.2 "FDI in Asia by Source Country and Year During 1995–2000" (www.aseansec.org/macroeconomic/cataloguing.htm [August 2, 2002]).

a. Breakout of Singapore from the ASEAN total.

non-ASEAN East Asian countries) over this period. More than other parts of East Asia, therefore, the ASEAN countries do appear relatively closely tied to one another and to the rest of East Asia through direct investment. But the fact remains that more investment comes from Europe than from Japan, and that American investment is roughly equal to that from Japan. Investment from other parts of East Asia total a sizable amount, but the amount from any individual nation other than Japan is relatively small.

A major issue for the ASEAN countries has been the fear that the opening of China, and especially its accession to the WTO, is leading to a redirection of direct investment from ASEAN countries to China. The overall evidence on capital flows certainly shows a decline in investment in

ASEAN while investment into China has increased. While investment in China increased from $27 billion in 1996 to $45 billion in 1999, investment in ASEAN dropped from $28 billion to only $11 billion. A superficial glance therefore might suggest that China, because of its low wages and the anticipation of its entry into the WTO, attracted more foreign direct investment at the expense of ASEAN countries.

However, investment in China does not seem to have come at the expense of the rest of Asia. China (including Hong Kong) claims 70 percent of the direct investment in the East Asian region other than Japan, but rising investment in China has, as one study notes, been accompanied by rising investment in South Korea.[12] The particular problem faced by ASEAN countries in the past several years has had little to do with China and much to do with their economic problems in the wake of the 1997 financial crisis. Much of the drop in investment in ASEAN from 1996 to 1999 occurred in two countries—Indonesia and Malaysia. Indonesia experienced a $7 billion net shift—from an inflow of $6 billion in 1996 to an outflow of $900 million in 1999. Malaysia experienced a $6.5 billion drop, from an inflow of $7.3 billion in 1996 to only $800 million in 1999. Thus out of the $17 billion drop in inflows to all ASEAN nations over these years, these two countries account for almost $13 billion. In the case of Indonesia, the financial crisis precipitated a political crisis, finally bringing an end to the increasingly corrupt regime of Suharto but leaving the country in a state of uncertain political stability for several years thereafter. Malaysia reacted to the crisis by imposing capital controls. While they did not affect direct investment, the government created a less hospitable environment for investment of any kind. In contrast, direct investment in some other ASEAN countries was not affected at all, including Singapore and the Philippines. Even Thailand weathered the 1997 financial crisis with little drop in inward direct investment.[13]

These data suggest, therefore, that fears of ASEAN permanently losing out to China on investment inflows are misguided. China provides certain advantages in terms of low wages and a potentially large domestic market. But investment location is motivated by many factors—size of domestic market, political stability, quality of supporting physical infrastructure and business services, robustness of the legal framework for commercial transactions, enforcement of intellectual property rights, ease of international travel, availability of housing and educational services for expatriate families, and a host of others. There is no reason not to expect that ASEAN nations will continue to attract foreign direct investment if they prove to be attractive locations on the whole array of factors affecting investment. To

Figure 4-14.  *Share of Direct Investment in Canada, by Source, 1990, 2001*

Percent

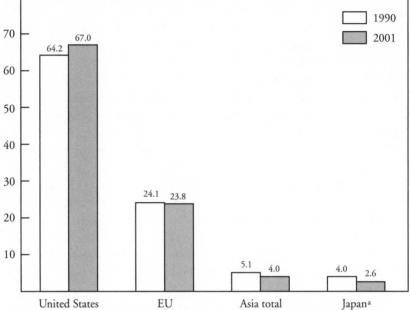

Source: Canada, Department of Foreign Affairs and International Trade, "Statistical Reports—Foreign Direct Investment in Canada" (www.dfait.gc.ca/eet [March 27, 2002]).
a. Breakout of Japan from the Asia total.

be sure, at the margin some foreign firms may relocate factories from ASEAN countries to China to take advantage of lower wages, and these anecdotal cases may play prominently in the media. The larger picture, though, appears rather favorable.

CANADA. Canada provides a useful contrast to the investment situation prevailing in Asian nations, underscoring the relative lack of regionalism in Asia. As the above data demonstrate, both the United States and Europe are major investors in Asia, and the region does not appear to becoming a more cohesive bloc in terms of any pattern of mutual investment. The contrast between Asia and Canada, a member of NAFTA, is striking. Figure 4-14 shows cumulative foreign direct investment in Canada in 1990 and 2001.

The United States dominates investment in Canada. It provided 64 percent of the total cumulative stock (rather than flow in these data) of foreign direct investment in Canada in 1990 and a slightly higher 67 percent in 2001. The EU countries are a distant second, providing 24 percent of investment. Meanwhile, Canada's ties to Asia are tenuous. The Asian countries considered in this study supplied only 5 percent of investment in 1990, and that fell to 4 percent by 2001. Japan is the largest of the Asian investors, but its share—which amounted to only 4 percent in 1990 and 2.6 percent in 2001—is miniscule compared with the total. The 1990 data in this figure follow, of course, the start of the U.S.-Canada free trade area that was the precursor to NAFTA, but since the agreement had only recently gone into effect, its impact on the cumulative value of foreign investment in Canada should have been marginal. Furthermore, the shares did not change much over the course of the 1990s. One Japanese strategy might have been to invest more in Canada in the 1990s to take advantage of somewhat lower wages and the lack of trade barriers, but that was not the case. The main point, however, is to reinforce the difference between Canada's very close investment ties with the United States, a huge economic neighbor with whom it has agreed to a preferential trade arrangement, and Asia. None of the Asian nations, not even South Korea, is as reliant on Japan as a source of inward direct investment as Canada is on the United States.

UNITED STATES. A rather different perspective comes from U.S. investment data. One very important difference between the American data on direct investment and those of most Asian countries is that they attempt to measure disinvestment as well as investment. Rather than attempt to survey actual financial flows, most countries derive their investment data simply from notifications of new investment by foreign companies. American data, for example, show a small net disinvestment by American firms in Japan in both 1996 and 1997, years for which Japanese data show a positive inflow of direct investment by American firms of $3.5 billion.[14] With that important caveat, the percentage shares of the total net outflow of American direct investment by region or country is shown in figure 4-15.

Over the years from 1985 to 2001, the total value of annual direct investment flows from the United States expanded from only $13 billion to $114 billion, peaking at $175 billion in 1999. Of this rapidly expanding dollar amount of direct investment around the world, 30 to 65 percent has gone to Europe (figure 4-15). While the share fluctuates widely from year to year, Europe has consistently absorbed the largest portion of American investment flows. Japan has absorbed very little—a long-standing

Figure 4-15. *Share of U.S. Foreign Direct Investment Annual Flow,
by Region*

Percent

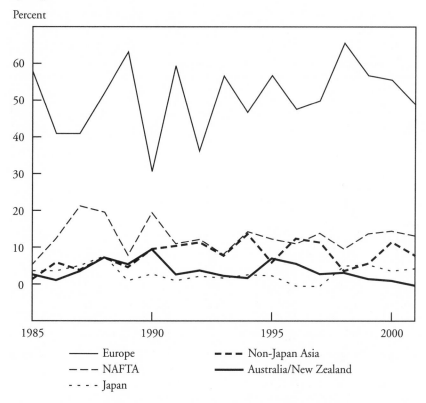

- Europe
- NAFTA
- Japan
- Non-Japan Asia
- Australia/New Zealand

Source: U.S. Department of Commerce, "U.S. Direct Investment Abroad: Balance of Payments and Direct Investment Position Data," individual pages for each year, 1994–2001 (www.bea.doc.gov/bea/di/di1usdbal.htm [July 16, 2002]), and printed tables from *Survey of Current Business*, August 1990, pp. 65–72; July 1993, pp. 101–04; and August 1995, pp. 99–100.

issue in bilateral relations. The very low level of American investment in Japan was once due to official restrictions, but since the early 1980s it has been the result of informal problems, including cartels among domestic firms that suggest that foreign firms would have difficulty penetrating the Japanese domestic market even if they invested in Japan. Only in the late 1990s (with the surge in investment in Japan from around the world indicated in figure 4-10) did American investment in Japan rise—to 4.8 percent of total American direct investments in 2001. Australia and New Zealand, two small economies in the Asia-Pacific region, absorbed more

Figure 4-16. *Share of U.S. Cumulative Foreign Direct Investment,*
*by Region, 2001*

Percent

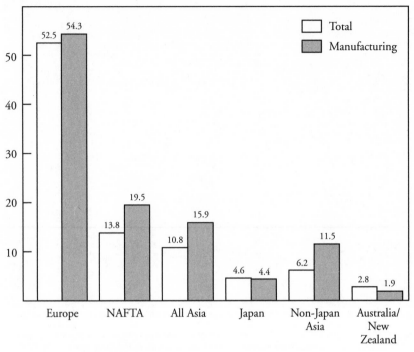

Source: U.S. Department of Commerce, "U.S. Direct Investment Position Abroad on a Historical-Cost Basis: 2001" (www.bea.doc.gov/bea/di/diapos_01.htm [July 16, 2002]).

American investment than Japan did in most years. The rest of the Asian countries considered in this analysis also have composed a somewhat larger destination for American investment. Throughout the 1990s, these countries took roughly 10 percent of annual American investment. Combined, Japan and the rest of Asia have been roughly as important a destination for American investment as NAFTA partners Canada and Mexico.

The overall picture from American data, therefore, is one in which Asia plays a relatively small role in direct investments abroad. This is confirmed by figure 4-16, which shows the location of the stock of American investment as of year-end 2001. Europe received 52.5 percent of all American investment, while NAFTA received just under 14 percent and all of Asia just under 11 percent. The picture for manufacturing investment (which constitutes 27 percent of all American investment abroad) is roughly the same, though in this case Asia receives 16 percent of the total.

These direct investment data are rather different from American trade data. American investment appears far more concentrated on Europe, and the data on annual investment flows do not indicate any strong long-term rise in the relative importance of Asian nations. Even with a surge of investment in Japan in the past several years, the most that one can say is that Asia is a relatively small but certainly measurable location for American investment, roughly as important as NAFTA.

The relative share of U.S. investment in Asia is not significantly different from that of Japan, with investments by Japanese firms heavily concentrated in other developed nations rather than in Asia. To be sure, in some years in the 1990s, Asia took more than 20 percent of Japanese new investments, but the 13 percent of American investment that went to Asia in 2001 is not far behind. The dollar value of the American investment flow also is higher than that from Japan because of the much higher value of the total flow of American investment to the world—$114 billion, in contrast to only $44 billion from Japan; moreover, the Japanese data are biased upward because they do not measure disinvestment. In 2001 American firms invested $9 billion in non-Japan Asia, while Japanese firms invested the equivalent of (at most) $6 billion. Japanese investments had fallen from earlier years, but even adding up investments over the whole decade from 1991 to 2001 (and adjusting the Japanese yen-denominated data for annual exchange rate changes), American firms invested a cumulative $92 billion in the region, while Japanese firms put, at most, $90 billion into the region. Thus American investment has been at least as large as Japanese investment—if not larger, considering the absence of any measure of disinvestment in the Japanese data. With the drop in the value of Japanese investments since the mid-1990s and the continued expansion of the annual dollar value of American investments, a relative shift is occurring away from Japan toward the United States as a source of direct investment in Asian countries. With direct investment as with trade, the notion that the region is becoming increasingly closely connected to Japan at the expense of the United States is simply untrue.

## Conclusion

Investment forms an economic linkage among nations every bit as important as that formed by trade, but it is studied less because of the lack of good data. The data that do exist, however, largely confirm the picture of Asia that emerges from the trade data: the region is not coalescing. Japan is the logical hub of any Asian regionalism based on investment. It is by far the region's largest economy and the world's largest net creditor nation, supplying investment funds to the rest of the world in a variety of forms. In addition, Japan is a very high-wage economy surrounded by lower-income neighbors that form a natural manufacturing "backyard" for Japanese firms.

A decade ago, a transcendent Japan appeared to be in the early evolutionary phase of building an East Asian regional economic bloc. As put by Kozo Yamamura and Walter Hatch in the mid-1990s, Asia was in "Japan's embrace."[15] In retrospect what was transpiring appears to have been a side effect of the domestic asset price bubble that affected Japan in the late 1980s. After experiencing high economic growth for five years and feeling flush with paper wealth, the Japanese government and private sector embarked on an orgy of overseas investment activity. Foreign aid, bank loans, and direct investment all expanded rapidly, and some was directed to Asia, thereby creating the image of an Asia that was becoming increasingly reliant on its enormous regional neighbor.

The data presented in this chapter indicate very strongly that the emerging trends of the late 1980s have not continued. Japan remains the world's largest net creditor, but since 1997 the rest of the region has moved away from being net absorbers of capital. It is not East Asia but the United States, with its persistent global and bilateral current account deficit with Japan, that has been the major absorber of net capital flows from Japan. Japan continues to send a high portion of its bilateral foreign aid to Asia, but the growth of its foreign aid came to a halt in the 1990s and is now in decline. Bank loans were rising rapidly in the early 1990s, to both the region and the world, but Japanese banks have been in serious retreat since 1997. Given their continuing troubles at home, a number of years will pass before they are ready to reenter international lending markets. Despite the emergence of moderately sophisticated capital markets, especially in places like Singapore and Hong Kong, the portfolio investments of the Japanese are overwhelmingly in the West, not Asia. Finally, Japanese direct investment abroad also is largely in the West, not Asia. That is true even for manufacturing investment, in contrast to the popular perception in Japan of a hollowing out of the manufacturing sector because Japanese firms are fleeing to Asia, and to China in particular.

The investment picture from the perspective of East Asian countries reinforces this story. For those countries receiving foreign aid, Japan has remained the largest single source, although the amount is no longer growing. More important, the lavish amounts of foreign aid that Japan dispensed to other Asian nations did not provide Japan with economic or political advantages in the region, given the trends in the trade data analyzed in the previous chapter and in the investment data considered here. Asian countries went through a period in the mid-1990s during which Japanese banks were their single largest lenders, but with the decline in Japanese lending, that situation has now changed dramatically. Moreover, American and European firms are as important as or more important than Japan as a source of investment flows. Indeed, Japan has become less important as a source of investment since the mid-1990s because Japanese firms have been beset with various problems at home that limit their expansion. And when Asian firms invest abroad, little investment goes to Japan, since Asian investors make up only a miniscule share of Japan's own, limited, inward direct investment.

In short, these data do not paint a picture of a region that has adopted an increasingly inward-focused investment posture. The private sector gross flows for which data from the region are available—bank loans and direct investment—demonstrate continuing close ties to the United States and Europe. Investment trends, therefore, do not point toward a narrow Asian region as a logical institutional grouping. As the next chapter shows, initial efforts to form a regional economic institution focused on the much broader Asia-Pacific region, including both the United States and Australia/New Zealand.

# 5 *Broad Regional Institutions*

Over the past forty years, several regional economic institutions have emerged involving the East Asian nations considered in this book. Behind these institutions has been the philosophy that groups of nations with significant economic links ought to engage in dialogue on the various issues and problems that those links entail. Implicit in this approach was the belief that certain issues are truly regional in nature and that separating discussion of them from the dialogue on global trade and finance was thereby justified. Furthermore, those advocating regional discussions in Asia Pacific believed that the governments and private sectors of countries within the region were extraordinarily ignorant about each other and that dialogue would provide a better base of understanding and information for policymaking.

This chapter considers those organizations whose conception of the region has been broad—those that include as part of an Asia-Pacific region the United States, Australia/New Zealand, and other nations not part of the East Asian region defined in this analysis. The evolution of these organizations has been slow, fraught with political difficulties stemming from the cold war. Initially, it was not possible to involve China or other communist countries, and then it was difficult to have both China and Taiwan in the same organization.

The organizations considered in this chapter are the Asian Development Bank (ADB), the Pacific Basin Economic Council (PBEC), the Pacific Trade and Development Conference (PAFTAD), the Pacific Economic Cooperation Council (PECC), and Asia Pacific Economic Cooperation (APEC). The Asian Development Bank is one of the regional development banks created in the wake of the World Bank. PBEC is a business group that began in the 1960s, bringing executives from around the region together once a year, but it has never evolved beyond a networking opportunity. PAFTAD is an academic group dating from the late 1960s that explores policy options for regional economic cooperation; it played a useful role in the eventual creation of APEC. PECC, created in 1980, is a government-business-academic group in which government officials participate as private citizens; it served as a stepping-stone in the formation of APEC. Finally, in 1989, APEC emerged as an official government-level group.

Since its inception, APEC has become the major forum for broad regional dialogue. The visibility of this dialogue was enhanced in 1993 when APEC added an annual leaders' meeting to its agenda. Equally important, in 1994 APEC adopted an ambitious target for eliminating trade and investment barriers throughout the region. While the gradual drift that eventually produced APEC and its policy goals is laudatory, the record of APEC's accomplishment is meager. Since APEC pertains to dialogue rather than negotiation, progress toward the goals of trade and investment liberalization has been quite limited.

This chapter traces the historical development of the broad Asia-Pacific dialogue undertaken in APEC. While there appears to have been a logical, useful progression toward a broad regional government-level institution that can increase the ease of doing business throughout the region, ennui characterizes the current situation. Mention of APEC in Washington often brings little more than a yawn. Because actual progress toward a liberalized trade and investment framework for the region has been so limited, Americans are impatient with it. On the other hand, some Asian nations, Japan in particular, have been unhappy that the Americans (and some others) have tried to use APEC to push aggressively for a set of liberal trade and investment goals.

Nevertheless, APEC remains an important institution, and it is a central part of this analysis. The alternatives to APEC, considered in the next three chapters, all exclude the United States and other economic players that would logically fit in an Asian regional organization. All the data in the previous two chapters suggest strongly that a regional dialogue including the United States, Australia, and New Zealand makes more sense than these narrower alternatives. The solution lies in finding an agenda for APEC that can satisfy both the impatient Americans and the cautious Asians and reenergize the broad dialogue.

## Asian Development Bank

The Asian Development Bank (ADB) might seem peripheral to the central theme of this chapter—the evolution of regional institutions promoting dialogue on regional economic issues. However, the ADB is important, for several reasons. First, it was the initial foray into regional cooperation at the government level. Second, economic development has always been an important regional issue because the region contains so many countries that are at different stages of economic development. Third, the history of the ADB provides some insight into the nature of Japanese leadership within the region.[1]

The ADB, formed in 1966, is part of the World Bank system, which includes two other regional banks, one for Latin America and one for Africa. The ADB extends beyond the Asian region as defined in this analysis, including among its borrowers South Asia and the Central Asian countries that emerged after the breakup of the Soviet Union. Over the years, the ADB has become a mid-sized lending institution ($5 to $9 billion in new loans per year) that makes subsidized loans (both "hard" loans at near-market interest rates and "soft" loans at near-zero rates) and offers small grants to developing countries in the region.

The initiative for forming the bank came largely from Japan. An advisory group to the Japanese government produced a detailed proposal for an Asian development bank as early as 1963, and while other Asian countries made similar early proposals, including a substantial one from Thailand in 1963, they faded in favor of the Japanese version.[2] One might imagine that the ADB arose from cold war concerns: by 1964 American involvement in Vietnam was exploding, and the promotion of economic development in a capitalist setting clearly was part of the U.S. cold war strategy. However, that does not appear to be the case. The bank was mainly the result of a very determined effort by the Japanese government to regain its regional prestige and reemerge as a regional leader. Japan's empire crashed with the end of the Second World War, but a number of officials, politicians, and intellectuals in the postwar period had wanted since shortly after the war to reconstruct Japan's regional leadership role. The ADB was the first realistic expression of that desire, and it focused on a liberal, cooperative development agenda that might be construed as atoning for Japan's wartime behavior.

This early effort at regional leadership was constrained by the very close and unequal postwar relationship between the United States and Japan. Whereas the African Development Bank's membership was composed entirely of countries within Africa, Japan proposed from the outset that the United States be a member of the Asian Development Bank and share an equal equity position with Japan. Nevertheless, the original Japanese proposal was for a bank that would be physically located in Tokyo, creating a visible symbol of power and prestige and putting the Japanese government in a much better position to play a dominant role.[3] One analyst of this period notes that although the Japanese government fought a desperate diplomatic battle to have the building located in Tokyo, it lost to the Philippine government and settled instead for presidency of the organization.[4] The fact that the initial effort focused on obtaining the building rather than the presidency lends some credence to the notion that Japan's objective was to increase its own stature rather than promote any moral or practical agenda for economic development. A focus on symbolism, not any real intellectual or practical agenda, has been a frequent characteristic of Japanese attempts at leadership in the region.

The starting point in 1966, therefore, was a bank with its headquarters in Manila, a Japanese president, and both regional members and members from Western developed nations. Japan and the United States had equal voting rights. From thirty-one original member countries, the ADB had grown to sixty members by 2001—forty-three from within the region and seventeen from outside the region. The voting shares for Japan and the United States remain essentially unchanged, with each country holding a 15.9 percent share in 2001.[5] Through a tacit understanding between the U.S. and Japanese governments, the president of the bank has been Japanese since the beginning (through similar tacit understandings, the World Bank president has always been an American and the president of the International Monetary Fund a European).

Like the World Bank, the Asian Development Bank maintains three financially separate operations. The bank makes "hard" loans at near-market interest rates from the ordinary capital reserves (OCR), "soft" loans at near-zero rates from the Asian Development Fund (ADF), and techni-cal grants from its technical assistance fund. Over time, the bank has grown to be a moderate-sized financial institution. In 2001 it had a total staff of 2,163 and total assets of $45 billion in the OCR and $20 billion in the ADF. Total assets included $29 billion in outstanding loans made through the OCR and $15 billion through the ADF. The technical assistance pro-gram is rather modest; $56 million in technical assistance grants was dis-bursed in 2001.[6]

These numbers should be put into some perspective. The total assets of the ADB (OCR plus ADF) are only 5 percent of the size of the largest Japanese commercial bank (Mizuho Holdings) and 6 percent of the size of the largest American financial institution (Citigroup).[7] ADB loans to the region also can be compared with total international bank loans. Exclud-ing Hong Kong and Singapore, the data in figure 4-4A show $222 billion in outstanding international loans to the region at the end of 2001. ADB data indicate that about $33 billion of its total loan assets (OCR plus ADF) in 2001 were loans to the East Asian countries considered here;[8] the ADB therefore supplied about 15 percent of international loans to the region. If one includes commercial lending to Hong Kong and Singapore (which, of course, are not eligible for ADB loans), the ADB share of total bank lend-ing to the region is only 8 percent.

As shown in figure 5-1, lending by the ADB was largely stagnant in the 1990s, except for a spike generated by the Asian financial crisis in 1997. These data track the gross value of new loans disbursed—that is, without subtracting the value of repayment of existing loans. On this basis, lending by the bank grew very quickly from the late 1970s through the 1980s, ris-ing more than fivefold, from less than $1 billion dollars in the 1973–77 period to $5 billion by 1992. The 1997 financial crisis led to a jump in new lending of more than $9 billion when the bank stepped in at the request of the IMF and creditor nations to provide emergency financing, and some of these loans were disbursed in 1998 and 1999. But following that burst of lending, the bank retreated. New loans in 2001 amounted to only $4 billion, no more than back in the late 1980s.

The Japanese government has exercised a voice in the ADB through means other than the presidency. While voting rights are evenly split with the United States (which also determines the allocation of financial contri-butions to the OCR), Japan actually is a much larger donor to the bank than the United States is. Japan provided an absolute majority of 51 per-cent of member government contributions to the soft-loan ADF as of the

Figure 5-1. *Annual New Lending by the Asian Development Bank*[a]

Percent

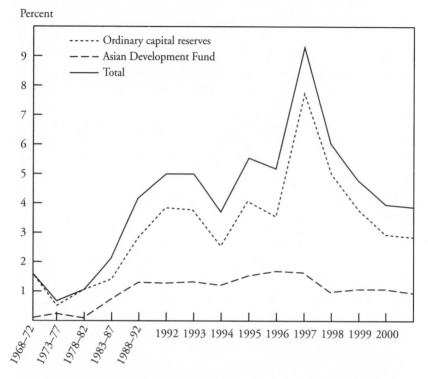

Source: Asian Development Bank, *Annual Report 1998*, pp. 264–65; *Annual Report 1999*, p. 252; *Annual Report 2001*, pp. 132, 162; and Edward J. Lincoln, "The Asian Development Bank: Time to Wind It Up?" in Mark Beeson, ed., *Reconfiguring East Asia: Regional Institutions and Organisations after the Crisis* (Routledge Curzon, 2002), p. 209.
a. Data for 1968 up to 1992 represent five-year annual averages.

end of 2001.[9] Furthermore, the ADB has a Japan Special Fund (JSF), which includes only annual donations from Japan. Technical assistance financed by the JSF came to $70 million in 2001, making it larger than the ADB's technical assistance special fund, which disbursed $56 million in 2001. In addition, the Japanese government wholly funded the temporary Asian Currency Crisis Support Facility, which disbursed $16 million in technical grants, interest payment assistance, and loan guarantees in 2001 and $241 million over its three-year lifespan. Of the total grants disbursed by the ADB in 2001, the Japanese government financed 61 percent.[10]

The Japanese government also has been able to increase its influence at the ADB by becoming actively involved in cofinancing. Eager to expand the leverage of its own modest funds, the ADB has actively courted cofinancing from its members since the early 1980s. As recently as 1999, $3.2 billion in ADB lending (OCR and ADF combined) involved deals in which cofinancing provided an additional $3 billion. Of that $3 billion, $1.7 billion (56 percent) came from Japanese sources.[11] The proportion was even higher than it was during the 1980s, when it varied considerably on an annual basis but generally ranged from 20 to 40 percent.[12] Virtually all of the Japanese cofinancing came from a single Japanese source—the Japan Bank for International Cooperation (JBIC), the principal Japanese aid loan agency, which arose from the newly amalgamated Exim Bank and Overseas Economic Cooperation Fund. Inexplicably, JBIC was not involved in any ADB cofinancing in 2001, although because the ADB approved less than half the amount of cofinancing deals in 2001 that it had in the previous several years, that was likely a fluke related to the timing of lending decisions rather than a change in policy by the Japanese government.[13]

Finally, the Japanese government has been able to increase its role through the new Asian Development Bank Institute (ADBI), a research organization focusing on economic development in the region. Established in 1998, the ADBI is entirely financed by the Japanese government, and it is located in Tokyo—a small victory some thirty years after Japan failed to get the entire ADB headquartered there. Although the research staff is largely non-Japanese, informal interviews lead to the conclusion that the ADBI was conceived as a vehicle to allow the Japanese government to propound its theories about Asian economic development as ADB doctrine.

The history of the Asian Development Bank yields two important conclusions of consequence to the issue of Asian economic regionalism. First, despite the involvement of the U.S. government, the de facto Japanese leadership of the organization has resulted in policies over the years that the U.S. government has found problematic. Through the 1980s, the American concern was that Japanese influence at the bank had resulted in an inordinate proportion of bank contracts going to Japanese firms. That concern has lessened in the past decade, although data on the national affiliation of companies getting contracts that show Japanese firms reduced to a minor role are somewhat suspect because Japanese firms often operate through local affiliates in which they do not have a formal controlling ownership interest.

More recently, the problem has been that the ideological position of the Japanese government on economic development differs fundamentally from the market capitalism espoused by the United States. The Japanese government has never believed in heavy reliance on market principles in economic development. Japan's own development—especially from the 1930s through the 1980s—relied on an intrusive government role and considerable restraints on markets. As discussed in chapter 2, the government was so alarmed at American pressure on the World Bank to attach market-oriented conditions to its loans during the 1980s that it financed *The East Asian Miracle*, a report produced by the bank, in hopes of demonstrating an alternative paradigm for economic development. The ADB, on the other hand, has provided more fertile ground for the Japanese government's pursuit of its vision of economic development. The ADB presidency, the higher number of Japanese nationals on the staff than at other multilateral institutions, the extensive cofinancing with the Japanese government's foreign aid loan agency, and the creation of the ADBI all helped Japan to pursue its agenda. Even with its equal voting rights, the U.S. government has had a much lower profile at the ADB, though U.S. officials often have disagreed with the policies of the bank.

Second, the ADB is an example of the extent to which Japan's leadership often focuses more on symbols than substance and operates cautiously in the shadow of the United States. As just noted, sometimes Japanese leaders have become involved in real issues—particularly in their disagreement with the United States over the process of successful economic development, with Japan championing a strong, intrusive role for government. However, much of Japan's involvement with the ADB has focused largely on the symbols of leadership. Having the presidency and having the research institute in Tokyo were important to the Japanese government. The president in 2002, Tadao Chino, a former vice minister for international monetary affairs in the Ministry of Finance, made a splash by declaring a new ADB agenda for "poverty reduction," though this "new" agenda was only a copy of an agenda change that occurred at the World Bank a full decade earlier. While Chino had a carefully crafted image as an innovative leader, the reality was more in keeping with Japan's tradition of symbolizing its importance by having its officials occupy prominent positions.

Central to these lessons from the history of the ADB is the nature of Japanese leadership at the regional level. The U.S.-Japan relationship—which involves both close economic ties and the bilateral security treaty that forms the core of Japan's foreign policy—certainly constrains the ability of the Japanese government to act in an independent manner at the regional level. This dilemma has continued despite the end of the cold war. Nevertheless, the government has long nibbled at the edges of the U.S.-Japan relationship, pursuing a quiet regional agenda at odds with American policy whenever it perceived that the U.S. government would not pay close attention or would not object strenuously. That pattern of behavior has often irritated the U.S. government. Although the Japanese government frequently tests the boundaries of tolerable behavior on issues ranging from trade protectionism to East Asian regionalism, the predominance of the U.S.-Japan relationship remains a core reality for Japanese policymakers. Their actions at the ADB have been sufficiently cautious that they have not become a major issue, although the American executive directors at the bank have frequently objected to particular proposals or actions. Japan's deference to the U.S.-Japan relationship while playing around the edges is a theme that is certainly visible in other aspects of Japan's recent role in East Asian regionalism—especially the ASEAN+3 central bank swap agreements considered in chapter 8. Japanese caution and deference to the United States also is obvious to other East Asian nations, which often have wanted the Japanese government to play a stronger role in pressing for regional policies that differ from those advocated by the United States.

Despite the problems with the ADB, it has the potential to play an important part in a revitalized APEC agenda. An important aspect of APEC has been its dialogue on economic and technical cooperation, which to date has concentrated mainly on what individual members might do. However, APEC could agree on a limited set of core projects and then use the ADB to provide the financing. If it does, it would usefully embed the ADB in the APEC process and make APEC a more forceful organization.

## The Pacific Basin Economic Council

The next step on the road to a broad regional dialogue on trade and investment was taken by the private sector, with the formation of the Pacific Basin Economic Council in 1967. The purpose of the PBEC was to create a forum for leading regional business executives to "create business relationships, encourage increased trade and investment, support open markets to lower trade barriers, and address emerging issues likely to shape the Pacific and global economies."[14] In short, the PBEC agenda combines networking (bringing together executives to meet one another for potential business deals) and lobbying members' governments for changes beneficial to business in public policies.

PBEC organizes a large annual international meeting; the location rotates around the region. Its membership consists of national committees, which work independently apart from the annual meeting. By 1999, PBEC had 1,100 corporate members in twenty countries around the Asia-Pacific region.[15] The members of PBEC are shown in table 5-1, along with those of other broad Asia-Pacific organizations. The U.S. national committee has forty-seven corporate members, representing some of the large U.S. corporations that do business in Asia, such as Boeing, Cargill, GE, Weyerhauser, and United Airlines.[16] While these are large corporations with major business interests in Asia, the breadth of American membership in PBEC appears quite limited.

In its early years, PBEC did not appear to have much purpose beyond its expressed goal of creating "relationships," bringing corporate executives into personal interactions that might not otherwise occur. With the advent of APEC, presumably PBEC has gained a somewhat more direct voice in aggregating business opinion and offering it to a government policy body. This is arguably more effective than relying on individual PBEC national committees to press their governments on PBEC policy proposals. In 2001, for example, PBEC played cheerleader to APEC on transparency issues. Noting that APEC had adopted a charter on standards for transactions between business and government, the group endorsed the APEC leaders' directive to their respective ministers to implement "APEC's agreed transparency principles," and it urged APEC economies to place priority on implementing transparency principles in trade facilitation, investment, government procurement, and trade in services.[17]

Nevertheless, the purpose of PBEC and its effectiveness are unclear. The limited American corporate membership suggests strongly that American firms do not see many tangible results from maintaining membership in the organization. To the extent that regional business networking is valuable, PBEC is useful but of only modest importance. Perhaps bringing executives together from across the broad Asia-Pacific region was more important in the late 1960s, when telecommunications and travel across the region were not as well developed. That also was an era in which American firms were actively seeking low-cost imports and a number of Asian nations were aggressively pursuing exports. Other American firms, such as

Table 5-1. *Membership in Asia-Pacific Organizations*

|  | PBEC | PAFTAD[a] | PECC | APEC |
|---|---|---|---|---|
| Australia | X | X | X | X[b] |
| Brunei |  |  | X | X[b] |
| Canada | X | X | X | X[b] |
| Chile | X |  | X | X |
| China | X | X | X | X |
| Colombia | X |  | X |  |
| Ecuador | X |  | X |  |
| Hong Kong | X | X | X | X |
| Indonesia | X | X | X | X[b] |
| Japan | X | X | X | X[b] |
| South Korea | X | X | X | X[b] |
| Malaysia | X | X | X | X[b] |
| Mexico | X |  | X | X |
| New Zealand | X | X | X | X[b] |
| Papua New Guinea |  |  |  | X |
| Peru | X |  | X | X |
| Philippines | X | X | X | X[b] |
| Russia | X |  | X | X |
| Singapore | X | X | X | X[b] |
| Pacific Islands Forum |  |  | X | O[c] |
| Taiwan | X | X | X | X |
| Thailand | X | X | X | X[b] |
| United States | X | X | X | X[b] |
| Vietnam |  |  | X | X |

Source: www.apecsec.org.sg [July 9, 2002]; www.pecc.net/members_listing.htm [July 8, 2002]; www.pbec.org/home/ [July 8, 2002]; http://sunsite.anu.edu.au/paftad/iscmem.htm [July 9, 2002].

a. Steering committee.

b. Founding member of APEC in 1989.

c. The Pacific Islands Forum has observer status in APEC.

Boeing and Cargill, were on the way to being global players in their industries and perhaps found the group useful for their rising business activity in the region. A broad regional business group may have helped them to initiate or enhance mutually beneficial business deals. However, by the beginning of the new century, many firms had their own connections across the region and had little need for an annual confab to pursue their business goals.

## PAFTAD

Given PBEC's limitations, the intellectual path to APEC really begins with the creation of the Pacific Trade and Development Conference, an academic conference series starting in 1968. The steering committee for PAFTAD is somewhat more restrictive than that of the other broad Asia-Pacific groups, as indicated in table 5-1. Neither the Latin American countries, Russia, nor some of the smaller Asian countries are involved, although academics from these countries may be invited as participants at some of the meetings. This group is the result of the efforts of Kiyoshi Kojima, a professor at Hitotsubashi University in Japan, with initial financial support from the Japanese government. Note that shortly after the creation of the ADB, the Japanese government was once again pursuing a modest regional agenda. Kojima's initial intent, and presumably that of the Japanese government, was to hold a conference to discuss the possibility of a free trade area among the advanced industrial nations in the Asia-Pacific region—that is, Japan, the United States, Canada, Australia, and New Zealand, not the Asia Pacific region more broadly. This was an interesting development in Japanese thinking. Rather than focusing on the geographical confines of Asia, the government focused on Japan's role as an industrialized nation and its major economic relationships with other industrialized nations across the Asia-Pacific region. (Japan's emerging reliance on iron and coal imports from Australia added to the existing strong U.S.-Japan relationship.)

From that narrow beginning, PAFTAD blossomed into an annual conference series that has brought together academics from around the region to discuss papers on a wide variety of economic topics, ranging from trade issues to economic development and the operation of financial markets. The principal actors in this series—Saburo Okita and Kojima in Japan, professor Hugh Patrick in the United States, and Sir John Crawford and professor Peter Drysdale of Australia—all were tireless advocates for eventual creation of a government-level dialogue in the Asia-Pacific region. Patrick noted that when APEC came into existence, many of the nongovernmental participants had been involved in PAFTAD conferences over the preceding twenty years.[18]

In the United States, proponents of a government-level Asia-Pacific economic dialogue like Hugh Patrick encountered considerable indifference in Washington, but both the Japanese and Australians found support in their governments. Both Kojima and Okita were close to the government; Okita had even served briefly as foreign minister at the end of the 1970s, a rarity for an academic economist. Drysdale and Crawford were at Australia National University, a government-funded academic institution in Canberra that also serves as a think tank for the government. When APEC finally came into existence, it was largely the result of the efforts of the Japanese and Australians, who had honed their ideas in PAFTAD, working with a still-reluctant United States.

## PECC

The next step beyond PAFTAD came in 1980 with the formation of the Pacific Economic Cooperation Council. PECC came about through the efforts of Saburo Okita and Sir John Crawford, who sponsored a seminar in Canberra in 1980 that launched PECC. Because of the difficulties in getting official government participation, PECC was established as a private nongovernmental organization with individual members from academe (including private research institutes), business, and government (with government officials "acting in their private capacity.")[19]

Formally PECC consists of separate committees in each of the member countries, buttressed by an international secretariat in Singapore. The important though modest step forward that PECC took was to engage government officials in addition to the business and academic communities, which made up the membership of PBEC and PAFTAD. Both of these precursor groups have membership in PECC, which also provides a sense of forward momentum. Although government officials participate in PECC only as private individuals, obviously they give PECC at least a quasi-official status. The unofficial status of this dialogue also has helped to circumvent the Taiwan-China problem, enabling participants, and most important, officials, of both to belong.

While PECC clearly represented a step forward toward government-level regional dialogue, its unofficial status meant that the group could do little more than discuss ideas. Formal meetings of the full membership occur only once every two years; PECC works mainly through task forces, which consider a range of regional economic issues. As an unofficial body, PECC cannot reach conclusions on the lowering of tariff and quota barriers, but it can recommend trade facilitation strategies to its member countries and address development issues.[20] As of 2001, PECC had seventeen task forces doing research and devising policy proposals on issues such as trade, energy, tourism, transportation, and corporate governance.[21]

PECC may be envisioned best as a stepping-stone between PBEC, PAFTAD, and APEC. With the advent of APEC, the role of PECC has become somewhat unclear. As an organization of individuals, however, it has adopted the role of advisory body to APEC, submitting policy proposals arising from its own deliberations. As noted in the PECC charter, it "provides information and analysis to the annual APEC ministerial meetings and supports the activities of APEC working groups."[22] At one point PECC saw itself in a more formal role, critiquing the annual progress within APEC toward accomplishment of its trade and investment policy goals, but this vision has not materialized.

## APEC

The final step toward forming an official intergovernment group occurred as the cold war was ending in 1989. The Japanese government had been pressing hard for such a group, fearful that the United States, ignoring Asia after the end of the Vietnam War, was turning inward and that the trend would worsen with the end of the cold war. The Japanese were further motivated by what they perceived as a rise in American protectionism, mainly because of the imposition of restraints on Japanese auto exports to the United States in the early 1980s and several other protectionist actions in the first half of the 1980s. These measures proved to be short-lived. But it was the Australians who made the formal proposal for Asia-Pacific Economic Cooperation (APEC) and convened the first meeting in 1989. Even with the cold war coming to an end, however, the initial members of APEC did not include China, Taiwan, or Hong Kong, whose inclusion took additional time to negotiate. (The original members of APEC are identified in table 5-1.)

Initially, APEC was composed of trade and foreign ministers from the member countries. Several years later, APEC took a major step forward in importance when the U.S. government added a leaders' meeting to the existing ministerial format. In 1993, President Bill Clinton invited the other APEC leaders to attend the annual meeting scheduled for Seattle. Although political complications have prevented some leaders from attending in some years, this format has continued. In addition, ministerial participation has expanded to include other ministers, such as finance ministers, whose ministries have an economic focus.[23]

In 1995, the APEC leaders' meeting established a permanent advisory group of business leaders consisting of three senior business people from each member country to "provide advice on the implementation of APEC action plans and on other specific business/private sector priorities."[24] Called the APEC Business Advisory Council (ABAC), it has submitted annual reports to the APEC meetings, but how effective these reports and the personal participation of the individual business leaders have been is unclear. The American business community does not regard ABAC as particularly effective, and ABAC members express some dissatisfaction with APEC's lack of responsiveness to their reports and proposals. ABAC's role also overlaps with the role of PBEC, although presumably, as a smaller group, ABAC can play a more effective part. However, even with only three individuals per member country, ABAC still has a somewhat unwieldy membership of sixty-two people.[25]

In 1993 APEC endorsed an education initiative calling for APEC study centers at universities in each of the APEC member countries. These centers, which are informally linked to one another, are engaged in research and education on relevant regional issues. Concerned about the diminished vigor in the APEC process, a subset of leading faculty members at the APEC study centers formed the APEC International Assessment Network (APIAN). This group, much like the eminent persons group (EPG) discussed below, has issued three detailed reports on how APEC might be revitalized. In addition to making recommendations on how APEC should function, the group sees itself as a source of independent, outside evaluation and pressure on APEC governments to carry through on their commitments.[26]

APEC began with no clear agenda other than to meet to explore issues of mutual interest. To help map out a vision of what APEC might accomplish, in 1992 the ministers established an eminent persons group that included government, private sector, and academic representatives, one from each of the twelve original APEC member countries. The American member of this group, and arguably its intellectual leader, was C. Fred Bergsten. The eminent persons group made a variety of recommendations a year later, but principal among them was a call for formation of an Asia-Pacific community characterized by free trade and investment throughout the region, accompanied by a vigorous trade facilitation program.[27]

The free trade proposal was adopted a year later at the APEC summit meeting in Bogor, Indonesia, in 1994. This proposal, dubbed the Bogor Declaration, called for APEC advanced nation members to achieve free trade status by 2010 and developing nation members by 2020. However, the Bogor Declaration failed to define free trade. The eminent persons group had advocated an "open region" in which regional members could work out an elimination of barriers among themselves but then extend these trade benefits willingly to any outside nations on a reciprocal basis. This would have contrasted with the usual free trade area approach of removing barriers only for other members of the group. The failure to define what regional trade would mean has not been resolved and remains a stumbling block.

The Bogor Declaration was followed a year later by the 1995 Osaka Action Agenda, which laid out a blueprint for achieving the broad goals of the declaration. The agenda specified that progress should occur on liberalization of trade and investment, business facilitation, and economic and technical cooperation (dubbed "ecotech"), but it did not resolve the problem of defining regional free trade. APEC chose to pursue liberalization of trade and investment through individual initiatives rather than real negotiations. By not defining free trade and by establishing a weak approach to liberalization, the Osaka Action Agenda has been largely responsible for the meager progress on liberalization since 1995. Weakness of process characterizes all aspects of APEC, since its underlying principle is voluntary action, not binding negotiation. Agreements and codes produced by APEC may or may not be adopted by individual governments, in striking contrast to the more binding commitments involved in WTO negotiations.[28]

Nevertheless, action on the Osaka agenda began in 1996 at the Manila meeting, where the initial reports from all member countries on their individual action plans (IAPs) to advance APEC goals were presented. A very diffuse set of ecotech issues was selected for "focused" attention: developing human capital, fostering safe and efficient capital markets, strengthening economic infrastructure, harnessing technologies of the future, promoting environmentally sustainable growth, and encouraging the growth of small and medium-sized enterprises.[29] Thus, outside the realm of tariff and quota barriers, APEC chose to pursue a rather broad range of trade facilitation and development issues.

Also in 1996, APEC members tried to jump-start the trade liberalization process by approving an information technology agreement (ITA) calling for complete elimination of tariffs on a wide range of information technology products, to be endorsed and forwarded to the WTO. Since a number of APEC members are major producers and consumers of such products, their agreement to this proposal represented a substantial kernel of support in kicking the proposal up to the WTO. At the subsequent WTO ministerial meeting, enough countries approved the ITA that it was

adopted. This success in using APEC as a source of innovative policy proposals for the WTO led some to hope that the process would continue.[30]

However, in 1997 a follow-on effort to bring about APEC acceptance
of an early voluntary sectoral liberalization (EVSL) agreement in fifteen
sectors foundered on Japan's refusal to accept the inclusion of fish and
forestry products on the list. According to APEC, the EVSL is a success,
but in reality it was a failure.[31] It marked the end of activism in trying to
accelerate trade liberalization in APEC, which has led to a sense of drift in
recent years. On the conventional trade liberalization front, the annual
IAPs have produced little besides a rehashing of existing WTO commitments. Observers writing in 2000 noted that "fresh doubts are emerging
from within the Asia-Pacific Economic Cooperation (APEC) forum about
its relevance."[32]

The sense of drift was accentuated by the fact that in both 1997 and
1998 the ministers and leaders were meeting against the backdrop of the
Asian financial crisis, concerning which they took little action. Because traditional trade interests were the primary reason for creating APEC, the
APEC finance ministers, who had not participated in earlier discussions,
met for the first time in 1994. Since that time the finance ministers have
met annually.[33] The Asian financial crisis presented something of a problem for the finance ministers. With the IMF acting as the key multilateral
organization in the crisis, there was no strong role for APEC to adopt. The
finance ministers, meeting in the spring of 1998 (their first since the out-
break of the crisis), did, however, establish several important points. First,
they debunked the notion that the crisis was caused by foreign speculators,
focusing instead on structural problems in the crisis countries. Second,
they endorsed the central role of the IMF (as had the leaders at their meeting in Vancouver in late 1997) and the secondary roles of the World Bank
and Asian Development Bank in handling the crisis. Third, they chose to
keep the APEC focus in longer-term efforts to promote development of
more robust financial markets.[34]

Arguably, the finance ministers could have done more. The Japanese
government, frustrated with IMF policies, proposed creating an Asian
monetary fund to make loans to crisis-hit Asian countries; when that proposal failed, the Japanese government proceeded to provide aid on its own.
It is at least conceivable then that APEC could have chosen to play a strong
role as a source of financing for the crisis countries. That it did not may
have been because the U.S. government and some others believed that the
existing institutions—the IMF, the World Bank, and ADB—were the

appropriate institutions to deal with the crisis. Nevertheless, the decision not to mobilize any short-term APEC initiative to help the countries led to some accusations that APEC was nothing more than a "Western-dominated club trying to push globalization and open markets down the throats of its less-developed Asian members."[35]

At recent APEC meetings—including both the 2001 meeting in Shanghai and the 2002 meeting in Los Cabos, Mexico—the economic agenda was overshadowed by global security issues. In 2001 the Bush administration was focused on lining up support for the war on terrorism and in 2002 for the upcoming war against Iraq. The economic agenda proceeded through a series of preparatory meetings and the annual ministerial meetings, but it was not a key component of the leaders' meeting.

The Shanghai meeting in 2001 illustrates the very modest accomplishments on APEC's economic agenda. The annual ministerial meeting just prior to the leaders' meeting produced the Shanghai Accord, which reaffirmed the goals of the Bogor Declaration, established a goal of reducing transaction costs associated with trade by 5 percent by 2006, and strengthened the peer review process for individual action plans. Beyond these actions, the Shanghai Accord consisted of diplomatic talk about the resolve to move forward on a host of other issues (so-called new economy policies, transparency principles, and strengthening "ecotech and capacity building"). About the only statement of any substance in the leaders' declaration was that welcoming the implementation of the Chiang Mai Initiative, the ASEAN+3 agreement in 1999 to strengthen bilateral swap arrangements among the central banks of their members. The only other significant action was to continue a moratorium on customs duties on electronic transmissions until a future WTO ministerial meeting—hardly a major step since all WTO members were supposed to abide by the moratorium. The rest of the document was a classic example of vague diplomatic talk without much content.[36]

The 2002 meeting in Los Cabos continued the pattern of taking modest steps. The leaders endorsed the start of the Doha round of WTO negotiations, but on the issue of agriculture they did not go beyond calling for the end of agricultural export subsidies or other export restrictions; they ignored the major sticking point, agricultural import barriers. But they also endorsed an APEC action plan for trade facilitation (with the goal of a 5 percent reduction in trade transaction costs), initiatives on APEC transparency standards, and "pathfinder initiatives" on such issues as simplification and harmonization of customs procedures, advance passenger information systems, and others. Appropriate to the times, the ministers and leaders condemned terrorism and discussed progress on counterterrorism actions, including APEC's action plan on combating the financing of terrorism.[37]

## Membership

Over time, membership in APEC has expanded, from the original twelve members to twenty-one by 2002. China, Hong Kong, and Taiwan entered simultaneously in 1991. Mexico became the first Latin American member in 1993, followed by Chile in 1994 and Peru in 1998. Papua New Guinea joined in 1993, while Russia and Vietnam joined in 1998. Some of these new members do not conform to the original concept of APEC, which was seen as including a set of market economies with close mutual economic ties.

Russia stands out as a new member with minimal economic ties with Asian countries other than China. All the Asian members of APEC absorbed only 10.3 percent of Russia's exports in 2000—2.7 percent went to Japan and 7.6 percent to the rest of East Asia. Meanwhile, an even lower 6.8 percent of Russian imports came from East Asia. Russia's main trading partner has been Europe, with the EU countries taking 36 percent of Russian exports in 2000 and supplying 33 percent of Russian imports. For the past thirty years, the Japanese have discussed stronger trade ties with Russia based on the development of Siberian resources (oil, gas, timber, and others) for export to Japan, but such ideas have yet to come to fruition. With its Pacific ports in Siberia, Russia appears to belong to APEC geographically, but its trade connections with the region are thin.[38]

The new Latin American members have somewhat stronger ties to East Asia. Peru shipped 19 percent of its exports to East Asia in 2000, but only 10 percent of its imports came from there. For Chile, the percentages were somewhat higher: 28 percent for exports and 16 percent for imports. Mexico's trade ties, as noted, are overwhelmingly with the United States. In 2000, for example, East Asia took only a miniscule 2 percent of Mexican exports.[39] Furthermore, in the 1990s the United States supplied 60 percent of direct investment to Mexico while Japanese firms supplied only 3.3 percent.[40] Of the three, Chile is the one whose trade links across the Pacific are most likely to justify its participation in APEC, but the primary trade and investment ties of these countries are with the rest of Latin America, the United States, and Europe.

Inclusion of these new members of APEC has contributed to the sense of drift. Expansion may have had a political logic, but the lack of strong economic links between the newcomers and East Asia has diluted the focus on economic issues. Some in the Japanese government, for example, feel that APEC has become unwieldy, that it has too many members with divergent goals to be able to achieve agreement. While that may be a problem, obviously kicking Russia or the Latin American members out of APEC is not an option.

### Assessment

Has APEC lost its relevance as a regional organization? It certainly has a number of problems, including the lack of a clear definition of "open regionalism" or "free trade and investment" and the weak voluntary process it uses to achieve those goals. However, APEC continues to serve a useful purpose, bringing together government officials in a regular dialogue and achieving some progress on trade facilitation and ecotech issues.

Consider first the problems. The main problem has been the failure to define the concept of open regionalism. The Bogor Declaration clearly stated that APEC was not to become an inward-focused or exclusive free trade area, but what it might be besides a free trade area was not defined. Without a clear concept to guide it, APEC's main activity has consisted of having members report on the trade liberalization measures that they agreed to in the Uruguay round of WTO negotiations or on unilateral measures that they planned to undertake anyway.

The eminent persons group proposed a set of definitions in 1994. In their view, APEC should adopt a four-part definition of open regionalism:

—Members should make maximum effort to lower their own barriers unilaterally on an MFN basis.

—While APEC works out intra-APEC liberalization, it should continue to reduce barriers to nonmembers. That is, APEC could be a free trade area, but one that is committed to moving forward with lowering barriers between itself and the rest of the world.

—APEC should be willing to extend its internal liberalization deals to nonmembers on a mutually reciprocal basis.

—Individual members of APEC should be able to extend APEC liberalization to nonmembers.

What the group had in mind was essentially for APEC to become a free trade area, but one that would engage the world liberally—with individual members and the group as a whole lowering barriers to the world and extending APEC benefits to those willing to reciprocate.[41]

Fred Bergsten further clarified and analyzed possible definitions of open regionalism in 1997. The EPG formulation avoided some of the practical problems with other definitions. For example, if open regionalism meant that all APEC members should unilaterally lower or eliminate their trade barriers on an MFN basis, the cost would be the loss of bargaining power in trade negotiations with states outside APEC, in which the offer to lower trade barriers could be used as leverage. This is a free-rider problem, in which nonmembers of APEC can enjoy the economic gains of lower import barriers negotiated among APEC members without having to increase the openness of their own markets. What the EPG and Bergsten were suggesting was "conditional MFN," in which APEC (or individual APEC members) would offer nonmembers the benefits of lower barriers if they reciprocate.[42] This was, for example, the essence of the 1996 ITA— the deal on eliminating tariffs on information technology products.

However, APEC has not adopted any definition of open regionalism. Other than the experiment with conditional MFN represented by the ITA, the result has been a de facto adoption of only the first of the four principles laid out by the EPG: encouragement of members to proceed with unilateral liberalization on an MFN basis. The outcome has been for members to do little more than report progress on implementation of their Uruguay round commitments.

A further problem has been the failure to define what free trade means. While it might seem obvious to Americans that the term should imply zero tariffs and no quotas, that is not the universal interpretation. The Bogor Declaration and the Osaka action plan speak of eliminating barriers but never specify how absolute that goal is. Indeed, as one commentator noted, in the narrowest sense, developing countries would "only have to lift bans or quotas on foreign products and investments"—that is, the removal of quotas, without any action on tariffs, might be construed to meet the requirements. And apparently the Japanese government felt that it was under no obligation to stop protecting the domestic rice market under the APEC goals.[43]

The final problem on the trade agenda is that the 1995 Osaka agreement established a liberalization process without recourse to traditional trade negotiations. Instead, each member is supposed to effect the unilateral, voluntary liberalization of its markets, with progress announced to the group each year in the IAPs, which are supposed to detail what each government is doing to move closer to the Bogor goal. These IAPs actually cover a broad range of APEC issues beyond tariffs, including many trade facilitation issues.

Theoretically, requiring members to present their IAPs creates peer pressure, since the plans are submitted and discussed at the annual ministers' meeting. Presumably because nations do not want to be viewed as undermining APEC goals, they will be inspired to produce annual progress that they can report to the group. PECC and other groups have periodically issued reports critiquing the quality of the IAPs.

Because the IAPs are lengthy documents and each APEC member submits one, evaluating each year's submissions is a daunting task. At the Shanghai meeting in 2001, APEC strengthened the peer review process. The new procedure involves taking a handful of IAPs each year for a formal review that involves outside experts and representatives from the private sector (members volunteer their IAPs for the review).[44] Greater formality and clarity in the review of the IAPs is a welcome step forward, one that the U.S. government actively pressed for in 2001.[45] But APEC remains stuck with a trade liberalization process in which individual, unilateral action is the only aspect of the EPG's four-part recommendation that has been put in place. The limitations that implies for progress in liberalizing trade is one reason members have turned to bilateral and subregional free trade negotiations.

The problems afflicting the trade liberalization agenda apply to other aspects of APEC as well. The guiding principle is voluntary action. Members either tell the group what they will do individually or engage in discussions that produce voluntary agreements or codes. While APEC can adopt trade facilitation codes and point favorably to members who adopt them, there is no real commitment. On ecotech issues, APEC has no financial resources for implementing any project ideas and relies entirely on the voluntary action of donor countries to adopt them. Linking the ecotech agenda to ADB financial resources as suggested earlier in this chapter would help APEC overcome this weakness.

The foregoing are the principal problems that have led to discouragement about APEC. But what about its positive accomplishments? There are at least four main achievements that continue to make APEC worthwhile.

First, APEC engages government officials across the region in regular dialogue and promotes a specific action agenda. As the breadth of the APEC agenda has widened, the scope of government ministries drawn into the process has grown. This involvement is particularly important for the developing countries in the region, which over time are building a cadre of career officials who regularly interact in a regional dialogue that pushes them in the direction of more liberal policies on trade and investment. APEC now has seventeen separate groups on trade and investment topics ranging from tariffs to intellectual property rights and the mobility of business people. The ecotech agenda has eleven working groups, and there are thirteen other task forces meeting on topics ranging from electronic commerce to sustainable development.[46] Even if specific accomplishments on APEC policy, especially reductions in tariffs, have been weak, the engagement of these officials in regular dialogue has a cumulative effect on their thinking about liberalization. The emerging codes and recommendations imply that officials must engage in action-oriented discussion or negotiation at APEC meetings, even if the outcome is nonbinding. This benefit of APEC may not be very important to American government officials, especially since the United States is an advanced industrial nation with rather open markets, but it is important for the developing nations of the region. Since these countries have many restrictions and rules that affect trade and investment or hinder the growth and development process, drawing their officials into discussions may slowly improve progress on these issues. The danger, of course, is that talk will never evolve into action. John Ravenhill, for example, labels the ecotech agenda as "a triumph of process over substance."[47] And even this author has worried in the past that much of APEC represented "activity masquerading as progress."[48] Nevertheless, exposing government officials from around the region to the value of trade liberalization, trade facilitation measures, and carefully constructed technical cooperation programs certainly has some positive long-term impact.

Second, APEC appears to be making progress on the trade facilitation agenda. To be sure, the goal of a voluntary 5 percent reduction in transaction costs related to trade may not be ambitious; nevertheless, it does represent a specific goal driving APEC discussions toward specific proposals. In many cases, trade facilitation measures do not have the political prominence of tariffs or quotas. Finding ways to expedite and reduce the cost of customs clearance procedures is less likely to irritate a domestic industry as much as lowering the tariff on competing products. But reduction of these costs may have a significant impact on easing access to the market. Therefore, the trade facilitation agenda has been a positive step that should be encouraged.

Third, the ecotech agenda could prove worthwhile as well. For a number of years the U.S. government was wary of efforts by Japan and others to enhance the importance of ecotech issues in the overall APEC agenda. Japan, after all, has been the largest provider of foreign aid to the region, and the U.S. government was reluctant to become involved in a dialogue in which it would be pressured to provide more aid or that would be dominated by a Japanese agenda. But the reality of APEC is that it includes both industrialized and developing countries. This means that APEC has an opportunity to address development issues for the mutual benefit of all—an APEC region characterized by rapidly growing and industrializing economies works to the advantage of all members, including the industrialized ones. This agenda gained greater salience in the wake of the 1997 financial crisis. If APEC was not to play an emergency financial role, then at least it could reinforce efforts to work with the developing countries to strengthen their financial and other economic infrastructure. If the ecotech agenda has a problem, it has been the proliferation of too many issues and a lack of unified funding. These problems could, as suggested earlier, be addressed by linking a core set of ecotech initiatives to ADB financing.

Fourth, the leaders' meeting has emerged as an important component of APEC even if the leaders are not always focused on the economic agenda that gave birth to APEC. APEC provides an opportunity for holding a number of bilateral meetings in addition to the formal group meeting. Some of those bilateral meetings might occur anyway, especially those between the United States and Japan, but many of the APEC members are very small, and bilateral summit meetings, especially with the United States, do not occur often. For example, it was very useful in 2001 for President Bush to press important issues related to the war on terrorism at both the APEC leaders' meeting and with individual leaders, especially China. On one hand, the noneconomic issues that may grab attention might detract from the centrality of the original economic rationale for APEC; on the other, the emergence of serious noneconomic issues gives the leaders' meeting some sense of importance and urgency, which helps to sustain the justification for APEC despite the disappointment concerning its very modest accomplishments on the economic front.

## Conclusion

APEC evolved out of a long campaign stretching back to the early 1960s that was led mainly by the Japanese and Australians. The Japanese were looking for ways to act as a regional leader in Asia, but they recognized the need to have the United States be part of the process—both to ease fears around Asia of Japan's resurgence and to assure the Americans that Japan was not abandoning its new relationship with the United States in favor of renewing Asian regionalism. The Australians needed to attach themselves to their geographic neighbors after losing their imperial trade preference when Britain joined the precursor to the EU in the 1970s. The Americans, on the other hand, initially appeared to be indifferent to an Asia-Pacific economic dialogue, placing their main emphasis on global trade, pushing for global trade negotiating rounds, and on bilateral trade, pushing Japan and some other regional governments to liberalize access to their markets.

Despite American official indifference, small steps led toward the eventual establishment of a government-level regional organization. The ADB created a precedent for a regional organization, made easier for the Americans by the previous establishment of the Inter-American Development Bank in the early 1960s. PBEC brought together Asia-Pacific business executives, starting in the late 1960s. PAFTAD developed the intellectual roots and policy proposals that eventually gave rise to government-level dialogue. PECC brought in government officials in a private capacity. Finally, the Japanese and Australians convinced the Americans to join in creating APEC at the end of the 1980s.

The data provided in chapters 2, 3, and 4 of this book imply that an Asia-Pacific approach makes sense if a regional organization brings together groups that have close economic ties. The United States has continued to be a close economic partner for Asian nations. Australia and New Zealand also have evolved close ties with their neighbors and with the United States. Meanwhile, the Japanese and others worried that the end of the Vietnam War and then of the cold war would cause a broader loss of American interest in Asia. They felt that unless the United States appreciated its strong trade and investment links with Asia, other aspects of American involvement in Asia, including the U.S.-Japan security treaty and the American military presence in South Korea, could be in jeopardy. Thus the movement toward a broad Asia-Pacific dialogue had strong roots in economic and security concerns.

Unfortunately, APEC did not live up to expectations. Its initial drive and energy certainly moved APEC in ambitious directions—elevating the annual meeting to the leaders' level, establishing a long-term free trade and investment goal, and mapping out a set of specific mechanisms and topics to achieve that goal. But after establishment of a weak process at the 1995 Osaka meeting and the failure of the EVSL proposal in 1997, the energy seemed to leak out of APEC. Disappointment over APEC has become an important reason for the proliferation of negotiations for free trade areas and subregional dialogue on financial issues. APEC remains important and relevant, however, and the final chapter explores how it might be reenergized.

Should APEC now be judged a failure and jettisoned in favor of other, newer regional institutions? No. APEC should not be judged entirely by its lack of progress on what, in retrospect, was an overly ambitious goal of free trade and investment. As Hugh Patrick notes, APEC should be judged by the degree to which general trade and investment liberalization continues to take place in the region, not by attainment of a particular goal.[49] Peer review may not lead governments to put more "action" into the annual IAPs, but peer pressure may be able to thwart new protectionist moves. Moreover, participating in the APEC process creates a cadre of government officials, especially in the developing economies of the region, who develop a commitment to trade and investment liberalization.

Meanwhile, APEC now has a well-entrenched process, composed of a number of committees, subcommittees, and working groups that are slowly grinding out progress on a variety of trade facilitation and ecotech issues that are modestly useful for the region. This process is quite bureaucratic, but at least it accomplishes more than would occur in the absence of APEC.

APEC thus has encouraged the move across the region in the general direction of lower trade and investment barriers and progress on trade facilitation. Discontent concerning APEC is rampant, however. The Americans are impatient with a flawed process for generating real progress on trade liberalization. The Japanese fear that APEC may become far more aggressive on liberalization than they envisioned in the late 1980s. China and the Southeast Asian nations want to shift the agenda away from trade and investment toward assistance on their economic development, a move resisted by the Americans. Everyone seems willing to find fault with APEC for not meeting its policy priorities. One consequence of this discontent has been the emergence of narrower approaches to economic regionalism in Asia, considered in the following three chapters.

# 6

## The East Asian Alternatives

Competing with the vision of a broad Asia-Pacific region embedded in APEC is a vision of a narrower East Asian region that has gained popularity in recent years. That vision, which dates back to Japan's establishment in 1940 of the East Asian Co-Prosperity Sphere, is certainly not new, and it was never entirely absent from the thinking of some bureaucrats and intellectuals after the war, especially in Japan. But the recent rise in consciousness of East Asia as a geographic entity deserving of some sort of institutional reinforcement dates mainly to the late 1980s, and it has been espoused by others besides the Japanese. The motives for creating a sense of East Asian regional cohesion and institutions to support it are complex, and any effort to bind the region together must overcome a number of economic and historical impediments. Nevertheless, that effort gained momentum over the course of the 1990s, and interest grew in the wake of the 1997 Asian financial crisis.

The effort has various elements, encompassing the desire for regional dialogue, specific bilateral or regional free trade agreements, and cooperation on exchange rate policies. One could argue that a narrow vision of regionalism began with the Association of Southeast Asian Nations (ASEAN), which dates back to the 1960s, although it did not adopt a strong trade agenda until the 1990s. The Japanese provided the initial impetus for a more broadly defined form of East Asian regionalism in the late 1980s, though it had no regional institutional component. They saw themselves as the self-appointed leader of East Asia, knitting the region together through aid, trade, and investment; however, that vision failed to materialize over the course of the 1990s. Prime Minister Mahathir Mohamad of Malaysia then proposed forming the East Asian Economic Caucus in the early 1990s. That concept also failed to materialize as he envisioned, but it resurfaced in the late 1990s in the guise of the ASEAN+3 dialogue. All of these versions of East Asian regionalism are considered in this chapter.

Throughout discussions of the need for East Asian regional dialogue and the form that it might take, an often unpleasant anti-American or anti-Western rhetoric has surfaced. Frustration over the perception of Western domination is certainly real and openly expressed, but one of the central conclusions of this book is that that rhetoric has resulted in less action to produce a regional bloc than one would expect. This conclusion is comforting, because a narrow form of regionalism based on strong anti-Western sentiments could yield a protectionist region detrimental to American interests.

## Motives for Forming a Regional Bloc

East Asia is economically, historically, and culturally divided. Economically, the nations in the region vary enormously in population, economic size, affluence, and openness to trade and investment. Historically, they were cut apart by several centuries of colonialism and then by the cold war. Culturally, they have a few common threads, but they exhibit far greater diversity than do the western European nations. Nevertheless, a variety of factors have driven a very active discussion of the region as a geographical area whose members should engage in dialogue. The following five factors stand out.

—*Social and economic commonalities.* East Asian economic and social commonalities are largely illusory, but they were pushed so vociferously at various times in the late 1980s and 1990s that they deserve some attention. On the social side, the argument was over "Asian values"; on the economic side, over the relevance of the Japanese economic model for the rest of East Asia.

The notion of Asian values asserts that East Asian societies are linked by common beliefs—for example, that the welfare of the group is more important than that of the individual—that are very different from "Western values." The two most vocal advocates of this view, at least in the Western press, have been former prime minister Lee Kuan Yew of Singapore and Prime Minister Mahathir of Malaysia.

The fact that the most vocal supporters of the concept of Asian values have been the leaders of Singapore and Malaysia suggests that emphasizing them was a means of building the identity of their own nations and achieving greater personal and national recognition than warranted by their nations' very small size. One American scholar, Donald K. Emmerson, casts the issue in exactly this light, writing that "the notion of 'Asian values,' for all its vast scope, originated in Singapore in the late 1980s and early 1990s as Lee Kuan Yew and his fellow ministers pondered their city-state's identity and how to strengthen it."[1] Singapore, a very small, polyethnic city-state, has felt a special need to create a coherent identity.

The concept of Asian values was based on selected tenets of Confucian ethics—emphasis on family, predominance of the group over the individual, respect for authority and order, and emphasis on education. "Respect for authority" easily became a self-serving argument used by autocratic leaders to justify their prolonged control of political activity and their suppression of freedom of speech. Although the press censorship problem has eased in Singapore and elsewhere in Southeast Asia in the past several years, the situation remains less than ideal.[2] However, order and discipline are by no means uniquely Asian values, as evidenced by authoritarian regimes elsewhere in the world.

Nevertheless, for a time the notion of Asian values had support as part of the explanation of why East Asian nations (or some of them, at any rate) managed to grow and industrialize so quickly in the past several decades. East Asia's economic performance was so truly remarkable that it appeared to require a special explanation, and ascribing a set of unique values to Asian countries was certainly one possibility.[3] The problem, of course, was that if "Asian values" were in fact taken from selected Confucian teachings, then how could they apply to countries without much of a Confucian tradition—including Indonesia, Thailand, and the Philippines?

Nevertheless, the concept reinforced the sense that the region was a unique or distinct geographical area, one whose constituents ought to be communicating. In a positive sense, this notion implies that like-minded countries ought to deal more closely with one another. In a negative sense, the idea of Asian values has an element of disdain for the decadence of the West, with its high crime and divorce rates, "excessive" freedom of the press, high unemployment, and other presumed ills. In this sense, the notion of Asian values feeds opposition to policy initiatives of the U.S. government or multilateral institutions such as the International Monetary Fund, which is dominated by the large industrialized nations of the West. Why, in this view, should East Asian nations listen to demands from the governments of decadent, poorly performing, immoral societies?

The concept of Asian values is not sufficient in itself to explain the evolution of East Asian economic dialogue. For starters, the concept was too much a creature of Singapore and Malaysia. Nevertheless, the idea led to other developments. The notion, for example, that moral superiority and superior norms of social conduct had produced a superior economic outcome in Asian nations fanned their willingness to denigrate U.S. and IMF policy at the time of the Asian financial crisis.

The period since the mid-1980s also has witnessed extensive discussion of whether the Asian economies that are basically capitalist in organization represent a different brand of capitalism. If they are different, then a regionalism that binds them closer together and insulates them from the negative impulses of Western capitalism would have more appeal for them. Certainly there are major differences between individual Asian countries and the United States and Europe in terms of how their economies are organized and operated. But the question is whether these differences are common across Asian countries and whether they are sufficiently important to justify forming a regional bloc of like-minded nations.

Back in the early 1990s, James Fallows wrote extensively about the distinctiveness of Japan and extended that view to the rest of Asia. In his view, these nations were focused on increasing "collective national strength" rather than the affluence of individual citizens and on making themselves "independent and self-sufficient" so that they did not have to rely on outsiders for their survival. He saw the political goal of national power rather than Western materialism as the force driving their economies.[4] While this view certainly accords with some of the rhetoric emanating from Asian countries, it is a flawed vision of the region. Asian economies certainly are organized and run differently from the U.S. economy, but they also vary widely among themselves.

Nevertheless, the Japanese believed this rhetoric sufficiently to mount a determined effort through the World Bank in the late 1980s to gain Western acceptance of the notion that Japan's economic organization and development process were distinctive and that the relative success of the Asian developing nations in the 1970s and 1980s came from borrowing the Japanese model. Japanese government officials involved with the World Bank, particularly Masaki Shiratori (the Japanese executive director of the bank, formerly a high-ranking official at the Ministry of Finance) became dissatisfied with what they viewed as an excessive focus on markets. Japan's own successful industrialization, particularly during the high-growth years from 1950 through the early 1970s—and its continued ability to grow faster than other industrialized nations after the mid-1970s (when Japan joined the ranks of advanced industrial nations) and on through the 1980s—occurred with substantial government intervention in markets. In their view, the neoclassical economists from the United States and elsewhere on the World Bank staff went too far in pushing developing countries to reduce government industrial policies.

The result of this pressure from Japan was a major research study issued by the World Bank in 1993 entitled *The East Asian Miracle.*[5] However, the report did not place as much emphasis on the role of industrial policy as the Japanese government had hoped, nor did it attribute the success of other nations in Asia to imitating Japan's development model. Indeed, the report emphasized the wide variety in the development experiences of Asian nations and the importance of "fundamentals" such as political stability and education. It also argued that industrial policy in Southeast Asian nations was a failure.

The Japanese government was very dissatisfied with the report and continued to produce its own research to convince the bank and the international community of the validity and success of the Japanese economic model. One major rebuttal was a World Bank discussion paper produced by the Japan Development Bank (a Japanese government organization) and the Japan Economic Research Institute, which forcefully stated that "[i]ndustrial policy played the key role in the reconstruction, stabilization, and high growth of the Japanese economy. Its most distinctive element as a response mechanism for promoting economic growth is the cooperative relationship between government and industry in the policy formation process—that is, the "public-private cooperative system."[6] The Japanese government continued to push its views through at least 1995, sponsoring a World Bank seminar in Japan at which the Japan Development Bank presented its own lengthy study of the Japanese economic model. At that meeting, Japanese government officials who had served at the World Bank made no bones of the fact that they were motivated by their contempt for what they saw as a naïve emphasis on simple "Western" neoclassical economic models at the World Bank and International Monetary Fund. Furthermore, they argued that neoclassical economic models are grounded in the Western notion that society is based on the free action of individuals—a notion that they felt did not characterize the societies of Japan or other Asian nations.[7]

The Japanese government's effort to push the validity of its distinctive economic model—as well as the notion that its model was, and should continue to be, imitated by the successful developing countries in Asia—conforms to the rhetoric of Asian exceptionalism, building at least the fiction that commonality of behavior exists among Asian nations. What is interesting about these notions is that their Japanese advocates seem to believe them much more than other Asians. Japan developed over the past century with unusually low dependence on foreign financing or direct investment and with very stiff import barriers that limited imports to a low percentage of GDP, at least after the Second World War. The rest of the Asian countries considered in this book, however, have adopted a quite different approach to trade and investment. They have been or have become (in the case of previously autarchic China) much more dependent on imports and foreign capital than has Japan. These differences alone ought to indicate that Japan's "model" of development has not been followed with any great devotion by the rest of the region. To be sure, most governments around the region have interfered with markets to a greater extent than the U.S. government has in the past half-century, but that is hardly a startling difference. European governments and governments of developing countries elsewhere in the world also have interfered with markets over the same period; government interference hardly constitutes a unique Asian characteristic.

The Japanese emphasis on an alternative form of capitalism also illustrates the sort of position the government might take as the leader of a tighter Asian economic bloc. Led by Japan, its dominant economy, an Asian bloc would likely pursue the notion that government economic policies could and should deviate from the strong market principles espoused by the IMF, the World Bank, and the United States. What is worrisome about this notion is that embedded in it is a basically illiberal view of international economic interaction that permits the government to control exchange rates, restrict international capital flows, and raise import barriers in order to guide the economy and limit the intrusion of foreign economic interests.

*—Japan's ascendancy.* A more cynical motive for claiming cultural commonality may have been the simple recognition by Southeast Asian nations of Japan's ascendance in the late 1980s. Seeing Japan as a rising source of foreign aid and direct investment, Southeast Asian nations may have perceived the need to solidify their emerging ties with Japan. On one level, they could reassure their citizens that Japan was a benign force, a follower of the same "Asian way" that they followed. On another level, they could reassure the Japanese that a sense of common purpose and culture justified Japan's new enthusiasm for East Asia. With the cash register open, the Southeast Asian nations were loath to have the Japanese shut it.

Notably absent among them, however, were China, South Korea, Hong Kong, and Taiwan. Either they were no longer eligible for Japanese foreign aid or received it but harbored animosity toward Japan over its actions during the colonial occupation and the Second World War. Still, the Japanese were pleased to have the Southeast Asian nations embrace them; Southeast Asia, too, had harbored anti-Japanese attitudes until at least the 1970s. The more practical attitude of Southeast Asian governments toward Japan was at least one of the factors that motivated and enabled East Asian dialogue. Of course, APEC also provided an opportunity to engage Japan, with the added advantage of having the U.S. government present to moderate the reactions of the region's nations to the Japanese government. Nevertheless, why not engage the predominant source of aid and presumed predominant future investor on their own?

The great disparity in size and affluence among East Asian nations has made it more difficult to create a regional trade bloc. However, the initial initiatives to establish a dialogue that included Japan did not deal with trade preferences. The disparities help to explain why regional institutions have been so slow to develop—and why the future of the various free trade areas considered remain uncertain. But the rapid increase in Japanese foreign aid in the 1980s and the surge in direct investment after 1985 gave some of the nations in the region a powerful reason to engage the Japanese government in a discussion that might help their domestic economies.

*—Exclusion from Western trade blocs.* In this view, East Asia needs its own regional force to counter the EU and NAFTA—and NAFTA's possible extension into a free trade area of the Americas (FTAA). The argument here flows from the trade diversion effects of free trade areas. If the EU and NAFTA imply a rising amount of trade among their members, East Asian nations, which have strong trade connections with both the United States and Europe, would be hurt. Forming a competing East Asian trade bloc

would be one way to combat their losses. For example, in 2001 Shinji Fukukawa, a former senior official at Japan's Ministry of International Trade and Industry (MITI)—which was later renamed the Ministry of Economics, Trade, and Industry (METI)—advocated the formation of a "free business zone" among Japan, China, and South Korea, justifying his proposal by noting that further EU integration and American interest in an FTAA made it necessary.[8] Much of the informal talk of Japanese officials about their own policy shift toward bilateral free trade areas mentions the fact that Japan was one of only three countries (with China and South Korea) that had not negotiated any such trade deals through the 1990s.

—*Anger over Western pressure.* The response of the United States and the IMF to the 1997 Asian financial crisis generated unease, frustration, and anger across Asia. On one hand, the initial American disinterest in the crisis renewed concerns about the lack of U.S. policy engagement with the region, despite the existence of APEC. On the other, when the IMF became involved, dissatisfaction arose over the stringent conditions attached to IMF assistance. IMF officials recognized that some of their initial policies were inappropriate and shifted their stance within a few months. But around Asia, this mistake in the IMF's initial response to the Asian financial crisis led to concern about unfair American or Western pressure and to a subcurrent of belief that the purpose of its policies was to help Western firms gain additional advantage in Asian nations. At its worst, the anger over Western policy became even more pointed. Prime Minister Mahathir blamed the devaluation of his own country's currency on George Soros—and more generally on a Jewish conspiracy—while stating that "great powers" were pressing reforms such as greater economic openness to the outside world as a means to "knock them [Asian countries] off as competitors."[9] This attributes a malicious intent to Western policy that easily serves as a regional rallying point.

More broadly, the Japanese and others have been reluctant objects of U.S., IMF, and World Bank pressure over the past two decades to reform their economies, lower trade barriers, open capital markets, and otherwise reform domestic economic rules and regulations in order to make their economies more like that of the United States. Japan has not been under much pressure from the IMF since it is a creditor rather than a debtor, but it has bridled at three decades of pressure on trade and structural reform from the U.S. government. Meanwhile, the World Bank has been advocating reforms to strengthen markets since the 1980s. The IMF also had been pressuring developing nations to strengthen their financial systems, and in the early 1990s it pressed them to liberalize international capital flows. Whereas Americans saw this as simply asking others to do what works—and thereby helping them overcome problems that lead to crises or poor performance—some in Asia saw it as an intrusion into domestic affairs and practices that have cultural roots. Culture and history aside, the small developing countries in the region later resented the pressure to liberalize their capital markets after the 1997 crisis demonstrated the dangers of liberalization when domestic rules governing the financial sector are weak. IMF officials learned this lesson too, and they took the blame for their earlier mistakes.

Frustration and anger over the Asian financial crisis is the core factor in the emergence of an East Asian economic dialogue. Because the frustration is so anti-Western, it also is profoundly disturbing. An East Asian dialogue intended to seek ways to fend off pressures from the U.S. government, the IMF, or the World Bank has the potential to increase tensions with the West. Furthermore, such an aim could lead to pursuing foolish policies under the banner of the "Asian way" that would perpetuate corruption, diminish economic performance, and leave the region vulnerable to further financial crisis.

—*Concern over American unilateralism and protectionism.* The notion of an economically and militarily dominant United States that cannot be trusted to listen to advice or bend its own policies to accommodate others around the region has been unsettling to regional governments. Even the Japanese have become deeply concerned over American unilateralism, especially since the start of the current Bush administration, on issues ranging from the breaking of the Kyoto Protocol on carbon emissions to, yet again, protecting the steel industry.

Some in Asia became even more concerned about the United States in the wake of the terrorist attacks of September 11, 2001. Deeply ambivalent about the quick and determined American military response to the attack, some see a broad economic and political disassociation from the United States as the logical response. While this view was particularly prevalent among radical Muslims in Malaysia and Indonesia, it was by no means confined to such groups.[10] The Japanese, for example, were deeply unhappy over many aspects of U.S. tactics, even though the prime minister continued to utter expressions of unconditional support for U.S. policies, including the war against Iraq.

Forming a regional dialogue from which the U.S. government would be excluded provides at least the illusion of being able to avoid or fend off

American pressures. In fact, whether acting unilaterally or not, the United States has been such a pervasive presence on so many issues that affect East Asia that the desire to get the Americans out of the room is understandable. East Asian countries might well enhance their bargaining power by caucusing among themselves. It is doubtful that the interests of the poorer developing countries and affluent Japan would be the same on very many issues, but the effort to establish a dialogue obviously has seemed worthwhile to the governments in the region.

A principal economic issue that brings Asians together is American protectionism. While the American market generally is quite open, there are exceptions. The Japanese have expressed concern about the United States becoming more protectionist since the early 1980s, when the Reagan administration put temporary restraints on the import of Japanese automobiles. Most recently, that concern has been stirred by the decision of the Bush administration in the spring of 2002 to slap punitive import duties on steel products from a number of countries, including Japan. In the view of one observer in Japan, the willingness of the United States to impose such duties demonstrated Japan's weakness in the global trading system and the need to "redouble its efforts to conclude bilateral free trade agreements with our Asian neighbors as soon as possible to achieve a unified Asian market with Japan as its hub."[11]

For others in the region the issue is textiles. And for all, the administrative procedures in American antidumping law are anathema. Japan and China have been frequent targets of antidumping cases. Of the 341 dumping and countervailing duty orders in effect in the spring of 2003, 15 percent involved goods from China and 9 percent from Japan, more than any other individual country. East Asian countries as a whole represented 41 percent of all dumping and countervailing duty cases.[12] Since the U.S. market is important for East Asian exports, concerns over actual or threatened American protectionist actions are strong. Regional dialogue provides the opportunity to coordinate responses—for example, to the antidumping procedures now on the table for the Doha round of WTO negotiations. Or, at the extreme, dialogue might lead to a regional free trade area that could lessen dependence on the U.S. market by enhancing intraregional trade.

## Forms of Regional Dialogue

The five factors discussed above provide a strong and understandable explanation for the desire of East Asian governments to talk among themselves without the participation of the United States. Much of it boils down to their visceral dissatisfaction over American policies and behavior, from general perceptions of the decadence of Western culture to resentment over specific issues, such as U.S. trade protectionism and pressure for reform after the 1997 financial crisis. No specific agenda of ideas or policies drove this process, but there was a desire to talk.

Individual manifestations of this desire are explored next. The first, the Association of Southeast Asian Nations, predates the trends just discussed, but during the 1990s it adopted a new economic agenda that is related to them. The other developments—Japan's implicit regional strategy, the East Asian Economic Caucus, and the ASEAN+3 dialogue—all came about in the 1990s. Today ASEAN+3 has emerged as the most formal regional forum, besides APEC, that engages the governments of countries in both Northeast and Southeast Asia.

## ASEAN

The Association of Southeast Asian Nations came into existence in 1967, consisting of five nations: Indonesia, Malaysia, the Philippines, Singapore, and Thailand. The original agreement to form the association speaks in broad terms of accelerating economic growth, social progress, and cultural development, but it does not speak specifically of what form economic cooperation might take.[13] The Vietnam War was under way at the time, and the primary purpose was to form an anticommunist coalition and allay the tension among some of the members. Singapore had just recently seceded from Malaysia, and the bloody overthrow of the leftist Sukarno regime in Indonesia had occurred just the year before.

Individually, each of these states is very small in terms of economic importance. Even in 2000 the ASEAN countries represented only 7.2 percent of the combined GDP of East Asia, and in the 1960s they had yet to undergo rapid economic growth.[14] Other than as suppliers of certain raw materials (oil and gas in Indonesia, tin in Malaysia, and rubber in several locations) these countries were not of much economic importance in the world, but they had recently escaped colonialism (except Thailand, which had never been formally colonized) and faced a common threat in the form of communist insurgency. As much as they were worried about fighting communism, they also were concerned about the vagaries of relying on the great powers to help them. They regarded the American-led Southeast Asian Treaty Organization (an attempt to partially replicate NATO in Southeast Asia) as a failure. The language of the preamble to the Bangkok

Declaration suggests that they also were concerned that the Vietnam War would bring an unwanted long-term American presence to the region, which its nervous, newly independent states might view as the precursor to a new descent into colonialism.[15] Individually, each of these five states was too insignificant to have much impact on the United States or other Western powers, but as one of the founding members of ASEAN put it, collectively they could strengthen their position and protect themselves against "Big Power rivalry."[16]

As a political association, ASEAN has been modestly successful. As the secretariat notes, "through political dialogue and confidence building, no tension has escalated into armed confrontation among ASEAN members."[17] That accomplishment should be recognized. ASEAN member states have had some internal political turmoil (especially Indonesia), but they have maintained largely amicable relations among themselves.

Over time, membership in ASEAN expanded: Brunei joined in 1984, Vietnam in 1995, Laos and Myanmar in 1997, and Cambodia in 1998, bringing total membership to ten countries by 2002.[18] While inclusion of these countries made ASEAN a true association of all Southeast Asian nations, it also diluted the original sense of commonality felt by a group of market-based economies that subsequently experienced high economic growth and industrialization. Other than Brunei, the new members represented countries that had been on the other side of the divide in the cold war and were only beginning the transition to capitalism and economic development in the 1990s. Myanmar, which has faced international sanctions due to the humans rights record of its heavy-handed military dictatorship, still was not on that path in 2003.

Simply by committing themselves to regional peace, these nations may have taken a useful step in the subsequent economic development of the region, but joint action was slow to materialize.[19] They began with a very low level of intraregional trade, estimated to have been around 12 percent when ASEAN was formed. As shown in figure 6-1, that percentage was not much higher at the beginning of the 1980s, when only 13 percent of the imports of the original five members of ASEAN came from within the group and only 17 percent of exports were sent to group members despite their geographic proximity. Note also that the percentages may be inflated in the same way as with Hong Kong, with Singapore serving as a port for products moving into or out of Malaysia. This low level of intra-ASEAN trade helps explain why preferential trade arrangements originally were not high on the ASEAN agenda. On the other hand, the group eventually

Figure 6-1. *Intraregional Trade among Original Five ASEAN Members as a Share of Total Trade*

Percent

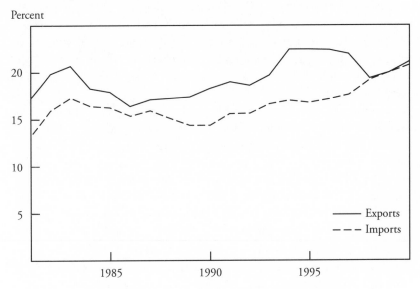

Source: International Monetary Fund, *Direction of Trade Statistics*, 2001, CD-ROM.

realized that preferential trade arrangements might help raise its trade shares and work to the mutual benefit of its members. The preferential trading arrangement (PTA) adopted in 1977 was replaced with an enhanced PTA in 1987.[20] Neither of these initiatives appears to have produced much real action, and they were superseded by the ASEAN Free Trade Area (AFTA) agreement in 1992.

One of the factors that held back intra-ASEAN trade cooperation for so long was the group's belief that its members' economic structures and trade patterns were more competitive than complementary. As low-income developing countries in the 1960s, these nations had manufacturing industries that tended to concentrate on simple products involving relatively little product differentiation (such as cotton textiles) or on raw materials that also involved little differentiation (such as rubber or palm oil). This belief was probably incorrect from the beginning; even products such as textiles involve considerable product differentiation. Furthermore, the potential group gains from the removal of trade barriers do not depend on any notion of complementarity; efficiency gains would appear if the most efficient producers expanded their market share and the share of the inefficient producers shrank. But obviously, ASEAN's members were reluctant to embrace this structural adjustment.

The long-standing reluctance of ASEAN's members to embrace regional free trade is unfortunate, in the sense that of all the narrow regional groupings considered here and in chapter 7, ASEAN has the strongest rationale. ASEAN, as an association of developing countries with substantial trade barriers (with the notable exception of Singapore), could have realized substantial efficiency gains by removing those barriers within the group. Furthermore, a strong, unified economic bloc would have given ASEAN a voice in regional and global trade negotiations that would have been considerably stronger than its members' weak individual voices.

At the macroeconomic level, cooperation has been minimal. The principle of noninterference in the domestic affairs of individual members has prevented ASEAN from adopting a policy of discussing and occasionally criticizing the performance and policies of member states, which is a core function of the G-7 (now G-8) group of major states. Therefore, while most of these countries were pegging their currencies to the U.S. dollar, the group had no mechanism for maintaining mutual surveillance and pressure on individual members to pursue economic policies consistent with their exchange rate commitments. Whether this situation is now changing is discussed in chapter 8, although the focus of the discussion is the slightly broader ASEAN+3 group.

## Japan's Implicit Regional Strategy

The second development in the region did not produce a new institution. Nevertheless, the Japanese government's strategy to make Japan the hub of a de facto economic bloc in the late 1980s and early 1990s was real. Either fearful of the U.S. government's reaction or confident that it could achieve its goal without formal institutions, Japan moved to bind the region more closely to itself through trade, investment, foreign aid, and diplomacy. Japan's actions in regard to the rest of the region during this period therefore represent an important step in the evolution of regional dialogue even though they did not occur in an institutional setting.

Beginning in the second half of the 1980s, the Japanese government developed a strong new interest in its East Asian neighbors, the immediate cause of which was the rapid and sharp appreciation of the yen in 1985. The region was a natural location for Japanese firms seeking lower-cost manufacturing bases. To ease the way for these firms, the Japanese government began to pump up foreign aid to developing countries in East Asia and assume a broader role as a regional leader.

To fuel this strategy, Japanese firms did invest more in East Asia, although Asia's share of Japanese foreign direct investments appeared to be relatively high for only a few years in the early 1990s. Japanese foreign aid to the region also expanded, and the prime minister made a show of visiting Asian countries in advance of the annual G-7 meeting so that he could claim to speak "for Asia." Foreign aid often was linked to specific Japanese economic interests, such as financing the industrial infrastructure needed by Japanese firms that wanted to locate factories in the region, including electric power, water supply and sewer systems, and harbor and other transportation facilities. Japanese diplomacy worked to avoid problems and build friendships. The government, for example, never downgraded its relationship with China as much as the Western nations did in the immediate aftermath of the Tiananmen Square massacre, and it moved back into a normal political relationship much more quickly. The Japanese prime minister was the first leader of an industrial nation to visit China after the incident, less than a year later. To reinforce its policies, the Japanese government pushed its concept of a unique Japanese development model, which, as discussed earlier, was advertised as the most appropriate choice for other East Asian nations. All of these developments indicated that the Japanese government was acting to build an informal regional network centered on Japanese economic interests. The trends in trade, investment, and foreign aid at the beginning of the 1990s suggested that this informal type of regionalism would continue to strengthen.[21]

However, those trends did not continue after the mid-1990s. Nevertheless, the Japanese government's presumption of regional leadership persisted, and it blossomed anew in the wake of the 1997 financial crisis. The most recent focus of the new Japanese regionalism has been bilateral or regional free trade areas. However, the free trade initiative is part of the government's broader, continuing desire to be the leader of the Asian region in other respects as well. The financing of the ADB's research institute in Tokyo is one manifestation of this. So, too, is the continuing talk in Japan of regional monetary cooperation, with advocates discussing an eventual single Asian currency. Moreover, in 2001 a Ministry of Economics, Trade, and Industry (METI) official argued that "it is very important for *Japan* to ensure a stable energy supply in Asia" (emphasis added), for example, by playing a "leading role" in cooperative relations between Asia and the Middle East.[22] This presumption of Japanese leadership in managing energy supply and demand in Asia is all the more interesting since the only formal institution for promoting cooperation on energy that has Japan's official support is a committee within APEC. This organization was formed in 1996 with Japanese money and Japanese support staff to work, in Tokyo, on issues such as supply and demand forecasting.[23]

What occurred within Japan was a very informal effort, devoid of institutions and formal agreements, to become the de facto leader of an Asian economic bloc. In this scenario, the Japanese government would play a paternalistic role, providing foreign aid and other forms of its largess to other nations, buying friendship, and helping Japanese firms. The rest of the region would prosper, but in the hierarchical fashion embodied in the popular notion of "flying geese," with Japan as the permanent head goose. The economic trends of the past decade, however, have militated against fulfillment of this vision. The more formal ASEAN+3 group has created a setting in which the Japanese government can continue to pursue its vision, but Japanese leadership in this forum has been weak or hesitant.

## The East Asian Economic Caucus

The first initiative for a formal East Asian institution broader than ASEAN came from Malaysia, not Japan. In 1990 Prime Minister Mahathir Mohamad proposed forming the East Asian Economic Group, which was quickly renamed the East Asian Economic Caucus (EAEC). Exactly what this group was to accomplish was never specified, although the shift in terminology from "Group" to "Caucus" was apparently intended to allay concerns outside the region that the group would become a trade bloc. Both the U.S. and Australian governments opposed the EAEC, and the U.S. government put considerable pressure on the Japanese government not to participate. The Indonesian government also was wary of the proposal.[24]

Concerns over the EAEC had two important elements. The first was that the group, coming in the immediate wake of the formation of APEC, might sap APEC's strength. The Australians were particularly interested in making APEC the dominant forum for regional economic issues. Second, Mahathir's proposal had a distinct anti-Western or racial slant, and the EAEC came on the heels of Singapore's and Malaysia's promotion of "Asian values." Creating a discussion or economic bloc based on an "Asia versus the West" approach would be a highly divisive move; at the very least, it could have led to active, coordinated opposition to American or Australian initiatives in APEC. More broadly, it could have fostered the deepening of "us versus them" thinking throughout Asia.

The U.S. government pressured Japan not to participate because Japan's natural economic interests lay with the developed nations and because Japan was the one key ally of the United States within the proposed EAEC membership, making it the only practical point of leverage. The Japanese government was well aware that its active participation in the EAEC could jeopardize its relationship with the United States. Furthermore, the proposal came at a time of high tension in Japan's trade relations with the United States, and the Japanese government needed to avoid intensifying the strain. But clearly the EAEC proposal was consistent with the thinking of some Japanese who envisioned Japan as leading a regional group independent of American participation. Prime Minister Mahathir did not completely drop the idea, but American pressure on Japan caused him to reduce EAEC's activity to a single breakfast meeting at the APEC leaders' meeting in 1994—enough for Mahathir to boast of an accomplishment but not enough to produce any meaningful policy discussion.[25]

## ASEAN+3

The EAEC eventually came into existence under a different name: ASEAN+3. The governments involved in the group initially met in advance of the inaugural Asia-Europe Meeting (ASEM), a summit meeting somewhat similar to APEC but designed to promote open-ended discussion, not an action agenda on trade and investment like APEC's. Unlike APEC, ASEM was more of a bilateral meeting between two groups. Because the Europeans could coordinate their participation through the institutions of the EU, the Asians decided to meet at the ministerial level in advance of the ASEM gathering to coordinate their views. The ASEAN governments asked Japan, South Korea, and China to participate in the discussions, which occurred in the second half of 1995. These ministerial meetings were supplemented several years later by a leaders' meeting in Kuala Lumpur, in the wake of the annual ASEAN leaders' meeting in December 1997. Perhaps recalling earlier American opposition, the Japanese government was reportedly uneasy about accepting the offer but felt it had little choice once the Chinese government had accepted.[26]

Whatever reluctance the Japanese government may have expressed in public, however, the idea dovetailed with the government's desire to take a regional leadership role without the U.S. government in the room. Furthermore, the Asian financial crisis in 1997 provided a perfect opportunity to press forward. Asian resentment over the behavior of the U.S. government and the IMF provided the Japanese government with an opening to distinguish itself from its primary developed-nation partners and to curry favor with its crisis-hit neighbors.

The ASEAN+3 concept brought together the leaders of almost all of the East Asian nations considered in this book. There were exceptions, however. Hong Kong and Macau, about to revert to Chinese sovereignty at the time, were not included as separate participants. Far more important was the exclusion of Taiwan. Without formal recognition as a nation-state, Taiwan could not participate in a leaders' meeting, but neither was it invited to participate at the ministerial level, in contrast to its ministerial-level participation in APEC.

After a second leaders' meeting a year later, the group agreed to make the dialogue an annual affair. Since 1999, the scope of the dialogue has expanded to include separate ministerial meetings under the rubric of ASEAN+3 rather than simply as preparation sessions for the ASEM meeting. Those meeting now include finance ministers, vice ministers of finance, deputy governors of the central banks, economic ministers, foreign ministers, and (by 2002) even tourism ministers.[27] The annual finance ministers' meeting occurs on the fringes of the annual Asian Development Bank meeting.

As was the case with the EAEC, the ASEAN+3 group began with no clear agenda other than the desire to talk about common interests in the wake of the financial crisis. The principal accomplishment of the group came at the finance ministers' meeting at Chiang Mai, Thailand, in 2000. Called the Chiang Mai Initiative, it advocated a series of agreements among the central banks to lend foreign exchange reserves to one another ("swap" agreements) to help them protect their currencies on foreign exchange markets. Since 2000, a number of these agreements have materialized.

## Conclusion

The evolution of a dialogue among East Asian nations has proceeded quite slowly. Three decades ago, there was little or no sense of common purpose among East Asian nations. The Southeast Asian region moved first, driven by regional security tensions, the Vietnam War, and geographical proximity.

However, in the early years its primary purpose was political, not economic. The economic ascendance of Japan in the 1980s created a new sense of informal regionalism centered on Japan's government and private sector behavior, but it was devoid of any formal institutions. Prime Minister Mahathir built on that informal regionalism with his EAEC proposal, but at that time the Japanese were not ready to irritate the U.S. government by participating. Only the 1997 Asian financial crisis provided sufficient incentive to bring an East Asian group together.

What has this evolution of an East Asian group produced, other than another series of discussions? Arguably, one outcome has been a gradual move toward an East Asian consciousness that may be beginning to overcome the many past impediments to regional discussion and cooperation. That consciousness and desire for regional dialogue received a strong boost from the 1997 financial crisis. In the broadest sense, these developments should be applauded despite the anti-Western slant that has characterized the rhetoric of some of the advocates of East Asian regionalism. Any regional forum in which neighbors discuss ways to enhance economic exchange may help lower barriers and reduce regional political tensions.

Whether this vague sense of common interests will be enough to move the East Asian region toward forming a tighter economic bloc remains doubtful. The following chapter considers what is happening on the trade front, where the move toward a regional group remains weak despite some activity. Actual regional accomplishments on cooperation on exchange rate issues also have been minimal. There has been an interesting evolution of East Asian dialogue carried out in a formal institutional setting, but the factors impeding tighter economic cooperation are still formidable.

# 7

## More Exclusive
## Trade Alternatives

Over the course of the 1990s, the East Asian nations watched regional trade blocs emerge and expand throughout the world. The further economic integration of the European Union was a major example; so too was the formation of the U.S.-Canada Free Trade Area and its expansion into the North American Free Trade Agreement (NAFTA), followed by talk of further expansion into a free trade area of the Americas. As put by Hew and Anthony, two Malaysian analysts, "To compete in this new century with regional superblocs such as the EU and FTAA, ASEAN, and others, East Asian countries must press ahead with the EAEC [East Asian Economic Caucus] process, with or without U.S. approval."[1] Simply put, if the rest of the world was doing it—especially the large Western trading partners of Asian nations—then the East Asian nations felt that they needed to pursue a similar strategy to compete.

These trade blocs are closed groups; their lower trade barriers apply only to the group's members, as in the EU or NAFTA. All such preferential arrangements involve economic costs and benefits, and this chapter begins with a review of what economics has to say about them. While debate on this subject continues, there are strong reasons to view regional trade preferences unfavorably, and there are political reasons to avoid them as well. This book therefore approaches the question of East Asian trade regionalism from the viewpoint that all such arrangements are undesirable in principle.

Undesirable or not, bilateral and regional trade preferences have become the policy flavor of the day. Examination of the arrangements emerging in East Asia suggests that so far they have had relatively limited success in eliminating trade barriers and that the political obstacles to their expansion remain strong. Surely the coming years will see further movement in this direction, but the movement is likely to be modest and slow.

With APEC stumbling, the East Asian nations put new energy into forming regional trade arrangements with a narrower geographic reach. This chapter and the one that follows somewhat artificially divide the discussion between trade and financial issues such as exchange rates, but both of these threads of Asian regionalism have the same origins.

## The Theory of Economic Regionalism

For half a century, economists have been exploring the implications of preferential bilateral or regional trade arrangements. In a world where almost all nations maintain trade barriers, is the world better off if some choose to remove the barriers among themselves? The global economy is obviously best off with universal free trade, something that economists have been saying for almost 200 years. For the past half-century, the GATT and then the WTO have provided a mechanism for lowering those barriers on a global basis—or at least among members of the GATT/WTO, who now constitute much of the world. Some nations have preferred to go much further, removing most or all barriers among themselves. This issue arose first with the 1952 formation of the European Coal and Steel Community, the precursor to what is now the European Union, which removed trade barriers on coal and steel products among its members.

The theoretical work by economists to explore what narrow bilateral or regional trade preferences might mean for global welfare began with Jacob Viner in 1950 and James Meade in 1955. They argued that the economic welfare effects of such arrangements depend on the interplay of two factors: trade diversion and trade creation. On one hand, a preferential trade bloc may divert trade from the most efficient producer as an importing member nation shifts its purchases from efficient producer outside the bloc to a less efficient producer within it. That is, if country A imports a product and charges a uniform tariff on all overseas suppliers, it will choose to import from the lowest-cost supplier abroad (call it country C). If A then eliminates all its tariffs with a favored trading partner (country B), A will import the product from B even if B's production costs are higher than those in country C—as long as the disparity in production costs between B and C is less than the tariff still levied on the producer in C. That is, if the landed price of the product from country C (which is the production cost plus the tariff) is higher than the landed price from country B (production cost with no tariff), country A will choose to import from B instead of the efficient C. Because production shifts from the efficient producer to a less efficient one, global welfare suffers.

Now suppose that the tariff imposed by country A is so high that its own inefficient industry supplies the entire domestic market. If the industry in country B is more efficient than that in A, then the creation of a free trade area will cause A to import the product from B. Because B is a more efficient producer than A, both countries gain through the creation of trade. Meanwhile, country C does not lose anything since it did not export to A anyway.

This example demonstrates the fundamental propositions involved in trade diversion and trade creation. Narrow preferential arrangements can divert trade from efficient producers of a product if those producers are outside the preferential arrangement, thereby worsening global welfare. But under certain circumstances, preferential arrangements can also create trade and improve global welfare. While the example is quite simple, economists have wrestled with this fundamental ambiguity for the past half-century, toying with the theory by adding various kinds of complications. Today, their conclusions remain ambiguous.[2]

Keep in mind that what appears to be a potentially positive result with trade creation in these models is still a decidedly second-best outcome. Consider again the simple trade case. Country A substitutes imports from country B for its more inefficient domestic production. Trade is created, but countries A, B, and C still experience a misallocation of productive resources relative to the ideal. On efficiency grounds, country C should be the producer and exporter to both A and B. Therefore, A is still paying too much for the product, B is misallocating its resources to producing the product, and C is allocating too few resources. On efficiency grounds, the world is still better off with global free trade than with narrow preferential arrangements.

Since the time of Viner and Meade, economists have explored issues such as the impact of economies of scale and imperfect competition on preferential arrangements. In industries characterized by economies of scale, the potential exists (depending on initial prices and production costs in the various countries) for the industry of one or more of the countries in the bloc to expand production and thereby lower production costs. More efficient firms outside the bloc lose (trade diversion), but the consumers of the firms within the bloc gain because of the lower costs and prices charged by their own firms. Again, the overall impact on global welfare depends on the size of the losses from trade diversion compared with the welfare gains within the bloc.

Trade theory, even in its current relatively sophisticated form, leaves out a number of complicating issues. First, the models are static. One can imagine another form of trade creation. If formation of a free trade area accelerates the economic growth of member nations, then their growth has the effect of bringing in more imports from the rest of the world. Potentially, this is a more important form of trade creation than that in the simple static models, if higher growth actually results from creation of a free trade area. But whether creation of a free trade bloc does in fact accelerate the economic growth of the participants is a question that does not yet have a definitive answer.

Economic models also deal only with merchandise trade, leaving out foreign direct investment. One can imagine two situations. If the bloc has barriers on inward investment from the rest of the world, then formation of the bloc enhances the possibility of expanding sales and reducing average production costs in domestic industries characterized by economies of scale. Should the economy-of-scale effect be sufficiently strong, then formation of the bloc could put firms within the bloc in a position to become low-cost sellers to the rest of the world. This possibility is simply a bloc version of what is known in economic theory as "strategic trade"—using import barriers to help bulk up a domestic industry to an efficient size in order to gain an advantage in global competition. Economics has generally been tolerant of strategic trade when practiced by developing nations, calling it protection of "infant industries." However, for economies beyond the initial stages of industrialization, the notion of strategic trade has been criticized as unfair.

If, on the other hand, the bloc does not have barriers on inward investment, then all producers, both within and outside the group, can benefit from the larger market scale within the bloc. Arguably, this has been the case within the EU. In this case, American and Japanese firms can take advantage of the scale of a unified European market, subject only to some disadvantage on rules of origin or from duties on imports of components from outside the bloc. Both the EU and NAFTA are open to inward investment, although outside firms do experience the disadvantage of paying tariffs on parts or components imported for assembly in their factories—an issue that Japanese firms have raised with their government concerning their factories in Mexico.

Theoretical economic models miss another important point. In all models of gains and losses due to formation of preferential trading blocs, economists compare gains for one group of countries (those within the bloc) with the possible losses of others (those outside the bloc). In the simple language of economists, if the gains outweigh the losses, then the bloc has an overall positive effect on global economic welfare. But this involves completely separate groups of people divided by national boundaries. If an increase in global welfare implies economic losses to people in one country and gains in another, the losers will be quite unhappy and their government will have no reason to look favorably on the formation of the trade bloc.

Because the welfare benefits of economic regionalism are ambiguous, many economists are skeptical of the economic efficacy of narrow preferential arrangements, and the evolution of a large number of such arrangements creates serious computational questions. For starters, consider the fact that in a free trade area, unlike in a customs union, each member continues to maintain its own individual tariffs on products from outside the group and those tariffs may vary considerably from member to member. An outside producer of a product that enters one country at a low tariff and then moves across the border to another member with a higher tariff must pay the differential—a requirement that involves more extensive paperwork to identify the ultimate origin of the product.

Further complicating the situation, consider the fact that in the contemporary world, a manufactured good may involve parts and assembly operations spread across several countries. A problem arises if a product enters a member country from the outside world at a low tariff, undergoes minimal processing, and then moves to another member country that has a much higher tariff on imports of this particular product from outside the group. Should the product cross the border duty free, as specified by the free trade area, or should it face the differential duty imposed in the cases of outside products moving from one member to another? This problem has led to complicated and varying rules of origin to specify which products are to be considered products produced inside the group. These rules and their calculation for particular products create further complications and arbitrariness in determining the import duty to be applied to any particular product entering a nation. Proliferation of free trade arrangements therefore imposes costs in the form of paperwork and verification of these complex production routes and their tariff implications. Depending on the level of tariffs, the incentive for cheating may be high, so free trade areas have the potential to create endless disputes. One group of economists has termed the proliferation of free trade areas and their differing rules as the "spaghetti bowl" phenomenon.[3]

These objections are important because some economists have adopted the view that customs unions and free trade areas will eventually overlap so much that they lead to a de facto global reduction in trade barriers. In their view, these narrow agreements are beneficial because broad global agreements on trade are so difficult to negotiate; if progress is slow and halting at the level of global negotiations and nations find it easier to negotiate with smaller subsets of their trading partners, then they should do so. However, this approach may not lead to a coalescing of narrow preferential arrangements into a global free trade. These arrangements could easily become a series of entrenched, enormously complex relationships that disadvantage some nations and benefit others, particularly if some nations end up being left out altogether.

Despite all the doubts raised here concerning bilateral and regional trade preferences, they are explicitly permitted under the rules of the General Agreement on Tariffs and Trade and its successor, the World Trade Organization. Article 24 of the original GATT (incorporated into the WTO) permits both customs unions (whose members allow free trade among themselves and adopt a common set of tariffs for the rest of the world) and free trade areas (whose members maintain their own individual tariffs for the rest of the world). However, in both cases, the GATT imposes two important requirements. First, the members of the group may not raise their tariffs or other barriers to the outside world while removing them among themselves. Second, any customs union or free trade area must remove "duties and other restrictive regulations of commerce" on "substantially all the trade between the constituent territories."[4]

The new General Agreement on Trade in Services (GATS) has a roughly similar clause governing free trade areas. Since services involve access issues that are more varied and complicated than the issues surrounding tariffs and quotas on physical products, the rule is not as clear. Instead, the GATS requires that members of a group liberalizing trade in services among themselves must include "substantial sectoral coverage" and provide for the "absence or elimination of substantially all discrimination."[5] That is, individual members may continue to regulate various service industries (such as the licensing of doctors or lawyers) as they wish, but they may not discriminate in such regulation against other members of the trade group— for example, a country might prohibit foreign lawyers from practicing law, but it would give lawyers or law students from countries in its trade group the opportunity to take the bar exam.

It is curious that regionalism would be condoned by an agreement intended primarily to establish a framework for nations to lower their trade barriers on a global basis or at least with respect to all other members of the WTO, which now comprises most countries in the world, with the notable exception of Russia. To understand why, it is important to recall that when the GATT was negotiated in the 1940s, a number of the major negotiating parties still had colonial empires characterized by internal free trade. Britain and France, for example, were not about to abandon the trade preferences they extended to their colonies. In addition, the initial stirrings of European regionalism were already in motion. Even the United States was motivated to accept any institutional moves designed to help rebuild war-torn Europe and knit its nations together in a more productive economic relationship that might reduce the kind of political tensions that had led to two disastrous wars in the previous thirty-five years.

In the first several decades of the GATT's existence, not very many customs unions or free trade areas were established. Until the early 1990s, less than fifty such agreements were in force. Since that time, however, the number has exploded; more than 150 agreements were in force by 2001. Some 60 percent of them involved European nations on the periphery of the European Union, or Central European and Central Asian states that had been part of the Soviet bloc. The WTO noted in its 2002 annual report that most of its members belonged to one or more regional trade agreements.[6]

As the popularity of free trade areas has grown, economists have attempted to model the economic impact of the proposed blocs. Empirical studies of possible free trade areas among various partners in East Asia find a combination of positive impact on participants (the trade creation effect) and negative impact on excluded economies (the trade diversion effect). For example, one recent study of the Japan-Singapore agreement yielded a tiny positive impact on the Japanese economy, a larger positive impact for Singapore (4 percent of GDP), but a negative impact on others, concentrated among Singapore's ASEAN neighbors. Despite the Singapore example, both the positive and negative impacts that emerge from these models are generally well under 1 percent of GDP. In a few cases, negative results emerge even for a participant, as in the case of South Korea in a simulation of a Japan–South Korea free trade area. The main point of such estimations is to underscore the ambiguity of narrow arrangements: while they may benefit the participants, they can hurt excluded countries.[7]

## Trade Blocs and Diplomacy

Diplomatic as well as theoretical economic issues arise with narrow free trade areas. To put it simply, if a nation chooses to form a free trade area with one trading partner, then its other close trading partners will be irritated. NAFTA, for example, has irritated Japan and other Asian trading partners of the United States. In 2001 Japanese manufacturers were particularly upset because the tariff preferences enjoyed by their Mexican assembly plants—which, under rules dating from the mid-1960s, imported parts tariff free as long as the output was exported—were eliminated as part of the phase-in of NAFTA.[8] The EU had negotiated a free trade area with Mexico but Japan had not when the tariff preferences were phased out. Suddenly, Japanese firms felt that they were operating at a disadvantage compared with their American and European competitors in Mexico. Pressure from the Japanese business sector led the government to begin negotiations with Mexico in 2002.

The Mexican example involves straightforward business interests, but free trade areas have a hint of broader discrimination. As the U.S.-Canada FTA and then NAFTA were negotiated, the Japanese government felt slighted. Why should the United States choose to play a free trade game with Canada and Mexico but demonstrate a distinct lack of interest in doing so with Japan? At various times in the late 1980s and 1990s, the Japanese government raised the question of a free trade area with the United States, but it went nowhere; policymakers in Washington felt that because the barriers in Japan were nontransparent, nontariff barriers, free trade negotiations were unlikely to make much difference in terms of access to the Japanese market. This experience left the Japanese government feeling that it occupied an inferior position as a friend and ally of the United

States. Those feelings of rejection would be reinforced if the U.S. government were to succeed in creating a free trade area of the Americas.

How serious are these diplomatic drawbacks? The possibility exists that they may actually have a positive effect. If the Japanese feel envious of NAFTA and are distraught over the loss of the import preferences for their factories in Mexico, then the negotiation of a free trade area with Mexico would be a positive response. Or perhaps the Japanese government might be motivated to strip away nontariff barriers at home so that even the U.S. government would consider forming a bilateral free trade area with Japan. That is certainly one possibility. The Japan-Mexico case is one example of an outsider in East Asia responding to trade blocs elsewhere by attempting to become an insider.

However, the rhetoric in East Asia about free trade areas reveals a strong tendency to view regional or bilateral blocs as competitors of blocs elsewhere in the world. Given the relatively high tariffs of developing countries in East Asia and the informal barriers in Japan, an East Asian bloc could involve substantial trade diversion. Furthermore, forming such a bloc would make a strong strategic statement about the region moving away from its close economic ties with the West. Accompanying rhetoric about creating an alternative to economic ties with the United States would reinforce the negative impact of this move on regional diplomatic relations with the United States.

So far, at least, an East Asian trade bloc is not emerging. But the bilateral and subregional deals that are appearing are creating complex diplomatic issues, especially concerning the relationship between Japan and China.

## Overview of Free Trade Agreements

In contrast to the global trend discussed earlier, bilateral or regional free trade areas were slow to develop in the East Asian region focused on in this book. In 1975, the United Nations Economic and Social Commission for Asia and the Pacific (ESCAP) brokered a minor deal known as the Bangkok Agreement, which has been signed by Bangladesh, India, South Korea, Laos, Sri Lanka, and, in 2000, China. However, the agreement does not appear to establish a full-fledged free trade area; it includes some regional trade preferences, but it is equally or more focused on policy studies, technical assistance, and advisory services.[9] The first major attempt at East Asian regionalism came within ASEAN, with the agreement in 1992 to create what is known as the ASEAN Free Trade Area (AFTA).

The latest wave of interest in free trade areas came after 1997. Table 7-1 presents the full array as of 2003 of existing agreements, ongoing negotiations, official study groups (a precursor to formal agreements), and informal public statements concerning potential free trade partners. Agreements actually signed and in the process of implementation include the old Bangkok Agreement, AFTA, and agreements between Japan and Singapore, Singapore and New Zealand, Singapore and Australia, Singapore and the United States, and Thailand and Laos. A number of proposed agreements are under negotiation, in particular other bilateral proposals initiated by Singapore, a Japan-Mexico proposal, and a recent China-ASEAN proposal. By late 2003, the U.S. government announced that it would start negotiations with Thailand, and Japan announced that it would do so with South Korea, Thailand, Malaysia, and the Philippines, but actual negotiations had not yet begun. Beyond these, various governments and business groups have floated ideas about agreements with other possible partners.

The following sections of this chapter explore AFTA, Japan's new FTA strategy, and the China-ASEAN negotiation in greater detail. The situation depicted in table 7-1 remains quite fluid, but it is possible to tease out some conclusions from what has happened so far and speculate on where the process is headed.

## AFTA

ASEAN gained a significant economic dimension in 1992 when its leaders agreed to establish the ASEAN Free Trade Area (AFTA). Beginning in 1993, reduction and removal of tariffs was to be conducted over a considerable time frame, with final elimination of all tariffs among members now scheduled to be completed by 2010 for the original six AFTA members and by 2015 for the other four (the dates in the original 1992 agreement have been accelerated by several years).[10] Of all the narrow regional groups proposed over the past decade, this one makes the most sense. First, while all these nations do not share land boundaries, they are reasonably close together in Southeast Asia. So like NAFTA and the EU, this is a group of close neighbors who choose to work together more closely, knowing that it is important for both security and economic reasons to foster productive relationships among themselves. Unlike in NAFTA or the EU, however, these neighbors do not have a long history of heavy intraregional trade; over the past 300 years, most of them were colonies of large powers, subject to the relatively exclusive trading patterns that came with colonialism. More recently, they have had a modest amount of intraregional trade. From 1981 to 2000, these countries' exports to one another have fluctuated between 16 and 22 percent of their total exports, without showing any clear upward trend. A free trade area may help provide an impetus to them to overcome the legacy of the past by reinforcing economic ties with their closest neighbors.

Second, ASEAN is a group of small economies, and all of them except Singapore are developing economies—although even among the developing members there is wide variation in per capita income. Formation of a meaningful free trade area should help the governments of this bloc speak with a more unified voice in bargaining with large industrialized nations such as the United States and Japan in international negotiations such as the Doha round of WTO talks.

Third, this particular region should benefit in terms of attracting foreign direct investment. Because the economies are small, a larger unified market makes investment more attractive, to the extent that the motive is to sell products in the local economy rather than ship them overseas. This motive has been enhanced by the sense of competition with China. As noted by former Singapore president Lee Kuan Yew, "to meet the economic challenge of China's attractiveness to foreign investments, the ASEAN countries will have to combine their markets in an ASEAN Free Trade Area. Without this, the ASEAN countries will be left out by international investors."[11] That is, by offering a unified market of more than 500 million people to foreign investors, Southeast Asia will look more attractive compared with China than it would if its economies are separated by high tariff barriers. Fears in Southeast Asia over the potential loss of new investment to China may be exaggerated, but a unified market certainly increases the region's attractiveness to investors.

The one oddity of ASEAN is the position of Singapore, which geographically sits at the heart of the ASEAN nations. However, how dedicated Singapore is to the ASEAN Free Trade Area is unclear. Singapore is a high-income, industrial city-state. Disappointed with the slow progress in dismantling trade barriers through both APEC and AFTA, Singapore has turned to signing free trade agreements with individual governments outside Southeast Asia. One of the first was with New Zealand, and Singapore's negotiation of this deal caused some consternation among other ASEAN members. As one observer put it, "Frustrated by foot-dragging fellow ASEAN members, Singapore hopes that by plunging outside ASEAN's free-trade area, AFTA, to cooperate with New Zealand it will shake the

Table 7-1. *Status of Bilateral and Regional Free Trade Areas, April 2003*

| | Japan | China | South Korea | Taiwan | Singapore | Other ASEAN |
|---|---|---|---|---|---|---|
| Agreement signed and implemented or in process of implementation | Japan-Singapore | Bangkok Agreement[a] | Bangkok Agreement Korea-Chile | | Singapore-Japan Singapore–New Zealand Singapore–United States Singapore-EFTA[b] Singapore–Australia | AFTA Thailand-Laos |
| Under negotiation | Japan-Mexico | China-ASEAN | | | Singapore-Mexico Singapore-Canada | ASEAN-China |
| Study group | Japan–South Korea Japan–Malaysia Japan–ASEAN | | Korea-Japan | Taiwan–United States | | ASEAN-CER[c] ASEAN-Japan ASEAN-India |
| Idea floated | Japan–Thailand Japan–ASEAN+3[d] ASEAN+5[e] ASEAN+5 plus India | | Korea-Mexico Korea–United States Korea-China Korea-Japan-China Korea–New Zealand | Taiwan-Japan Taiwan-Singapore Taiwan–New Zealand | | ASEAN–United States Thailand–United States |

Source: Author's compilation from various sources.

a. Bangkok Agreement = Bangladesh, India, South Korea, Laos, Sri Lanka, and China.

b. EFTA = The European Free Trade Area, comprising Iceland, Liechtenstein, Norway, Switzerland (that is, a group of European nations not belonging to the EU).

c. CER = Closer Trade Relations Agreement (Australia and New Zealand).

d. ASEAN+3 = ASEAN plus Japan, China, and South Korea.

e. ASEAN+5 has had two variations in Japanese speeches. In December 2001, Prime Minister Koizumi defined it as ASEAN plus Japan, China, South Korea, Australia, and New Zealand; in April he substituted Taiwan and Hong Kong for Australia and New Zealand.

group into finally exploring free trade with outsiders."[12] At the mid-November 2000 ASEAN summit meeting, criticism of Singapore's go-it-alone approach on FTAs popped up again, on the grounds that such behavior would undermine solidarity within ASEAN. One Malaysian analyst argued that such bilateral deals could derail the AFTA process.[13]

The dissatisfaction of Singapore reflects the bumpiness of the road to free trade within ASEAN. Although the date for bringing AFTA into force has been moved up, incomplete tariff elimination has been a problem due to strong reluctance among members of even this small group to fully open their markets to one another (with the exception of Singapore, which does not have tariff barriers).

At the beginning of 2002, the six original members of AFTA had lowered most tariffs to 5 percent, a target originally set for 2008. The other four members (Cambodia, Laos, Myanmar, and Vietnam) had until 2006 to reach that target. Although complete tariff elimination remains a goal, implementation will be slow. At a September 1999 meeting, the six original AFTA members agreed to advance the original goal for complete tariff elimination to 2010, while the other four members are to reach that goal by 2015 rather than 2018. Some sensitive products will be allowed to remain on the 2018 schedule.[14] Thus the ASEAN member governments have managed to accelerate dates for achieving trade liberalization—a move that gives the surface appearance of success.

That impression is somewhat misleading. The main problem has been the incomplete elimination of tariffs, enabled by many loopholes. Member governments can "temporarily" exclude some products to shield infant industries, as Malaysia has done with its national car project.[15] In fact, the exclusions extend far beyond the temporary category. Member countries establish an inclusion list, a temporary exclusion list, a sensitive list, and a general exception list.[16] When AFTA began in 1992, the member states included an average of 87 percent of their tariff lines in the list of tariffs to be reduced—called the Common Effective Preferential Tariff Scheme (CEPT); the percentage ranged from 74 percent to 98 percent among the six original ASEAN members. Of the remaining 13 percent, 10 percent were temporary exclusions, and by implication the remaining 3 percent were sensitive and general exclusions.[17] Rice, for example, is one of the sensitive products.[18]

Since that time, ASEAN has become more reticent about releasing information on how many products have shifted categories or what percentage of existing trade the tariff lines represent. According to other sources, backsliding has occurred. In 2000, for example, Malaysia announced that it would delay liberalizing its protected domestic car industry until 2005, to the deep concern of other ASEAN nations. In retaliation, Thailand threatened to postpone liberalizing trade in palm oil, a major Malaysian export. The temporary exclusions were not fixed at the outset in 1992, and more crept in over time, giving the appearance of disarray and backsliding.[19] These exclusions matter. Malaysia has tariffs of up to 300 percent on imported automobiles and an inefficiently small production level—some 222,000 cars for the whole industry, produced by two companies.[20]

The four newest members of ASEAN—Laos, Myanmar, Vietnam, and Cambodia—have left a considerable portion of their own tariff schedules off the inclusion list. When entering in 1997, Laos placed only 15 percent of its tariff lines on the inclusion list, 79 percent on the temporary exclusion list, 2.7 percent on the sensitive list, and 2.9 percent on the general exception list. Myanmar placed 43 percent on the inclusion list, 54.6 percent on the temporary list, 0.4 percent on the sensitive list, and 2 percent on the general exception list. Cambodia initially offered to place 45.6 percent on the inclusion list, 51.6 percent on the temporary exclusion list, 0.8 percent on the sensitive list, and 2 percent on the general exclusion list.[21]

Where do all these exceptions leave AFTA's movement toward free trade? Skeptics abound. As one observer put it, AFTA "is riddled with exceptions, multiple deadlines and other confusing elements that have made selling the concept to outsiders difficult."[22] Nevertheless, at least the average tariff on goods traded among ASEAN has fallen. When the process of lowering tariffs began in 1993, the average tariff among the ASEAN nations was 13.4 percent.[23] There is no doubt that ASEAN countries have made considerable progress in lowering their tariff barriers from that starting point, although the process remains incomplete. By 2001, the average intra-AFTA tariff level had fallen to 3.96 percent, and in 2002 it fell further, to 3.57 percent.[24] The average tariff in 2002 was 2.89 percent for the original six members of the AFTA agreement and 6.77 percent for the four new members.[25]

Even among products on the inclusion lists, however, the reduction in tariffs has been quite uneven. Figure 7-1 shows the dispersion of tariff levels of the six major ASEAN members for products on the inclusion list. By 2000—eight years into the implementation of AFTA—the six original AFTA members imposed no tariff on only 41 percent of the 52,563 line items in their tariff schedules and tariffs of 5 percent or less on another

Figure 7-1. *Percent of Total Tariff Lines of Items on Inclusion List, by Tariff Rate, 2000*

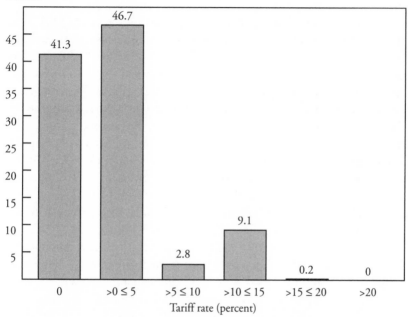

Percent

Source: Calculated from ASEAN Secretariat data on twenty-one separate groups of Harmonized System tariff categories (www.aseansec.org/economic/afta/afta_trw.htm [April 18, 2003]).

46.7 percent. However, 2.8 percent of tariff lines were in the 5 to 10 percent range, 9.1 percent in the 10 to 15 percent range, and 0.2 percent in the 15 to 20 percent range. This picture is somewhat biased by the fact that Singapore imposes no tariffs on any products on an MFN basis, and Brunei is largely tariff free, with 72.5 percent of its tariff lines at zero and the remaining 27.5 percent at 5 percent or less. If these two countries are removed from the total, only 24.2 percent of tariff lines were at zero, and the Philippines had yet to lower any tariffs to zero. These pockets of higher tariffs for goods on the inclusion list were supposed to be eliminated by 2003 for the original six AFTA signatories, so that all products on the list would be subject to tariffs of 5 percent or less. Data on compliance with this goal were not yet available in the spring of 2003. However, Indonesia announced in 2001 that it would postpone achievement of the 2003 goal, and in 2002 the Philippines announced that it intended to remove some petrochemical products from its inclusion list.[26] Although average tariffs were falling, doubts continued as to the commitment of AFTA members to meet their original goals.

Clearly AFTA has had some impact in reducing tariffs and facilitating trade among ASEAN members, even though a decade after its start tariff levels were not yet at zero. The big unknown for AFTA is whether its members will be able to meet their final obligations to end the temporary exclusions, reduce tariffs to zero, and reduce or eliminate the list of sensitive and general exception products. While the number of tariff lines represented by these products is small, they may be important. The best one can say is that the ASEAN countries have achieved a record on tariff reduction roughly similar to that achieved by the industrial nations under the GATT/WTO system—a low average tariff level, with many products at zero, offset by some exceptions at higher tariff levels.

The ability of the ASEAN countries to make the agreed-on future moves may be in considerable trouble. Because of its inclusion of the poorest countries in the region, ASEAN became both larger and more diverse in terms of its members' economic interests, reducing their willingness to fully open up their markets.[27] Part of the problem also relates to the 1997 financial crisis. Some ASEAN nations went through a difficult time economically and politically for several years. Indonesia faced political instability in 1998 and after; in the Philippines, President Joseph Estrada was impeached and removed from office; in Malaysia, Prime Minister Mahathir Mohamad's grip on power was shaken by the scandal surrounding the ouster of Finance Minister Anwar Ibrahim. And in 1997–98, ASEAN was unable to coordinate or provide help on large economic issues because of its policy of noninterference in domestic affairs.[28]

AFTA provides an important window on the problems facing all Asian regional trade propositions. Of all the efforts considered in this chapter to pursue greater market openness on a narrower East Asian basis, AFTA is the one that has the clearest rationale, both economically and politically. Certainly some progress on lowering barriers among the ASEAN nations has occurred. However, the incomplete nature of market opening and the doubts about its eventual realization indicate the fundamental difficulty East Asian nations have had in embracing free trade. In economic theory, the full benefits from bilateral or regional free trade areas come from eliminating barriers, driving a wedge between the region and its trade with the rest of the world. Ability to behave as a bloc in WTO negotiations also depends on demonstrating bloc solidarity. This group of nations has been unable—at least so far—to form a true free trade area.

In addition to AFTA, ASEAN has begun to explore other free trade areas. Its negotiations with China are discussed later in this chapter, as is the proposal for an FTA with Japan. Beyond these, proposals are under study for FTAs with Australia/New Zealand and India. Finally, the Bush administration announced the Enterprise for ASEAN Initiative in October 2002, offering to negotiate free trade areas with individual ASEAN members. The tactic of dealing with individual members rather than ASEAN as a whole sidesteps the problem of Myanmar, which is subject to American trade sanctions, and possibly other members not considered suitable partners.[29] At the annual APEC leaders' meeting in October 2003, President George W. Bush announced the start of the first of these individual free trade negotiations, with Thailand.

### Japan's Approach to FTAs

A decade ago the intent of the Japanese government was to foster a more exclusive relationship with the nations of East Asia. Its motivation was the desire or need of Japanese firms to relocate production abroad after the yen appreciated in 1985; the "grease" came from Japanese government foreign aid and diplomatic overtures to make other nations in East Asia receptive to Japanese investment. However, this new approach was informal, and it involved no new institutional arrangements. On the trade front, the Japanese government remained a formal supporter of the global GATT/ WTO approach and the open regionalism of APEC. The government had informally floated the idea of a U.S.-Japan free trade area in the late 1980s when the U.S.-Canada agreement materialized but dropped it quickly in the face of American opposition, maintaining instead its formal commitment to globalism. That approach changed suddenly and dramatically at the beginning of the new century, when the Japanese government began to embrace bilateral free trade areas. Although the new policy did not focus exclusively on other East Asian countries, it has a strong regional orientation.

The Japanese government had flirted with narrower versions of regionalism in the early 1990s when Prime Minister Mahathir of Malaysia floated his vague concept of an East Asian Economic Caucus, but it backed away under American pressure. By 2000, the government was once again embracing Asian regionalism. A senior Ministry of Economics, Trade, and Industry (METI) official speaking on the record in late 2000 in San Francisco spoke disparagingly of APEC, saying "to be frank, APEC has become sort of [an] incarnation of bureaucracy." He went on to speak very favorably of the ASEAN+3 framework as an alternative. He noted that as an ally of the United States, Japan had "no choice" but to maintain good relations, but his enthusiasm for Asian regionalism outside the grasp of the United States was obvious.[30]

JAPAN-SINGAPORE NEW AGE ECONOMIC PARTNERSHIP.  The Japanese government's first foray into free trade areas involved an agreement with Singapore negotiated during 2001 and signed in January 2002. This agreement was an obvious, easy way to begin because Singapore has no tariffs and exports few agricultural products. In fact, it is not entirely clear whether Japan initiated the process or Singapore approached Japan as part of its ongoing effort to build a web of free trade areas outside of ASEAN. As easy as the negotiations should have been, the process was more difficult and the outcome considerably less robust than anticipated.

According to the two governments, the outcome of the agreement would be an increase in duty-free exports from Singapore to Japan, from 84 percent to 94 percent of the total value of total exports. The number of tariff lines that would be duty free was scheduled to rise from 34 percent to 77 percent. Most of the decreases in duties that were to drop to zero took place immediately upon initiation of the agreement in 2002, and duties on ten petrochemical products were to be liberalized gradually by 2010. In theory, agriculture was not entirely excluded from the agreement. The Japanese government proudly announced that although only 2 percent of Singapore's exports to Japan were agricultural products, the government did "not exclude any sector from tariff elimination and tariff concessions cover both industrial and agricultural products." Technically, the agreement resulted in a 14 percent increase in the number of Japan's zero-tariff line commitments on agricultural products beyond its commitments in the WTO.[31] One METI official claimed that a total of sixty-eight "controversial" products were included in the agreement—including some agricultural products and some chemicals.[32]

That is the official story. Looked at carefully, the agreement is modest at best. Consider first the overall elimination of tariffs for products exported from Singapore to Japan. The rise in duty-free exports from Singapore to Japan from 84 to 94 percent of total exports means that only 10 percent of Singapore's exports to Japan would be positively affected by the agreement. Put another way, the free trade negotiations managed to eliminate tariff barriers for only 62 percent of those exports from Singapore to Japan that currently faced duties. Put in that context, Japanese government negotiators made few concessions.

The big story, however, concerns agriculture. Both Foreign Ministry and Ministry of Economics, Trade, and Industry officials told the author during the negotiations that they hoped the trivial amount of Singapore agricultural exports to Japan would enable them to win the political battle with the Ministry of Agriculture to include all agricultural products in the agreement. Having established a precedent, they could then negotiate free trade areas with other countries whose agricultural exports to Japan might be more important. Of course, Ministry of Agriculture officials and farm groups would have had to have been blind and deaf not to have seen through that tactic. The result was fierce opposition to any significant concessions.

Nongovernment observers noticed immediately that the agreement did not include duty-free access for all products from Singapore, especially in the areas of petrochemicals and agriculture. The excluded agricultural products seemed quite minor—tropical fish, tuna, orchids, and coconut milk—leading to some disappointment and dismay among advocates of more open trade.[33] The Chinese government immediately denounced the agreement as "unfair and biased" because of the incomplete coverage and the exclusion of agriculture in particular; New Zealand's trade minister, Jim Sutton, also criticized the agreement for excluding agriculture—in contrast to New Zealand's own, broader, free trade agreement with Singapore signed in 2001.[34] In the United States, Fred Bergsten joined the chorus of complaints concerning the exclusion of agriculture. But Singapore's trade and industry minister, George Yong-Boon Yeo, dismissed such complaints from the United States as simply American anxiety about being "locked out of the western Pacific." Echoing the common themes coursing through the rhetoric on East Asian regionalism, he added that countries like Japan had no choice but to turn to free trade areas because of the American emphasis on a free trade area of the Americas and the continuing consolidation of the EU.[35] His comments may have been intended to needle the U.S. government at a time when it was in the midst of its own negotiations with Singapore to establish a free trade area, which have since been concluded successfully.

According to one analysis, of 2,277 agricultural product categories in the nine-digit Harmonized System (the standard classification of products for tariff purposes), the Japanese government included only 486 in the agreement. Of these, 428 were products on which Japan had already agreed to eliminate tariffs in the WTO, and fifty-eight were for products on which the tariff rates already were "effectively zero," meaning that while the WTO "bound" rate was above zero, the "applied" rate was already zero.[36] The bilateral agreement did nothing to provide Singapore with more open access to Japan's markets for agricultural products than was available to any other exporting nation. The main observation is not that the agreement included some agricultural products, but that opposition from the Ministry of Agriculture prevented any meaningful removal of tariffs. It even protected products as trivial as goldfish.

The agreement also contains extensive language on issues other than tariffs; the focus on service sector issues and trade facilitation is what led to the "new age" designation in the title. For example, it provides for possible cross-recognition of electrical safety standards, acceptance of college credits earned in either country, and closer cooperation between the stock exchanges.[37] However, the reality is that the nonmerchandise trade aspects of this treaty consist largely of vague statements of cooperation and plans for the establishment of committees with no clear mandate or deadlines. For example, Article 93 of the agreement calls for recognition of professional qualifications of individuals from the other country, but the only action taken was to establish a joint committee whose mandate was "reviewing and discussing" the issues involved, without any deadline or goal. This pattern of making nonspecific references to "cooperation" and establishing joint committees without clear mandates applies to most other areas, such as intellectual property rights, competition policy, financial services, science and technology, human resource development, promotion of trade and investment, promotion of small and medium-sized enterprises, broadcasting, and tourism.[38]

Perhaps more important than the lack of specifics in these aspects of the agreement is that many of these areas already were subject to discussion and negotiation within APEC, which may be a more appropriate institutional vehicle for handling them. For example, the Japan-Singapore agreement calls for establishing a joint committee to look into "paperless trading"— the use of electronic documentation to eliminate the paperwork involved in customs procedures and other business transactions. The committee is to report on the issue by 2004.[39] However, paperless trading involves new software technologies and procedures that make sense only when deployed on a general basis, not just in a bilateral setting. As noted by Fred Bergsten, "It might be technically feasible, but extremely costly and surely foolhardy, to erect differential customs procedures and product standards."[40] APEC has a subcommittee on customs procedures and by 2000 already had developed the "APEC Blueprint for Customs Modernization" as well as the "APEC Blueprint for Action on E-Commerce." According to APEC, these initiatives are only part of a broader global discussion of these issues through the World Customs Organization and the United Nations.[41] At the 2001 APEC summit meeting, commitment to paperless trading was reinforced, with individual action plans on this topic due in 2002.[42] The Japan-Singapore agreement therefore is unlikely to produce any progress on paperless trading that would occur significantly earlier or on a broader basis than action under APEC.

Overall, the Japan-Singapore agreement hardly represented a bold new step toward a "new age" form of bilateral free trade area. From Japan's standpoint, the failure of the Foreign Ministry and METI to browbeat the Ministry of Agriculture into accepting more duty-free agricultural products had to be a major disappointment. More important, the exclusion of agriculture introduced a precedent of a different sort: it bent WTO Article 24 rules about inclusion of substantially all products. The overall increase in duty-free products was not extensive and did not result in complete tariff elimination, though probably no WTO members will challenge the agreement as a violation of Article 24. Other free trade areas also have excluded small amounts of trade from zero tariffs (also usually agricultural products), and the coverage of 94 percent of Singapore's exports to Japan appears to be within the range of other agreements. The problem will come when Japan negotiates with other countries where agriculture is a more substantial part of trade.

Meanwhile, the trade facilitation and service sector aspects of the agreement were largely without serious content. The various committees established might produce real agreements to eliminate barriers and harmonize standards; nevertheless, the lack of clear objectives is obvious. The committees could easily yield only recommendations for further study or a variety of half-measures that do not really eliminate barriers. Cross-recognition of undergraduate university credits may emerge, but cross-acceptance of licensed lawyers (long a thorny issue pressed by the U.S. government with Japan) probably will not.

Nonetheless, the Japanese government has continued to explore other free trade areas. As of late 2003, how far these proposals would go or how fast they would mature was uncertain given the failures of the Japan-Singapore pact, although some movement occurred.

JAPAN-MEXICO TALKS. Interestingly, Japan's next trade negotiations were with Mexico. As indicated earlier, these talks were prompted by the phase-out of the preferential tariffs for Japanese factories in Mexico under the *maquiladora* system, in which foreign-owned firms could import parts duty-free for production of goods that were to be exported. With NAFTA, American firms continued to be able to import duty-free parts, as did the Europeans following a recent Mexico-EU free trade pact. This left Japanese-owned manufacturing plants in Mexico at a disadvantage relative to their American and European competitors.

After informal discussions between President Vicente Fox and Prime Minister Junichiro Koizumi when Fox visited Tokyo in June 2001, Japan and Mexico launched a study group in September to report by summer 2002 on the feasibility of a trade agreement.[43] Both the Foreign Ministry and METI were cautious about this initiative, arguing that they had less negotiating experience with Mexico than with other Asian countries.[44] Despite their caution, the study group issued a favorable report, and a subsequent summit meeting between Fox and Koizumi in October 2002 produced an agreement to launch formal negotiations.[45] By spring 2003, two negotiating sessions had taken place, and the intent was to complete negotiations by the end of 2003.[46]

In October 2003, talks temporarily broke down. The key problem was agriculture; even the joint study group report had made note of it. The Japanese indicated that agriculture would be a "sensitive" sector and that "there is difficulty in liberalizing this sector," while the "Mexican side expressed its view that certain agricultural liberalization is indispensable in the final package."[47] One development that encouraged the Japanese government to begin these negotiations was the fact that the Mexico-EU agreement excluded several agricultural products.[48] However, some agricultural products were important to the Mexican government in the negotiations with Japan. The breakdown in talks was caused principally by Japan's refusal to include port and bananas in the free trade framework.

The negotiations failed during a visit to Japan by President Fox. A summit meeting usually results in compromise because of the pressure on both sides to conclude the meeting on a positive note; the failure therefore was significant. However, it remained possible that negotiations would resume and an agreement emerge. Whether an agreement would include any serious Japanese concessions on pork or other agricultural products remained to be seen.

EAST ASIA. The rest of Japan's initiatives have been aimed at other East Asian nations. In spring of 2002, there was a flurry of announcements of agreements to establish study groups with various bilateral partners to evaluate the possibilities for free trade agreements.

Japan and Thailand agreed to such a study in April 2002 during a summit meeting on the fringes of the Boao conference, an informal regional conference of officials, business leaders, and academics initiated by the Chinese government and held in China.[49] Thai prime minister Thaksin Shinawatra was enthusiastic enough about a possible agreement with Japan to tell Japanese reporters in the spring of 2003 that a three-stage process—in which sensitive issues such as agriculture were postponed to the final stage—might be feasible.[50] However, subsequent bilateral talks to explore the possibility of negotiations stalled over agriculture despite the apparent flexibility of the Thai prime minister. He insisted that elimination of tariffs on agricultural products—including the sensitive categories of rice, poultry, and sugar—would have to be included for negotiations even to start. By late 2003, agreement to start negotiations was finally reached.[51]

At a Japan–South Korea summit in March 2003, an agreement for a similar study was reached, although it was puzzling since a somewhat similar study group had already produced a report in 2000.[52] In this case, the two countries announced at the October 2003 APEC meeting that formal negotiations would begin.

A meeting between Koizumi and Prime Minister Mahathir of Malaysia in December 2002 produced an agreement to establish another study group.[53] A bilateral Japan-China leaders' meeting at the Boao conference, however, yielded only a commitment to a broader general dialogue on economic matters.[54] In fall 2002, the Japanese Foreign Ministry adopted a very cool stance toward China in its formal strategy statement concerning free trade areas. The report states that "while the possibilities for an FTA could be considered from the standpoint of ultimately working out an economic partnership in East Asia centering on Japan, China, and the Republic of Korea, plus ASEAN, for the present we should continue to closely monitor China's fulfillment of WTO obligations."[55] Similar coolness characterized Japan's approach to Australia. When Prime Minister Koizumi visited Canberra in late April 2002, he agreed to a study group to explore a possible free trade area;[56] the proposal, however, appears to have come from Australia.[57] The Japanese Foreign Ministry strategy statement welcomed the study group but characterized the possibility of a free trade area with

Australia and New Zealand as a "longer-term task." In fact, similar caution and coolness has applied to all potential new partners other than South Korea and Mexico. For Taiwan, the official concern was that an agreement "would not produce major benefits." Language concerning other areas of the world is more definitely negative: Chile would be "a mid- to long-term task," and Mercosur, Russia, South Asia, Africa, and North America and the European Union "would be very difficult." Overall, therefore, the government appeared to be sticking to a limited approach in which South Korea stands out as the only preferred candidate besides Singapore and Mexico.

Not all of the flurry of activity on free trade areas by the Japanese government occurred at a bilateral level. A major issue was whether the government would offer to negotiate a free trade area with ASEAN. In April and September 2001, Japanese ministerial officials met with ASEAN officials and agreed to establish a study group on this issue, to report back in 2002.[58] In part, consideration of this possible free trade area was intended to counter China's separate offer to ASEAN to form an FTA, making it more reactive than proactive. But the big story on the Japan-ASEAN free trade area has been its slowness to materialize.

A key step in the Japan-ASEAN process was a major diplomatic trip by Prime Minister Koizumi to several ASEAN nations in January 2002. When Koizumi made his trip, his hosts widely expected him to offer to begin negotiations on a free trade area. The *Jakarta Post,* for example, touted the advisability of an Indonesia-Japan free trade area just prior to the prime minister's speech.[59] In Thailand, the *Bangkok Post* wrote that "Thailand is keen to pursue its proposal for a bilateral free trade agreement with Japan."[60]

The Japanese government encouraged such expectations by claiming that the trip would be as significant as that in 1977 of Prime Minister Takeo Fukuda, whose Fukuda Doctrine launched Japan's major expansion of foreign aid to the region. Even the Japanese press had been reporting that an "action plan" to start free trade area negotiations with ASEAN was supposed to be under development prior to the trip, although in the action plan timetable, Prime Minister Koizumi was to make general comments during his trip and the plan was to be ready for presentation at the ASEAN+3 summit in Cambodia in the fall of 2002.[61]

Koizumi's major policy speech in Singapore contained only vague platitudes about "cooperation" and not a single concrete proposal on trade or anything else. He called for cooperation in five areas: education and human resources, designation of 2003 as the Year of Japan-ASEAN Exchange, an initiative for a Japan-ASEAN comprehensive economic partnership, a proposed conference on initiatives for development in East Asia, and cooperation between Japan and ASEAN on security. None of these five areas, least of all the comprehensive economic partnership concept, included any specific proposals for action. Even by Japanese standards, this represented a very vague speech.[62]

Koizumi reprised his Southeast Asia performance with a speech at the Boao conference in April 2002. Delivering the keynote address at this "Davos-East" gathering, Koizumi again stuck to vague generalities on cooperation and made them even more diffuse by including central and west Asia in his call for expanded cooperation. At least he referred to the flurry of study groups concerning bilateral and regional free trade areas that he had recently agreed to, but he stuck largely to broad-brush, vague notions encompassing such areas as energy supply and foreign aid.[63]

The sense of disappointment in the region was palpable. The *Jakarta Post* noted somewhat plaintively that "no new aid pledges or projects were proposed by the Japanese side during the visit."[64] A day later, in response to Koizumi's likening of his vague concept of an East Asian community of cooperation to an opera, the same paper opined rather peevishly that "if Japan intends to sing the main aria in this new East Asian opera, it should also clearly indicate the funding commitments it is willing to make to ensure [the opera's] success."[65] The *Bangkok Post*, which also had been so hopeful of an offer from Prime Minister Koizumi, wrote that Japan "spurned" the idea of an FTA.[66] A Malaysian academic teaching in Japan warned in a newspaper op-ed that "unless Japan squarely tackles such important issues [as agriculture] to further strengthen economic cooperation with ASEAN, it will be left in the dark in the move to advance regional economic integration."[67] The fact that Koizumi's trip did not go well did not seem to filter through to the Japanese themselves. One of Japan's leading newspapers, *Asahi Shimbun*, labeled his initiative a "worthwhile cooperation plan" and dutifully followed the Foreign Ministry's lead in comparing his trip to Prime Minister Fukuda's trip of 1977.[68]

A year later, in the spring of 2003, little further progress had occurred. Japanese and ASEAN officials meeting in March 2003 agreed only "to expand economic cooperation, including possibly creating a free trade area."[69] This left the issue about where it had been in 2001, two years after China had already begun negotiations with ASEAN on its own free trade initiative. While it is possible that actual negotiations might materialize in another year, the slowness of the Japanese government in coming to terms with the issue suggests the difficulty of the agricultural problem. Concern over losing leadership in the region to China should have been a powerful incentive for the Japanese government to move forward with this proposal.

Meanwhile, various Japanese government officials have floated alternative, broader free trade proposals. In May 2002, a METI advisory council on industrial competitiveness proposed an East Asian free trade area that would encompass the ASEAN+3 members. The new twist in this (as well as the Japan-Singapore agreement) was the notion that greater regional trade integration was necessary to "increase Japanese industrial competitiveness."[70] That is, the liberalization mandated by the agreement would help force Japanese firms to restructure, thereby hopefully regaining international competitiveness. Meanwhile, some METI officials began to float balloons in the press about a possible ASEAN+5 free trade area, including Taiwan and Hong Kong in addition to the ASEAN+3 members.[71] The inclusion of Taiwan was encouraging, but it may simply reflect indecision in the Japanese government on what countries to include. This approach was at least consistent with comments in Koizumi's speeches in Singapore and Boao about the need to view the region expansively—and in sharp contrast to China's approach to the region.

PROSPECTS. By spring 2003, the Japanese government's approach to bilateral or regional free trade areas appeared to be somewhat muddled. The government had one agreement in its pocket, another in negotiation, one round of negotiations slated to start in 2004, and a variety of proposals for other candidates on which it had not taken action. Proposals involving South Korea, Thailand, Australia, ASEAN, and ASEAN+3—and two involving ASEAN+5—were talked about, but there was little forward motion. Underlying the lack of action has been Japan's fundamental inability to cope with the agricultural problem. Leaving most agricultural products out of the Singapore agreement might have been acceptable, but none of the other candidates is likely to tolerate such exclusions. The opposition from negotiating partners may be more important than Article 24 of the WTO. Since other free trade areas have excluded some products without being challenged at the WTO for Article 24 violations, Japan—which was encouraged by the exclusion of some agricultural products from the Mexico-EU agreement—might be able to do the same. Mexico has at least entered into negotiations with Japan, but what it and other countries will accept as agricultural exclusions and what the Japanese government has in mind may be quite different. The Japanese agricultural ministry may be adamant about a total exclusion, as it was with Singapore.

Even Foreign Ministry officials, often on the liberal side of this debate with the Ministry of Agriculture, seemed to agree that free trade areas with developing countries would be "difficult."[72] Japanese farmers, the most heavily subsidized and protected in the world, would lose sales to agricultural products from lower-wage free trade partners. Even the manufacturing sector appeared to have pockets of opposition to opening the market to favored bilateral partners, as was the case with petrochemicals in the Singapore agreement. Agreements with developing countries also would accelerate the decline of some labor-intensive industries that have shrunk but remain in business and support the Liberal Democratic Party.

The outcome of these pressures is that Japan's bilateral and regional free trade strategy is proceeding rather slowly. The experience of negotiating with Singapore was a sobering one for METI and Foreign Ministry officials who thought they could crack the opposition of Japan's agricultural ministry. At the end of 2003, the Japanese government announced it would begin negotiations with Korea, Thailand, and Malaysia in 2004 (and with ASEAN as a whole in 2005). Nevertheless, the government's approach to these upcoming negotiations was likely to be cautious.

### China

China also has recently entered the game of regional trade negotiations. During the 1990s, its principal policy goal was to enter the WTO, and it finally achieved that goal in the fall of 2001.[73] The process involved lengthy and difficult negotiations with the United States, the EU, and Japan that eventually resulted in considerable movement toward lowering barriers to foreign firms in China. At the regional level, in 1991 China became a member of APEC, along with Taiwan and Hong Kong. For China, a large nation with global economic and political interests, taking an approach that emphasizes global trade and keeps APEC's open regionalism on the side seems suitable. Nevertheless, the Chinese government made a somewhat unexpected offer to negotiate a free trade area with the ASEAN countries in 2000.

At a side meeting during the ASEAN+3 summit meeting in November 2000, the leaders of the ASEAN countries agreed with China to study the possibility of creating a free trade area. An expert group made a report on the desirability and feasibility of closer cooperation, including establishment of a formal free trade area, that was submitted in time for the 2001 ASEAN+3 meeting. At that meeting the leaders agreed to move forward with negotiating a free trade area, to be completed within ten years. Since this ten-year period is just under way, it is too early to predict any details of the outcome. Nevertheless, several factors suggest that an agreement will not create a significant economic bloc under Chinese leadership.

To begin with, the existing trade and investment ties between ASEAN and China are quite thin. Despite their geographical proximity, the ASEAN countries supply only 10 percent of China's imports and absorb only 7 percent of its exports, while China is the source of only 5 percent of ASEAN's imports and absorbs only 3 percent of its exports. The investment ties also are weak: Chinese enterprises have not invested much abroad, and the tiny amount of investment in ASEAN is concentrated mainly in the countries bordering China—Vietnam, Laos, and Myanmar. In the years from 1995 to 1999, Chinese investment represented less than 1 percent of total ASEAN inflows (except in 1998, when China represented 1.7 percent), a miniscule amount.[74] ASEAN investment in China may be more substantial—especially that of ethnic Chinese firms in ASEAN.

So why form a free trade area? Part of the answer may lie in the very fact that the trade and investment flows are relatively small: neither side will be heavily affected. A sophisticated econometric simulation predicted that formation of the free trade area would substantially increase trade: a 48 percent estimated increase in ASEAN exports to China and a 55 percent increase in Chinese exports to ASEAN. However, since these flows are small to begin with, the overall impact on the economies also would be quite small. Indonesia, Malaysia, and Singapore were estimated to experience a 1 percent increase in GDP as a result of the elimination in trade barriers, and China's close neighbor Vietnam to experience a 2 percent increase. The GDP boost for China would be only 0.27 percent, while the cost to Japan and the United States from lost trade would be less than 0.1 percent of GDP.[75] Thus the economic implications for all parties would be small. That would make an agreement easier to negotiate because fewer inefficient domestic industries would oppose it, but the deal would have little economic significance. Nevertheless, all parties can gain political benefits because they can employ the rhetoric of regional cooperation without having to bear economic adjustment costs or worry about economic gains.

The official simulation exercise also predicted substantial trade diversion but little trade creation. That is, ASEAN-China trade would increase as estimated, but at the cost of reduced trade with other parts of the world. Even though the impact on U.S. or Japanese GDP from trade diversion would be low, particular industries would certainly feel its impact—a fact that could lead to considerable consternation among American firms. Thus this particular study reinforces the point made earlier in this chapter about the overrating of trade creation by proponents of narrow free trade agreements.

The projected favorable economic impact of the free trade agreement between China and ASEAN members, as limited as it is, could be overestimated. The study used 1995 data for its base line, and China subsequently engaged in considerable trade liberalization on a global basis as part of its preparation for entry into the WTO. Furthermore, even as the free trade area with ASEAN is under negotiation, China's global barriers will fall further as it implements its WTO entry commitments. Thus while the ASEAN countries would undoubtedly see their trade with China increase as a result of negotiating a free trade area, the increase would take place in the context of falling Chinese global barriers. The marginal impact of the agreement beyond the benefits of China's broader liberalization would certainly be considerably smaller than estimated.

Meanwhile, the ASEAN-China study group advocated a variety of trade facilitation measures, such as enhanced transparency, simplification of customs procedures, mutual acceptance of standards, promotion of e-commerce, and others.[76] As with the Japan-Singapore agreement, this list sounds very much like the trade facilitation agenda of APEC. Therefore it is unclear what, if anything, an agreement between ASEAN and China would accomplish that would go beyond what APEC could accomplish during the decade in which the negotiations would proceed.

Besides the small economic impact involved, the main reason for negotiating this free trade area is politics. With China entering the WTO, the ASEAN countries appeared to be concerned about a possible adverse impact on their economies. Inviting the ASEAN countries into a free trade area was a way for China to reassure them of a positive, cooperative relationship in which they would have preferential access to the Chinese market. For ASEAN, acceptance of negotiations appears to represent the beginning of its recognition of China as the de facto future leader of the region, with whom they might as well collaborate.

ASEAN's concern about China's entry into the WTO has a strong investment element. The ASEAN countries have been worried that foreign firms will favor China—where wages are lower than in most ASEAN nations and the domestic market larger—for direct investment. Indeed, the report of the joint study group on an ASEAN-China free trade area made much of the fact that the inflow of direct investment into ASEAN countries declined sharply from 1997 to 2000, while investment flowing to China remained above $40 billion during the same period.[77] Much of this concern about investment was exaggerated; nevertheless, it became another reason for the ASEAN countries to embrace a free trade area with China. The obvious advantage was that foreign firms might keep their factories in ASEAN countries or build more if they have duty-free access to China from them. Wages might be lower in China, but ASEAN's more advanced infrastructure and, in parts of ASEAN such as Singapore, its more cosmopolitan atmosphere could well cause foreign investors to remain deeply invested in at least some ASEAN countries.

Oddly, the study group report takes up a very different possible investment benefit: a potential increase in Chinese investment in ASEAN. The argument suggests that as China grows and its industry becomes larger and more international, Chinese enterprises will engage in more investment around the world themselves. With the open environment provided by the free trade area, they will choose to invest in ASEAN.[78] However, it is not at all clear why that would be the case. To the extent that foreign direct investment is driven by a search for lower labor costs, China's costs will remain below those of most ASEAN countries for years to come. The other main motive for Chinese investment would be to serve overseas markets through sales, repair, and other after-sales services. If that is indeed a motive for Chinese enterprises, then their major investment markets will be Japan, the United States, and Europe, not ASEAN. The notion that the agreement could generate a wave of Chinese investment in ASEAN countries therefore appears to be mainly a bit of political fluff to help ASEAN governments sell the idea at home.

Some Japanese, not surprisingly, have taken a dim view of the ASEAN-China proposal. Yoichi Funabashi, a leading newspaper commentator on international affairs, fretted that manufacturing industries in Southeast Asia could be "hollowed out." In addition, he believed that while ASEAN was willing to start negotiations, it was very worried about "China's true motive."[79] Such views are in keeping with the generally negative cast to Japanese attitudes toward China. In addition, an ASEAN-China free trade area would undermine Japan's role as a leader in the region unless Japan were to counter it with a similar move itself. This chapter has already discussed the failure of the Japanese government to make such an offer so far.

With a ten-year negotiating horizon, it is too early to predict whether the China-ASEAN free trade negotiations will succeed or what the details might be. The preliminary evidence presented here, however, suggests that it will be concluded, given the relatively small economic importance to both sides of existing trade. What such an agreement would do to the flow of direct investment is difficult to predict, though ASEAN fears of losing inward investment to China—with or without a free trade area—are overblown. The more important implication of this agreement is that it represents the first serious foray of the Chinese government into regional leadership on economic issues.

### Taiwan

The final economy that has recently embraced the free trade area strategy is Taiwan. The main concern of the government of Taiwan since the 1970s had been its isolation in the world. As the United States and others gave China diplomatic recognition, they withdrew recognition of Taiwan and adopted instead a variety of nondiplomatic relationships. In multilateral organizations, Taiwan was ejected as the representative of China and China was admitted. Taiwan's membership has been an issue even for broad regional organizations, although it is a member of the Asian Development Bank and APEC. In the GATT, neither Taiwan nor China had membership. However, the simultaneous entry of China and Taiwan in the WTO in fall 2001 opened new opportunities. With membership, the Taiwanese government felt that it had an institutional basis for seeking free trade areas with important trading partners, even though it was considered not a nation-state but a "customs territory," designated "China, Taipei" in accordance with the nomenclature adopted in APEC and the Asian Development Bank to finesse this thorny political issue.[80] The government's hopes were based on the presumption that the legitimacy conferred by WTO membership would make Taiwan an acceptable free trade area partner for countries that might otherwise shy away for fear of offending China.[81] Accordingly, the Taiwanese government established a task force in 2001 to explore free trade areas with countries such as the United States, Japan, Singapore, and New Zealand.[82] Of those countries, apparently the primary target in 2002 was New Zealand.[83] The exclusion of Taiwan from narrow East Asian regional discussions raises important security concerns, shifting the delicate political balance of the past quarter-century in an undesirable direction. Successful in getting its neighbors to spurn Taiwan, the Chinese government could be emboldened to pursue a harsher diplomatic and military policy toward Taiwan. Such an outcome is in the interest of no one, including the United States.

These moves seem quite similar to those of Japan and other countries wanting to jump on the bandwagon to avoid being left out of free trade areas and to gain whatever benefits accrue to members of such groups. However, Taiwan also has a critical political motive—lessening its political isolation. That concern was heightened by the announcement of the China-ASEAN agreement—a free trade area that had the potential to harm Taiwan economically through trade diversion and politically by improving the bond between the Southeast Asian countries and China.[84] Negotiating free trade areas with Japan and the United States therefore became particularly important to the government.

In the spring of 2002, one Taiwanese government official noted that a free trade agreement with the United States would "promote their shared values of democratic and economic freedom," a claim that one does not hear often in the justifications of other countries around the region for their forays into regionalism. The Taiwanese government took comfort from some signs of positive response in both the United States and Japan. In the United States, the International Trade Commission (ITC)—an independent regulatory body that rules on injury in trade disputes brought under U.S. trade law and conducts studies on trade policy—conducted a study on the feasibility of a free trade area with Taiwan in 2002. This study, done in response to a request from the Senate Finance Committee and fourteen members of the House, found a small but positive impact on both economies.[85] The Taiwanese government was highly pleased also with positive statements about a Japan-Taiwan free trade area made in Japan by Noboru Hatakeyama, a former high-level government trade negotiator heading the quasi-governmental Japan External Trade Organization (JETRO). Although Hatakeyama did not speak for the government and Taiwan had not been included in the list of bilateral partners with whom the government was eager to enter negotiations, his statement was received warmly.[86] Taiwan's government also was quite pleased when the Japanese government made comments in the spring of 2002 about an ASEAN+5 free trade area that included Taiwan.[87]

Whether any of the feelers put out by the Taiwanese government would actually lead to negotiation of free trade pacts remained unclear in 2003 despite the small signs of interest shown by potential negotiating partners. The ITC report, for example, reflected only the interest of a handful of legislators, not of the Bush administration. If, however, the strategy actually worked with significant Asia-Pacific countries such as Japan, the United States, or even Singapore, it would provide at least some of the stronger institutional membership that the government wants to bolster its legitimacy. If not, then Taiwan faces the prospect of obvious exclusion while China becomes an increasingly active participant or leader in regional developments.

## Conclusion

Clearly something new has been happening across East Asia, paralleling developments elsewhere in the world. After decades of focusing on global trade negotiations through the GATT/WTO system, a number of East Asian economies have embraced the concept of bilateral and regional free trade areas. Even if one agrees with this book's conclusion that bilateral and regional free trade areas are undesirable or only a second-best approach to liberalizing trade, the new enthusiasm of many governments—including the United States—is a reality. Recent developments suggest several conclusions.

First, despite the enthusiastic talk of free trade areas and the proliferation of studies, in most cases the spread of negotiations and agreements has been cautious. Singapore, apparently hoping to distance itself from its ASEAN neighbors, appears to be most active in pursuing free trade areas as a strategy, signing agreements with Japan, the United States, New Zealand, Australia, and non-EU western European countries while negotiating with Mexico and Canada. Others have moved more slowly. ASEAN as a whole has been very slow to implement the ASEAN free trade agreement, which was signed over a decade ago. Japan has embraced the rhetoric of free trade areas but has completed negotiations only with Singapore, and serious questions remain concerning its will or ability to successfully complete negotiations with Mexico. Prospects for upcoming negotiations with Thailand, Malaysia, and the Philippines (or ASEAN as a whole in 2005) are also quite uncertain. China has started negotiations with ASEAN but has not indicated much interest in doing so with others.

Second, some governments in the region continue to have difficulty with the concept of opening up completely, even to a small group of partners. Although Singapore has no import duties, other ASEAN members, principally Malaysia and the Philippines, are experiencing difficulty in fulfilling the spirit of the ASEAN Free Trade Area. The Japanese government failed to get concessions from its own agriculture ministry in the Singapore negotiations, a precedent that creates a problem in its negotiations with Mexico, South Korea, and other potential partners. As with other free trade areas approved by the WTO, the incomplete nature of those in East Asia will probably not result in WTO censure. Nevertheless, the inability to open markets completely will surely restrict the initiation of some negotiations because governments are reluctant to start negotiations when they cannot meet the other side's minimum expectations for reciprocity.

Third, the partners involved in actual or possible free trade areas are by no means restricted to other East Asian economies. Singapore has reached outside the region to New Zealand, Australia, the United States, Canada, and Mexico. Japan's second foray into negotiation has been with Mexico. The South Korean government's first completed agreement is with Chile, and it has floated the United States, Mexico, and New Zealand as possible partners. At this level of bilateral deals, actual or possible, East Asia does not appear to be turning inward to itself.

Fourth, there is little evidence that a broad East Asian trade bloc will emerge. To be sure, a China-ASEAN free trade area would bring together a large geographical chunk of the region. But an ASEAN+3 free trade area does not appear to be under serious consideration. Parallel negotiation of an ASEAN-Japan agreement might provide something resembling the functional equivalent of an East Asian bloc, but the Japanese government remains reluctant to move in this direction and has explicitly declared its lack of interest in pursuing an agreement with China. Despite expressions of desire in the region to build a bloc to compete with or imitate the EU or a possible bloc of the Americas, East Asian governments are not ready to move forward in a regionwide effort of their own. The exclusion of agriculture was not a deal-breaker in Japan's negotiations with Singapore, for example, but clearly it is an element in the reluctance of the government to propose negotiations with ASEAN.

Since this book is skeptical of the "building block" concept of bilateral and regional free trade areas, in which they coalesce to create open global markets, the very cautious approach of most East Asian governments is encouraging. However, the fact remains that free trade areas are proliferating around the world. For one set of countries to generally eschew this approach implies that they will be saddled with the impact of trade diversion without having some favored partners of their own to provide trade creation benefits. Concern over being left out of the emerging global trend is clearly a motivator for East Asian governments, and it certainly was a key motivator in the Japan-Mexico negotiations.

The enthusiasm for bilateral and subregional trade deals has eclipsed the attention given to APEC. It would be easy to conclude that the failure to move forward strongly to achieve the Bogor Declaration goals in APEC means that East Asian governments are abandoning APEC to pursue separate deals. The caution with which governments in the region have approached bilateral and subregional negotiations suggests, however, that that conclusion might be premature. In addition, these separate negotiations open the possibility of a new role for APEC as a watchdog. Since the WTO has not been very active or critical in ensuring that free trade deals comply with its requirements, APEC certainly could take an active role in doing so among its members.

# 8

## East Asian Monetary Cooperation

Problems in East Asia in maintaining fixed exchange rates during the 1990s—and particularly during the 1997 financial crisis—put cooperation on monetary issues squarely on the regional agenda. Spurring discussion has been deep dissatisfaction with the International Monetary Fund and the U.S. government. Believing that Western financial speculators caused the 1997 crisis, that the U.S. government's response was too slow, and that the IMF's demands made the crisis worse, East Asian governments began to explore the possibility of banding together to defend themselves.

Overall, the picture that has emerged is one of considerable talk but little action. Proposals have run the gamut from adopting a unified Asian currency to pegging regional currencies to the yen, establishing a "basket" system for setting exchange rates, or simply cooperating to help one another defend whatever exchange rate regime each country has in place. Ideas for new institutions have included an Asian monetary fund, a regional equivalent to the IMF that might provide the region with some independence in helping crisis countries, but the main practical outcome so far has been a set of bilateral swap agreements between some of the central banks in the region.

One of the main undercurrents has been the idea that closer trade and investment links in East Asia should result in currencies that are less reliant on the U.S. dollar. The Japanese had long advocated that the yen play a more substantial role in the exchange rate policies of their neighbors, and in the wake of the 1997 Asian financial crisis, Japanese interest in that idea increased. But the reality is that little movement toward a "yen bloc" has occurred. A number of countries whose currency had been fixed against the U.S. dollar have begun to allow greater flexibility. In some cases that flexibility might reflect new policies to manage the exchange rate against a basket of other currencies, a shift that would increase the role of the yen in regional exchange rate policies. Such developments, however, are hardly a first step toward a yen bloc.

Discussion of monetary cooperation appears to be largely rhetorical. Substantial differences in the levels of economic development and conduct of monetary policy in the region continue to act as a major obstacle to a yen bloc or anything resembling the currency unification in Europe. The swap agreements represent a real policy development, but they are largely meaningless. In fact, the most important development since 1997 has been the shift of some East Asian nations to floating exchange rates, and that trend may continue.

## Currency Issues

Reducing or eliminating currency fluctuations has had enormous appeal throughout history. International trade and finance obviously are facilitated by certainty concerning future exchange rates. Any transaction that involves a delay between an agreement and payment across national boundaries carries the risk that one party or the other might suffer a loss if the currency exchange rate shifts in the interim. Most recently, the Bretton Woods system, set up in 1944, attempted to produce quasi-fixed exchange rates among the major nations. That system collapsed in the 1971–73 period, followed by floating exchange rates among major nations. However, most of the members of the European Union agreed to unify their currencies in the 1990s, producing the euro at the beginning of the new century. Small developing countries often fix their exchange rates to that of a major currency, most often the U.S. dollar.

As appealing as the idea of reducing or eliminating currency fluctuations may be, it is difficult to do, as the collapse of the Bretton Woods system demonstrated so dramatically in the 1970s. At the core of the problem is the existence of independent monetary authorities and policies in nations attempting to coordinate exchange rates. Faced with multiple policy objectives—domestic economic growth, inflation, and the exchange rate—governments and their monetary authorities cannot accomplish all of them. Often there is a conflict between, for example, the desire to accelerate growth by lowering interest rates and the need to prevent depreciation of the currency, which would occur if interest rates fall relative to those of other countries. In a system such as Bretton Woods, governments were supposedly obligated to defend their currencies at the expense of other domestic policy objectives. In reality, sovereign nations cannot be counted on to pursue such policies despite international agreements. Sometimes they do (as in the case of Hong Kong sticking to its U.S. dollar peg in 1998 despite strong pressures), and sometimes they do not (as in the case of the U.S. government in 1971).

One approach to this dilemma is for governments to maintain tight restrictions on capital flows into and out of their economies, as many of the Bretton Woods signatories did in the 1950s and 1960s. However, the general trend has been to liberalize capital markets. Developing countries needing or wanting foreign funds to raise domestic investment and economic growth have liberalized their rules, at least for direct investment. The IMF in the 1980s and 1990s also encouraged developing countries to liberalize, in the name of efficiency and in the hope of fostering more robust financial sectors. However, maintaining a fixed exchange rate while liberalizing capital flows is difficult because rising capital flows can overwhelm a government's ability to defend its currency. A poorly developed domestic financial sector may exacerbate the problem by putting foreign money into dubious investments, as was painfully learned in the 1997 Asian financial crisis.

Therefore the only way to ensure that policies are consistent with currency stability is to establish a single monetary authority, as the Europeans did with the euro. Any other efforts to limit market-determined fluctuation of exchange rates run into problems if the market perceives that a government is pursuing a fixed exchange rate policy that is at odds with its monetary policy or other economic policy actions. However, the good news is that three decades of experience with floating exchange rates has led to both expanded use of market tools to reduce risk for the private sector (such as forward exchange markets, which enable exporters and importers to hedge their risk) and a general acceptance of the risk involved in international transactions.

Currency policies in East Asia embody these difficulties. Currency stability has long had political appeal in Asian countries. The Japanese government resisted the move to floating rates in the early 1970s and frequently has expressed the desire to reduce the fluctuations of the yen against the dollar. Others in the region pegged their currencies to the U.S. dollar, either tightly or within relatively narrow bands of variance. For some of those countries—especially Thailand, Indonesia, and South Korea—the dangers of policy conflict between pegged exchange rates and domestic policy objectives became painfully clear in the 1997 Asian financial crisis. That experience heightened discussion among East Asian countries on how they might cooperate more among themselves to cope with such crises and generally reduce exchange rate fluctuations or even to move to some sort of regional fixed currency.

The choices are legion. East Asian nations could adopt a single currency, as the Europeans did. They could abandon their dollar pegs for yen pegs. They could jointly agree or independently choose to peg their currencies to a "basket" of other currencies that would include both the dollar and the yen. They could avoid agreeing to any currency regime but cooperate to help any member of the region whose currency comes under speculative attack. This final form of cooperation could take the form of a new regional monetary fund, a series of bilateral cooperation agreements, or simple reliance on the region's wealthy giant—Japan—to unilaterally come to the rescue of others.

All of these choices run into the dilemmas outlined here. Any choice that limits the movement of an exchange rate involves subordinating domestic monetary policy to exchange rate goals. Establishing the regional central bank required to adopt a common currency was difficult in Europe and would be even more difficult in East Asia. Like Germany, Japan would expect to dominate the central bank, but the poor record of the Japanese government in managing its own economy in the past decade surely diminishes the willingness of other governments in the region to accept Japan in this role. Lesser forms of regional cooperation also can be problematic. Choosing to help one's neighbor defend its currency or help with the aftermath of a currency crisis implies either agreeing with that nation's policies or imposing conditions on the help.

## Historical Background

Many nations in the region had currencies tightly or loosely pegged to the dollar, and they experienced a major shock when markets overrode their efforts to maintain those rates in 1997. That experience and others over the past decade have stimulated discussion of cooperation on exchange rates and other financial issues. Japan moved to a floating exchange rate in 1973 when the Bretton Woods system finally collapsed; even so, the government has actively intervened in foreign exchange markets since that time and has frequently made statements on what it considers to be an appropriate exchange rate. The yen exchange rate is officially listed by the International Monetary Fund as an "independent floating" rate, although a strong case can be made for government policies aimed at keeping the yen weaker against other currencies than pure market forces would indicate.[1] Most other governments around the region have engaged in some form of official limitation of currency fluctuation. Table 8-1 shows the status of currency arrangements in 1996 and 2001, at least as officially reported to the IMF. Consider first the situation in the 1990s before the onset of the 1997 financial crisis.

Six countries, including Japan, claimed to have floating rates, three had officially managed floats, and six had fixed rates (either pegged or administered through a currency board). Thus the idea that the region generally had pegged rates before 1997 is not entirely accurate, although certainly a majority claimed to restrict exchange rate movements to some degree. Principal among these were the countries hit with the 1997 currency crisis—Thailand (pegged), Indonesia (managed float), and South Korea (managed float).

The implications of these various arrangements are evident in figure 8-1A, which shows currency fluctuations against the dollar for these currencies (other than the yen) in the period from 1990 through 1996, indexing each of them to 100 at the beginning of the period. Hong Kong maintained a strict peg to the dollar, and Thailand came very close to it, allowing its currency to vary by only a few percentage points of its pegged value. Malaysia permitted a somewhat greater band of fluctuation, of about 10 percent. Indonesia permitted its currency to fall against the dollar, but it did so in a very controlled, steady fashion, as indicated by the downward sloping straight line of its currency. The currency movements of the Philippines and Singapore appear to be consistent with the floating rate regimes they claimed to maintain, with their currencies fluctuating on a monthly basis; the Singapore dollar appreciated over the period and the Philippine peso depreciated somewhat. South Korea permitted some depreciation early in the period but then appeared to keep its currency in a narrow band, at 85 to 90 percent of its value at the beginning of 1990. China actually allowed its currency to

Table 8-1. *Official Exchange Regimes*

| Country | Exchange arrangement | |
| --- | --- | --- |
| | *1996* | *2001* |
| Brunei[a] | Currency board arrangement[b] | Currency board arrangement |
| Cambodia | Managed floating | Managed floating |
| China, Mainland | Pegged | Pegged |
| China, Hong Kong | Currency board arrangement | Currency board arrangement |
| Indonesia | Managed floating | Independent floating |
| Korea | Managed floating | Independent floating |
| Japan | Independent floating | Independent floating |
| Laos | Managed floating | Managed floating |
| Malaysia | Managed floating | Pegged |
| Myanmar | Pegged | Pegged |
| Papua New Guinea | Independent floating | Independent floating |
| Philippines | Independent floating | Independent floating |
| Singapore | Managed floating | Managed floating |
| Thailand | Pegged | Independent floating |
| Vietnam | Pegged | Pegged |

Source: International Monetary Fund, *Annual Report on Exchange Arrangements and Exchange Restrictions 1996*, special supplement, and the 2001 annual report.

a. Brunei's peg is to the Singapore dollar, not the U.S. dollar.

b. Currency board arrangement is a form of strict pegging.

fluctuate until 1994, when it was officially devalued and then maintained at a fixed rate.

Among the smaller Asian nations (figure 8-1B), most tried to maintain exchange rates pegged to the dollar, with varying degrees of success. Macau, like its neighbor Hong Kong, maintained a strict fixed rate. Vietnam allowed a major devaluation of 50 percent in 1990–91 but then kept the rate fixed. Cambodia experienced an even greater devaluation—80 percent in 1992–93—and then maintained a fixed rate. Laos had a mild devaluation of 20 percent in 1995. Myanmar allowed its rate to fluctuate modestly in a 20 percent band around the target level. Papua New Guinea maintained a fixed rate until mid-1994 and then allowed its currency to appreciate 40 percent, where it stabilized. This experience among the smaller nations illustrates the problem with pegged rates: governments often resist making necessary adjustments in the exchange rate (for example, because inflation is much higher at home than abroad) until a large depreciation

Figure 8-1A. *Exchange Rates, Larger East Asian Nations, 1990–96*[a]

Index

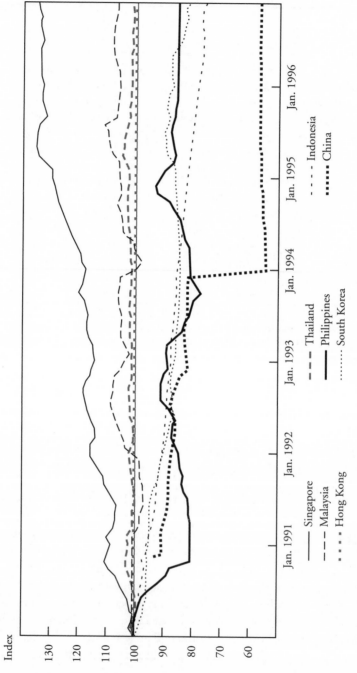

Singapore
Malaysia
Hong Kong

Thailand
Philippines
South Korea

Indonesia
China

Source: International Monetary Fund, *International Financial Statistics*, various years, CD-ROM.
a. Local currency versus the U.S. dollar (January 1990 = 100).

Figure 8-1B. *Monthly Exchange Rates, Other Asian Nations, 1990–96*[a]

Index

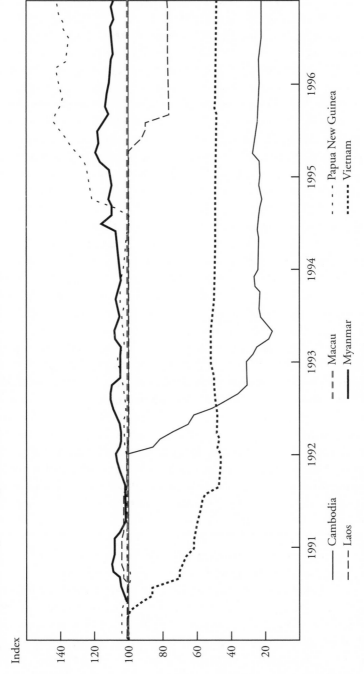

Source: International Monetary Fund, *International Financial Statistics*, various years, CD-ROM.
a. Index (January 1990 = 100).

becomes necessary. The fact that only one tiny city-state out of this collection of smaller economies managed to maintain its fixed rate throughout the period indicates the difficulty governments have in subordinating domestic monetary policy completely to exchange rate goals.

Overall, the picture that emerges from these data is one of a region that had a number of nations whose exchange rate was fixed against the U.S. dollar or managed in a way that limited or smoothed its movement against the U.S. dollar. On one hand, knowledge of these exchange rate policies lessened the risk to borrowers in these countries in tapping international capital markets. They could borrow in dollars, convert the proceeds to local currency, and assume that they could acquire dollars to repay the loans at roughly the same exchange rate. But some of these countries were liberalizing their capital markets, making it easier for domestic firms to raise money abroad. In Thailand, for example, domestic borrowers raised foreign money to speculate in real estate—a business activity that generated no foreign exchange revenue. Without a stream of foreign exchange revenues, these borrowers faced a problem if their assumptions about the fixed nature of the exchange rate proved to be untrue—and that is exactly what happened in 1997 when existing exchange rates became untenable.

The causes of the Asian financial crisis continue to be debated. A common view in Asia has been that the crisis was caused by Western speculators, hedge funds in particular, that chose to mount an "attack" on particular currencies. For example, Eisuke Sakakibara, a professor at Keio University who was vice minister for international monetary affairs at Japan's Ministry of Finance during the crisis, places blame on a report from Goldman Sachs in the spring of 1997 that warned investors that the Thai government would soon have to devalue the currency; he maintains that the report had a pernicious effect on the behavior of Western investors.[2] More independent analysis finds that hedge funds and portfolio equity investors were not to blame. Instead, the crisis was precipitated by the withdrawal of funds by banks—including Japanese banks, which were the largest lenders to the region at that time.[3]

Most of the currencies included in figure 8-1 experienced sudden and sharp declines against the dollar in 1997—with the notable exceptions of China and Hong Kong, both of which maintained their strict pegs (the Chinese, however, had devalued their currency substantially back in 1994). As indicated in figure 8-2A, among the major developing nations, Thailand was hit first, and its currency fell by just over 50 percent against the dollar at its lowest point. Indonesia's currency, however, experienced a far larger fall, losing 83 percent of its value from the beginning of 1997 to the summer of 1998. South Korea followed a pattern quite similar to Thailand's, while both Malaysia and the Philippines saw their currencies drop 40 percent at their lowest point. Even Singapore, which weathered the crisis in its neighbors quite well, experienced a 20 percent drop in the value of its currency.

This experience was obviously a shock for those countries that had proclaimed that their exchange rates were either fixed or heavily managed. Borrowers in Indonesia, Thailand, and South Korea had to repay foreign currency loans that had become vastly more expensive in terms of their local currency. In Indonesia, for example, loans were five times larger in the local currency, creating an impossible repayment problem for any borrower who did not have a stream of foreign exchange revenues.

The real economic shock that followed the sudden depreciation in local currencies is well known. In many ways, the currency movements were a result rather than a cause of these countries' rising domestic economic problems. Nevertheless, the experience of both exchange rate gyrations and tense relations with the IMF and creditor country governments was traumatic. Since Asian governments tended to place much of the blame on Western financial speculators for their initial plight and on the IMF for later problems, they began to think more in terms of regional cooperative action to protect their currencies.

The experiences of the smaller countries in the region continued to vary (figure 8-2B). Like Hong Kong, Macau continued to maintain a strictly fixed exchange rate. Myanmar appeared to narrow the degree of fluctuation it permitted in the first half of the decade, with its currency varying in a narrow 5 percent band; however, a black market exists for its currency. Papua New Guinea kept its rate fixed until late 1997 and then allowed it to float up. Laos experienced a large steady decline of 80 percent, while Vietnam and Cambodia experienced milder, slower slides of 20 to 30 percent and returned to stability by late 1998. One important conclusion that emerges from the experience of these smaller economies is that the 1997 financial crisis was not a general phenomenon among Asian countries; it was very much contained in the crisis countries. Laos experienced a large depreciation, but it occurred more gradually over the whole period.

A second issue in the region concerns Japan and the yen—a currency not included in figures 8-1 and 8-2. If pegging currencies to the dollar turned out to be a problem, why not switch to the yen? This simple notion has arisen from two perceptions: that regional trade and investment patterns in

Figure 8-2A. *Monthly Exchange Rates, Major Asian Nations, 1997–98*[a]

Index

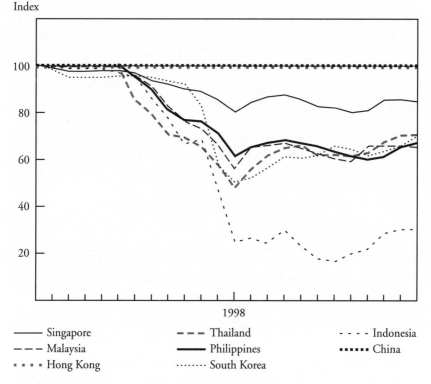

1998

——— Singapore     ▬ ▬ ▬ Thailand     - - - - Indonesia
– – – Malaysia     ▬▬▬ Philippines     ▪▪▪▪▪▪ China
▪ ▪ ▪ ▪ Hong Kong     ········ South Korea

Source: International Monetary Fund, *International Financial Statistics,* various years, CD-ROM.
a. Local currency versus the U.S. dollar (January 1997 = 100).

the early 1990s were gravitating toward Japan, a large industrialized neighbor, and that the U.S. government was behaving in a manner inconsistent with ensuring the stability of the dollar. That, for example, is the central thesis of a recent book by C. H. Kwan, an economist with the prestigious Nomura Research Institute in Tokyo. Kwan argues that "problems associated with the prevailing floating rate system can be attributed to the United States abusing its privileges without fulfilling its responsibilities as a key-currency country, as manifested by the wide fluctuation of the dollar's exchange rate against other major currencies."[4] In his view, a global system in which the euro bloc and a yen bloc offer strong alternatives to the dollar would force the United States to accept more economic discipline. In addi-

Figure 8-2B. *Monthly Exchange Rates, Other Asian Countries, 1997–98*[a]

Index

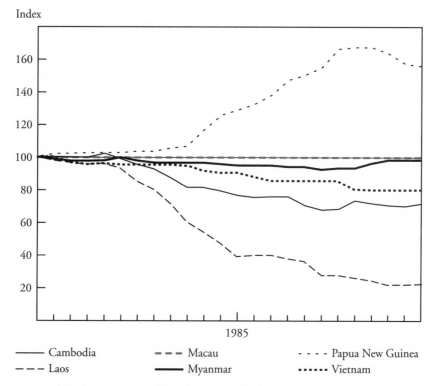

Source: International Monetary Fund, *International Financial Statistics,* various years, CD-ROM.
a. Index (January 1997 = 100).

tion, Kwan argues that exchange markets are susceptible to herd behavior, which causes high volatility and misalignment, thereby aggravating business cycles at the macroeconomic level, particularly in small, open economies.[5]

In this view of exchange rates, the alternative is some system that ties Asian currencies to one another. Kwan claims that pegging exchange rates more closely to the yen would "contribute to macroeconomic stability in Asia's developing countries" and especially in the more advanced economies in the region (South Korea, Hong Kong, Thailand, and Singapore).[6] He also predicts that the region would receive more direct investment and financing from Japan, encouraged by exchange rate certainty.[7] Such reasoning is quite seductive, and expressions of this sort have become common around the region. But this view of the exchange rate problem facing Asian countries is largely wrong and prescribes the wrong solutions.

First, the notion that the dollar is unusually volatile (against all currencies) because of American profligacy is unfounded. Over the last half of the twentieth century, the United States had moderate inflation, reasonable fluctuation in interest rates, relatively strong economic growth, highly developed financial markets, and political stability. To be sure, differences in inflation and productivity growth between the United States and other industrial nations made the fixed value of the dollar in the old Bretton Woods system untenable, and there was some legitimate concern that the American current account deficit was becoming dangerously high in the mid-1980s. However, what appears to be high dollar volatility when viewed from Tokyo turns out to be mainly a problem of the yen, not the dollar.

Figure 8-3 shows the fluctuation in market exchange rates for major currencies against the dollar over the period from 1973, when generalized floating among major currencies began, through 2000. To provide a meaningful comparison across exchange rates, the fluctuation is expressed in terms of the standard deviation as a percentage of the average value of each exchange rate over the period.

What figure 8-3 shows is that on an annual and quarterly basis, the yen has been more volatile than other major currencies against the dollar. On a monthly basis, Norway and Italy were somewhat more volatile, but with those exceptions Japan was again more volatile than the others. Short-run monthly fluctuations are easily hedged by businesses, and it is the longer-term swings, especially the annual movement of exchange rates, that matter to the private sector. On this basis, the standard deviation of the yen-dollar rate as a percentage of the average value during this period was 70 percent higher than that of the German mark, the benchmark European currency before the euro.

For East Asian nations, these data should be disquieting. They have a strong economic relationship with both the United States and Japan, but they happen to be stuck with a yen-dollar exchange rate that has gyrated more over time than have other currencies. Pegged to the dollar, they faced unusually wide variation against the yen, affecting their substantial trade and investment relations with Japan, such as the price competitiveness of their exports to Japan and the willingness of the Japanese to invest in their countries. Pegged to the yen, these nations would have faced the same unusual volatility in their economic relations with the United States. For

Figure 8-3. *Standard Deviation of Exchange Rates against the U.S. Dollar as a Percentage of the Average Value of Each Exchange Rate, 1973–2000*

Percent

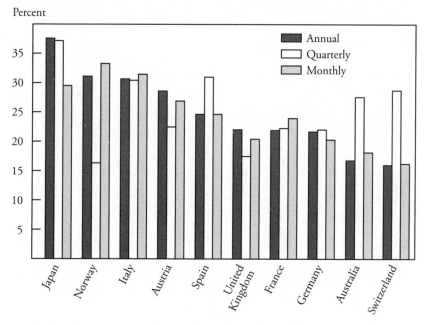

Source: calculated from data in International Monetary Fund, *International Financial Statistics*, 2001, CD-ROM.

no reason other than their historical trade and investment links, East Asian nations have been stuck with coping with this volatility between their two largest economic partners.

That volatility can be viewed more broadly through the movement in nominal effective exchange rates. The effective exchange rate, as defined by the International Monetary Fund, is a weighted geometric average of exchange rates of the currency in question against the currencies of the nation's trading partners, with the weights determined by the size of trade flows.[8] For example, if a country traded equally with Japan and the United States (and no other countries), its nominal effective exchange rate would be calculated as an equally weighted average of its currency's value against the dollar and the yen. This rate is expressed as an index since the weighted average has no meaning as a particular raw number. This index provides a measure of the overall fluctuation of a currency and a broader picture of

Figure 8-4. *Standard Deviation of Flucuations in Nominal Effective Exchange Rates as a Percentage of the Average Value of Each Currency, 1973–2000*

Percent

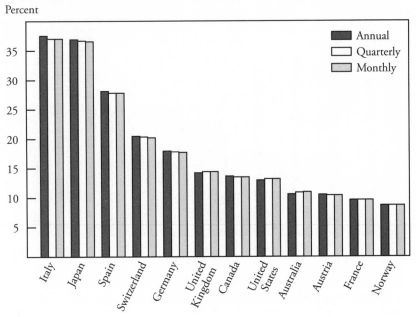

Source: Calculated from data in International Monetary Fund, *International Financial Statistics*, various years, CD-ROM.

volatility than can be seen by simply looking at its exchange rate against the dollar. Figure 8-4 presents the same measure of volatility as in figure 8-3 for the indexes of nominal effective exchange rates over the 1973–2000 period for the same set of countries, plus the United States.

According to figure 8-4, the nominal effective exchange rate of the yen has been much more volatile than that of the dollar. Only the Italian lira was as volatile as the yen over this period. The standard deviation of the yen's fluctuations around its average was 180 percent higher for monthly movements and 188 percent higher for annual movements than that of the dollar's. In comparison with the standard deviation of the fluctuations of the German mark, the standard deviation of the yen's fluctuations was 109 percent larger.[9]

Consider what this overall volatility implies for Asian nations. Would they prefer to bind their exchange rates closely to the yen, a currency that was particularly volatile over the past three decades, or the dollar, which was much more stable? The real answer is that they should not have pegged to any currency; they should have let their currencies float. But given the rather incomplete institutional development of capital markets in some of these countries, they chose to peg, and the dollar was a more sensible choice than the yen.

Why has the yen been so much more volatile than other currencies? The answer lies in the interplay of four important factors. The first is poorly developed financial markets in Japan (especially short-term markets), which have prevented the yen from being a more attractive currency in general due to concern over lack of liquidity in holding yen-denominated instruments. American financial markets, in contrast, have been broad and deep. Had Japanese financial markets been better developed and more fully integrated into global markets, then it is likely that the gyrations in the yen would have lessened. Although the problem diminished over time as deregulation prompted the development of new financial instruments and international participation in the market broadened, the relative thinness and peculiarities of Japanese financial markets made them more prone to influence by relatively small shifts in the behavior of international investors.

Second, the consistent desire of the Japanese government to suppress the value of the yen to help Japanese exporters also has increased volatility. That is, while the government's general policy has been to keep the yen weaker against the dollar than the markets would, periodically that policy has failed. When it has failed, the yen has tended to move up very quickly, overshoot the dollar, and then move back. Had the Japanese government not pursued an active policy to manipulate its exchange rate, then it is quite likely that the yen would not have been so volatile against the dollar and other currencies.[10]

Third, the Japanese government engaged in wide gyrations in monetary policy and overall economic performance over the past twenty years. The government pursued a disastrously loose monetary policy in the second half of the 1980s, which was designed to offset the strong appreciation of the yen that occurred in the 1985–87 period. The outcome was Japan's "bubble economy," with its speculative tripling of stock market and urban real estate prices. That was followed by too much monetary tightening in the opening years of the 1990s to combat the "bubble" and then by record low nominal interest rates in the second half of the 1990s to combat economic stagnation.

Fourth, the Japanese private financial sector also engaged in erratic behavior over the past two decades. Financial institutions rushed into global markets in the first half of the 1980s as the government liberalized regulations, only to lose enormous sums when the yen rose so rapidly and so high after 1985. They also lost heavily in unwise investments in the United States—for example, by buying trophy buildings at any price during the peak of the market in the late 1980s. Then in the 1990s, they redirected some of their investments to Asia and became a major source of international bank loans, only to lose again in the 1997 Asian financial crisis. Now they have substantially withdrawn from the Asian lending market. This pattern of herd investment and disinvestment abroad contributed to the gyrations in the yen as well.

Given the much higher volatility of the yen than of the dollar, as well as the highly visible problems in Japan's economy and monetary policy, would pegging to the yen have made much sense for other Asian countries? Certainly less movement of their own currencies against the yen would provide greater certainty in their dealings with Japan, but it would come at the expense of added volatility in their dealings with other parts of the world. For Asian nations, therefore, tying their currencies to the yen was never a realistic or sensible choice.

The bigger issue is that pegging per se is not a good strategy for East Asian nations. Given the fact that these countries are linked economically to both Japan and the United States and given the wide fluctuations in the yen-dollar exchange rate, their interests are best served by adopting a flexible exchange rate to moderate the impact of the yen-dollar movements on their economies. These countries are not faced with an either-or choice between Japan and the United States, and they would be foolish to take such a route on the basis of dissatisfaction with the U.S. government or the IMF in the wake of the 1997 financial crisis. Floating rates are now advocated by the International Monetary Fund, which stated recently that "for most emerging market countries, primarily in Asia and Latin America . . . floating exchange rate regimes appear to be the increasingly relevant choice."[11]

Adopting freely floating rates is not the only option for East Asian nations. There are a number of alternatives: each country can peg to an individual basket of currencies, or the nations of the region can peg to a common basket of currencies or create a common currency (like the euro) that would float against other major currencies. For a variety of reasons, these alternatives entail problems that make floating rates the rational choice.

Pegging a currency to a basket of other currencies involves a nation's central bank focusing not on a single currency but on a collection ("basket") of currencies and calculating—on the basis of some economic model—an appropriate exchange rate for each individual currency in the basket. If, for example, a nation adopts the yen and dollar as its basket and the yen rises against the dollar, the government might allow its exchange rate to fall a bit against the yen and rise a bit against the dollar. Such a procedure avoids the problems of pegging to a single currency, but it leaves the government in control of exchange rate policies. The presumed objective of this interference in markets is to smooth exchange rate movements by letting the exchange rate slide in response to "fundamentals" such as differences in inflation or productivity growth among trading partners—but without the spikes in a purely market-determined exchange rate that temporarily deviates from those fundamentals. Countries choosing a basket approach have two choices: to maintain a common basket with all members of a group, who move their exchange rates in tandem, or to select an individual basket.

A common peg involves the nations in a group agreeing on a common formula for calculating the exchange rate. Political problems may arise because no consensus exists on how to devise basket pegs—should they be based, for example, on the trade shares of the basket currency countries in the exports of the pegging countries or on some weights based on similarity of economic structure? Different members of the group may feel that one formulation works to their advantage (or disadvantage), making agreement difficult. Disagreements over the appropriate procedure for devising the basket also imply that defections in the face of particular economic shocks are likely.[12]

The other alternative is for each government to determine a separate basket for itself. C. H. Kwan is an advocate of this approach for East Asian nations. Even though he emphasizes the goal of a "yen bloc" when discussing the region in general terms, he ends up advocating pegging currencies to baskets that include both the yen and dollar, among other currencies. He proposes picking basket weights for each country based on an economic model designed to minimize the fluctuation in domestic output due to foreign exchange fluctuations.[13]

For small economies that are not ready for freely floating exchange rates but are uneasy about the demands of pegging to a single currency, the basket approach makes some sense. Particularly for East Asian economies, the basket approach reduces the problem of being tied economically to both Japan and the United States. However, even this approach entails problems. Even if the central banks keep their models secret, analysts can still figure out the weights used in the baskets and bet against the government's exchange rate choice if the existing rate appears to be badly out of line with economic data. Furthermore, the economic models for determining the baskets matter. For example, Kwan's proposal for choosing baskets to minimize the impact on domestic output is problematic. A domestic impact may be exactly what is required to bring a country into better balance with the outside world. That kind of mistake in objectives increases the probability that foreign exchange investors would discern a difference between the existing exchange rate and economic fundamentals and thereby defeat the government's attempt to maintain the rate it has chosen.

Floating exchange rates avoid the problems involved with pegged rates, common baskets, and individual baskets. To be sure, market-determined exchange rates do introduce uncertainty because the private sector cannot predict what will happen to the rate in the future and cannot count on the government to ensure that the movements are slow and smooth. Nevertheless, the private sector has devised sufficient means to cope with that uncertainty. While hedging exchange rate risk is not costless, the costs are not so high as to seriously affect international trade and investment. Floating exchange rates actually provide the most sensible alternative for East Asian nations as their domestic financial markets become more sophisticated and they remove international capital controls.

Consider the implications of market-determined exchange rates in light of the 1997 crisis. The large capital inflow into the crisis countries was premised on fixed exchange rates; there was to be no exchange risk involved in the loans. The huge devaluation that occurred in Thailand, Indonesia, and South Korea created major repayment problems, especially since many of the loans were for projects that did not produce exports and thereby could not earn foreign exchange. Floating rates eliminate both problems. With floating rates, foreign investors and domestic borrowers are aware from the outset of exchange risk and work out mechanisms to hedge that risk. This foreknowledge also makes international capital flows somewhat more cautious. Under floating rates the Asian crisis countries might have received less capital inflow, but that would have been to the good—reducing, for example, international loans for speculative projects. Furthermore, floating rates vary continuously, diminishing the sharp changes that characterized the devaluation of pegged rates and allowing lenders and borrowers to continuously reappraise their situations so that they can back out of relationships before they become untenable.

The strong conclusion of this book, therefore, is that freely floating, market-determined exchange rates are the most sensible choice for most countries in the region. Some, of course, are still in the early phases of building private financial sectors of any degree of sophistication. Laos, for example, which has adopted a managed float, may not be ready for a fully floating exchange rate. China has kept a pegged rate and extensive capital controls, even though its institutional structure is becoming more sophisticated. But many in the region are certainly ready. In fact, some Asian nations moved to floating rates in the wake of the 1997 financial crisis. As the Chinese economy and its financial markets continue to develop, it is likely to move to a floating exchange rate and liberalize capital flows.

Despite the reality that the region is actually moving to wider acceptance of floating exchange rates, the dialogue among East Asian nations since 1997 has concerned how governments might cooperate to limit exchange rate movements or ameliorate their impact. Proposals have included the Japanese suggestion for an Asian monetary fund, a unilateral Japanese plan to assist its crisis-hit neighbors (the New Miyazawa Initiative); an ASEAN+3 agreement to pursue expanded foreign currency swap agreements among its central banks; and general talk of further currency cooperation.

## The AMF Proposal

When the Asian financial crisis occurred, the Japanese government, dissatisfied with the initial policy response from the U.S. government and the IMF, launched a vague proposal to create an Asian monetary fund (AMF) in the fall of 1997. Never fully sketched out, the AMF theoretically would have complemented the IMF in dealing with any regional Asian financial crises. This proposal was a purely Japanese initiative, pushed by the vice minister for international monetary affairs, Eisuke Sakakibara, and his deputy, Haruhiko Kuroda. They floated their proposal in mid-September and discussed it with U.S. and IMF officials immediately after at the annual IMF/World Bank meeting.[14] The proposal called for a fund with $100 billion available to bail out crisis countries; however, a written proposal was never produced and details such as membership, sources of funding, criteria for providing assistance, and governance were never spelled out.[15]

This proposal was quickly criticized by the U.S. government, and even some Asian countries, particularly China, were not enthusiastic about it. Faced with strong, overt opposition from the United States, the Japanese government dropped the proposal. The AMF concept failed, in the view of Sakakibara, not because it was a bad idea but because Japan had "failed to lay adequate ground work with the United States and China." He believed that the United States government (that is, Lawrence Summers, deputy secretary of the treasury) saw the AMF proposal as a Japanese challenge to American hegemony over Asia that "wounded U.S. pride" more than it should have.[16]

This interpretation, always popular in Japan, misses the mark. As originally proposed, the AMF was simply a bad idea. When a financial crisis strikes, it is critically important for the creditors to speak with one voice. If the creditors are divided, then incentives exist for one group of creditors to advance their own interests at the expense of others. Different creditors may differ on the conditions of their assistance, providing a debtor a chance to play one against the other. Financial institutions in the United States and Europe are among the major creditors of firms in Asian countries. To set up a new organization that excluded the United States or Europe would have opened the way for exactly the kind of detrimental outcome that flows from speaking in more than one voice. The initial Japanese proposal not only excluded the United States but also allowed for action independent of the IMF, raising legitimate concerns about the role the organization would play.

These concerns were intensified by the sort of anti-Western or anti-IMF rhetoric that pervaded East Asia at the time. As C. H. Kwan puts it, "an AMF can be interpreted as an attempt by Asian countries to escape domination by Washington and to achieve financial independence."[17] The Japanese government also had taken other moves to distance itself from the then-current stance of the U.S. government. Sakakibara proudly claims that he went out of his way to support Prime Minister Mahathir's decision to impose capital controls in Malaysia, making Japan the only G-7 nation to do so.[18] The Japanese AMF proposal—even if the eventual details would have been formally consistent with or subordinate to IMF policies—came from a government that was signaling its displeasure and disagreement with ' American policy. Having that government play the major role in establishing and running an independent AMF was anathema to U.S. officials.

The point here is not whether the U.S. government and the IMF were entirely correct in their initial approach to the crisis. Controversy over the appropriateness of IMF policies continued to reverberate for years after.[19] What mattered, for better or worse, was that in the midst of a major international financial crisis, one of the major creditors, Japan, was behaving very much as though it intended to play a separate game with the debtors, to the possible disadvantage of other creditors and to the potential detriment of the global financial system. Through such actions as Sakakibara's quick approval of the capital controls imposed by Malaysia, for example, the Japanese government reinforced the impression that it would endorse nonmarket solutions.

More broadly, the AMF proposal raised strong concern that under Japanese leadership the organization would not impose any conditions on the financial assistance it extended to Asian nations in crisis. The lack of conditions or pressure for reforms has been characteristic of Japanese foreign aid to and general foreign policy toward other East Asian nations. Furthermore, noninterference in domestic affairs has been a hallmark of ASEAN, and the Japanese government would be likely to endorse this principle in any AMF in order to curry favor with Southeast Asian governments. Indeed, the inability to force strong action has been apparent in the Japanese government's handling of its own banking sector—an unfortunate fact that has drawn out and worsened the huge nonperforming loan problem that has plagued Japan for the past decade. The Asian crisis nations were clearly in need of reform—since the ultimate cause of the crisis stemmed from problems in their economies—so the indulgent "leave them alone" attitude of the Japanese government was justifiably unsettling in Washington.

Faced with strong American opposition, the Japanese government quickly dropped the AMF proposal. However, in 2000 the Institute for International Monetary Affairs (IIMA), a research institute in Tokyo that is very close to the Finance Ministry, and the Thailand Development Research Institute (TRDI) proposed a Framework for Regional Monetary Stabilization (FRMS). The new proposal included a secretariat, surveillance and research functions, and liquidity support in times of crisis. This proposal was careful to include conditions on support during crises as well as "consultations" with the IMF. The membership envisioned for the FRMS was the ASEAN+3 group. The proposal was presented in the summer of 2000 at an international meeting of finance experts from the ASEAN+3 member countries plus observers from the IMF. Interestingly enough, some participants suggested that both Hong Kong and Taiwan ought to be considered for membership—and perhaps the United States, given its participation in other regional institutions such as the Asian Development Bank.[20]

A separate panel of prominent Japanese in 2000 also endorsed the idea of an AMF-like organization in which Japan would play the major role. As their report states, "there have been growing calls from many Asian countries for the establishment of such an institution *under the leadership of Japan*" (emphasis added).[21] The group also endorsed the notion of a "yen sphere" in Asia. Following proposals from C. H. Kwan, who participated in drafting the report, the group's official short-term recommendation on Asian exchange rates was to take a basket approach, in which the yen would have a strong role. However, they argued that in the longer run "the world as a whole will see the formation of a tripolar [U.S. dollar, euro, yen] currency system.[22]

More recently, the East Asia Study Group—a group established at the urging of Kim Dae-Jung, then the president of South Korea—included an AMF-like proposal in its report to the ASEAN+3 summit meeting in 2002. This proposal called for a regional institution to "provide financial resources to supplement IMF programs in the region" as a medium- to long-term goal but cautioned that in considering such an institution, "East Asian countries need to be in harmony with the discussion of reform of the financial system at the international level."[23]

The concept of an AMF, therefore, has not disappeared at all, although it does not currently exist as a formal proposal of the Japanese government or the ASEAN+3 group. Discussion could proceed on a general level for several more years before reappearing as a concrete policy initiative. If it does reappear, the East Asia Study Group approach is likely to prevail, with a regional institution serving to provide supplementary financing under IMF guidance. The desire to diminish the appearance or reality of Japanese dominance in an AMF could conceivably lead to inclusion of the United States or other nations. This would effectively turn an East Asian financing facility into an APEC initiative.

## The New Miyazawa Initiative

One year after the defeat of the AMF proposal in 1997, the Japanese government announced a unilateral plan to offer financial support to Asian countries hit by the crisis. It was dubbed the New Miyazawa Initiative,

Table 8-2. *New Miyazawa Initiative*[a]

| | Medium- and long-term support | | | |
| | Hard loans | Soft loans | Short-term support | Total |
|---|---|---|---|---|
| Indonesia | 1,500 | 1,430 | | 2,930 |
| Korea | 3,350 | | 5,000 | 8,350 |
| Malaysia | 900 | 950 | 2,500 | 4,350 |
| Philippines | 1,100 | 1,400 | | 2,500 |
| Thailand | 1,350 | 1,520 | | 2,870 |
| Total | | 13,500 | 7,500 | 21,000 |

Source: Ministry of Finance, www.mof.go.jp/english/if/e1e042a.htm [May 30, 2002].
a. Financial support announced February 2000, in millions of U.S. dollars.

after then-finance minister and former prime minister Keiichi Miyazawa; the "new" was to differentiate the plan from one concerning the financial bailout of Mexico in the 1980s that also bore his name. Announced at a G-7 finance ministers' meeting in Washington in October 1998, the plan was for $30 billion—$15 billion in short-term financial support and an additional $15 billion in medium- to long-term financing.[24] These funds had no special conditions attached to them, but the Japanese government noted that they were being made available "in line with" IMF policies toward the involved countries.[25] In a sense, the Japanese government was doing unilaterally what it had intended the AMF to do, although on a considerably smaller scale.

Table 8-2 shows the actual provision of funds. Of the $30 billion announced, some $21 billion was used—or less, depending on how much of the short-term credit made available to South Korea and Malaysia was actually used, a detail not indicated in the Ministry of Finance's data. The short-term credits to these countries were in the form of swap arrangements with the Bank of Japan. Since the currencies of these countries had stabilized by the time the Miyazawa plan came into effect, it is likely that the short-term credit lines were not used at all. In addition, some of the projects listed in the longer-term financing category were traditional foreign aid projects not directly related to the 1997 financial emergency. Leaving these official development assistance (ODA) loans out is appropriate, since, as indicated in figure 4-5 (chapter 4), no large increase occurred in the Japanese foreign aid budget in the 1998–2000 period. Subtracting the ODA loans

Figure 8-5. *Net Change in Japan Bank for International Cooperation Loans to Asia*[a]

Billions of yen

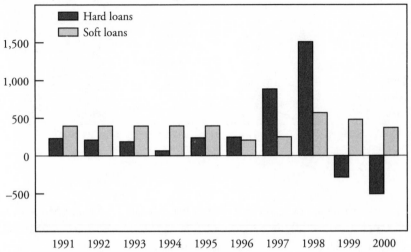

Source: Japan Bank for International Cooperation, *Annual Report 2001*, p. 112; Japan Export Bank, *Annual Report 1999*, 1998, 1996, 1995 (www.jbic.go.jp [October 24, 2003]); Overseas Economic Cooperation Fund, *Annual Report 1998*, 1997, 1996, 1995, 1991 (www.jbic.go.jp/english/oec [October 24, 2003]).

a. The value for the net increase in soft loans in the years 1991 through 1995 is the average annual increase over the period.

brings the total down to $16 billion. How much of even this amount represented new lending that would not have otherwise occurred is unclear. However, most of the Miyazawa money would have had to flow through the Japan Bank for International Cooperation (JBIC), which is responsible for making both hard loans (for trade and investment financing) and soft loans as part of Japan's bilateral foreign aid program. Figure 8-5 shows what happened to the net change in lending by the bank to Asia (although the definition of Asia used includes more than East and Southeast Asia). Rather than showing new commitments or gross disbursements, the figure shows new loans minus repayments on existing hard loans to Asia.

Figure 8-5 shows a definite large increase in hard loans in 1997 (before the Miyazawa Initiative was announced) and 1998. However, those increases were largely offset by absolute decreases in lending in 1999 and

2000. Also consider the increase that occurred from the base level, prior to the crisis. From 1991 through 1996, the average annual increase in net hard loans to Asia was ¥197 billion ($1.8 billion). Subtracting this from the increases in 1997 and 1998 results in an increase in net lending of ¥2.0 trillion (just over $15 billion) above and beyond what probably would have occurred otherwise. That is less than the $22 billion claimed by the government for trade financing, and it is a generous estimate since it does not include the absolute drop in lending that occurred in 1999 and 2000.

Soft lending by JBIC also shows some increase in 1998 and 1999, but not as much. In this case, the average net increase in ODA loans to Asia from 1991 through 1997 amounted to ¥348 billion (or $2.5 billion). Immediately following the crisis, the net increase bumped up to ¥353 billion (about $3.5 billion). By 2000 the net increase was back to the levels that prevailed before the crisis. Therefore the increase in soft loans that might be attributable to the Miyazawa Initiative was on the order of $1 billion.

These data imply that a significant increase in Japan's official lending, both hard trade and soft foreign aid lending, did occur, but that it was not as much as claimed by the government. Part of the disparity is due to the counting of hard and soft lending that would have occurred anyway. The rest is due to actions that did not necessarily involve any expenditure by the government—such as offering loan guarantees and expanding swap agreements with other central banks. Hyperbole aside, the experience of the Miyazawa Initiative yields several conclusions.

First, the government does deserve credit for stepping up to provide financial assistance to its neighbors, both through the IMF and on its own. And in a policy sense, the government deserves credit for emphasizing to Washington the seriousness of the emerging crisis. One could argue that the AMF proposal was not really serious, that it was intended to get the U.S. government to focus on how devastating the crisis was and how dissatisfied governments in the region were over the very limited American and IMF response in the opening months.

Second, despite the positive effort, the amount and disbursal of the Miyazawa money left much to be desired. As noted above, actual disbursements were no more than half the advertised amount. Equally important, the money was slow to materialize. The New Miyazawa Initiative was not announced until the fall of 1998, more than a year after the crisis broke, with disbursements presumably occurring until 1999. For example, soft loans going to Indonesia under the Miyazawa Initiative were not even announced until March 1999.[26]

Finally, the extent to which the Miyazawa funds contributed to helping the recipient countries is unknown. Obviously some of the money, as intended, helped governments in crisis. However, some cynics believe that a considerable portion of the unilateral assistance probably went to pay off Japanese firms or financial institutions owed money from firms in crisis countries; if that is true, then the aid had a large element of self-interest. One would be surprised if Japanese firms were not the beneficiaries of some of these funds, since all governments behave in this manner. Nevertheless, this detracts from the altruistic, eleemosynary behavior claimed by the government.

In summary, this episode created an image of Japanese regional activism. It reinforced Asian governments' belief that Japan would be their cash register and stand up for them against the Americans and the IMF, even though the Japanese government had not truly challenged IMF policies. American government officials were obliged to express their appreciation to Japan for playing a helpful role in aiding the crisis nations while they harbored considerable uneasiness because of the Japanese government's continued promotion of a regional approach that could be detrimental to American interests.

## ASEAN+3 Swap Agreement

In May 2000, the ASEAN+3 finance ministers reached an agreement—the Chiang Mai Initiative, named after the Thai city where the ministers' meeting occurred—to have their central banks create or expand agreements to swap foreign exchange holdings. In such an arrangement, one central bank lends some of its holdings of foreign exchange to another, expanding the resources available to the borrower to defend its currency. Over the next two years, a number of specific bilateral swap agreements between pairs of central banks were negotiated. The Japanese government even tried to stimulate the process by announcing that it would provide ¥100 million (roughly $900,000 at then-current exchange rates) to finance "administration" of the swap arrangements, although exactly what this entailed was not at all clear.[27]

By 2002, a number of bilateral swap agreements had been signed or were under negotiation (table 8-3). The total value of all these agreements (that is, the total value of foreign exchange funds made available) was $31 billion. Overall, this package of agreements represents very little in

Table 8-3. *ASEAN+3 Foreign Exchange Swap Agreements*[a]

| | Lender | | |
|---|---|---|---|
| Borrower | Japan | South Korea | China |
| South Korea | 2 | | Under negotiation 1 |
| China | 3 | 2 | |
| Malaysia | 1 | Under negotiation 1 | Under negotiation 1 |
| Thailand | 3 | Under negotiation 1 | 2 |
| Philippines | 3 | Under negotiation 3 | Under negotiation 1 |
| Indonesia | 3 | | |
| Singapore | Under negotiation 3 | | |
| Sum | 18 | 7 | 6 |

Source: C. Randall Henning, *East Asian Financial Cooperation* (Washington: Institute for International Economics, September 2002), p. 20 table 3.1; "Joint Ministerial Statement of the ASEAN+3 Finance Ministers Meeting," May 10, 2002 (www.mof.go.jp/english/if/as2_020510e.htm [April 29, 2003]); "Japan Agrees to $3 Billion Foreign Exchange Swap Pact with Indonesia," *Japan Digest*, January 23, 2003, p. 3.

a. Billions of U.S. dollars.

terms of meaningful cooperation on foreign exchange and financial matters, for several very important reasons.

First, the total amount of funds is actually quite small compared with the amount of foreign exchange reserves held by the central banks in the region (the total for the region is more than $1 trillion).[28] The Japanese government, for example, made very little of its huge hoard of foreign exchange reserves available to its neighbors on a temporary basis in order to deal with their exchange rate problems. Of the $496 billion in foreign exchange reserves that the Japanese government had amassed by March 2003, only $18 billion, less than 4 percent of the total, was involved in swap agreements (table 8-3).[29] Unless all of the nations with which Japan had signed agreements needed to activate their swaps simultaneously, only a portion of even the $18 billion would be tapped during any crisis. This caution on the part of the Japanese government is all the more interesting given the image of generosity created by the New Miyazawa Initiative.

Second, the amount also was small compared with the size of intervention that might be necessary if a central bank intended to seriously defend a pegged exchange rate. This is particularly true considering that the sum available through these agreements to any particular country is actually quite small. What matters is not the sum total of the agreements but the amount available to an individual country, which is only a subset of the total. The largest amount, for example, is the $6 billion available to Thailand from Japan, China, and South Korea.

Third, the fact that these swap agreements are independent bilateral arrangements implies that nothing resembling a regional approach to currency policy has yet emerged. One Japanese analyst, for example, noted that the effectiveness of the swaps was lessened by the lack of any multilateral arrangement; in times of need, a borrower would have to deal separately with each lender.[30] Optimists may believe that this very limited and uncentralized set of agreements might evolve into something more coherent that would represent a first step toward an AMF or some other form of real coordination of exchange rates. While that is possible, there is no particular reason for them to lead to anything more.

Fourth, the swap arrangements were not buttressed by regional willingness to share important data on capital flows, which would be important if East Asian governments were to act in a coordinated fashion. This issue came up at the ASEAN+3 finance ministers' meeting in the spring of 2002, but nothing was produced beyond a pledge for more "cooperation." At this meeting, the group announced that only seven of the countries—Brunei, Indonesia, Japan, Korea, the Philippines, Thailand, and Vietnam—were willing to share data on short-term capital flows; Singapore, Malaysia, China, Laos, Myanmar, and Cambodia demurred. Nor was the group ready to consider any independent institution to monitor the performance of its members' economies.[31] This reluctance came despite a Japanese effort to promote such sharing by having announced the previous October (prior to an ASEAN+3 summit meeting held just after the APEC summit in Shanghai) that the Ministry of Finance would help ASEAN countries set up systems to monitor short-term capital movements. The Ministry of Finance budgeted ¥200 million (about $1.7 million at then-current exchange rates) to provide assistance, specifically naming the Philippines, Vietnam, and Laos as recipients.[32]

Fifth, the ability of these swap arrangements to allow Asian countries to defend their currencies without interference from the IMF turned out to be very limited. The Chiang Mai Initiative included a provision to have each bilateral agreement specify that only 10 percent of the amount of the swap could be activated simply by the agreement of the lending bank; access to the other 90 percent is explicitly tied to approval from the IMF. This limitation was a disappointment to advocates of a more independent

Asian stance. One Japanese analyst, for example, argued that if the swap arrangements were to have any real value, they needed to address "the financing needs of the borrower in accordance with the situation *before* the country goes to the IMF" (emphasis added).[33] He was hopeful that the 10 percent restriction would be lifted in the future. But the call for the limitation came from the analyst's own government: Japan appeared to be playing its usual cautious political game by trying to portray itself as a regional leader by championing the swap arrangements, while not provoking strong criticism from Washington.[34]

The sixth and by far most important point is that the swap arrangements are essentially meaningless. Swap agreements between central banks are marginally useful devices when governments are committed to maintaining fixed exchange rates and face some delay in activating support from a multilateral institution—that was the motivation for a number of such agreements in the days of the Bretton Woods system. With floating exchange rates, such agreements have little value. Governments can intervene in the market anyway (as the Japanese government has done on numerous occasions in the past thirty years, usually to suppress appreciation of the yen), but the consensus among economists is that most such direct intervention is futile. With the Asian region drifting toward greater reliance on floating exchange rates, the ASEAN+3 group has entered into bilateral agreements that are not really needed or useful. To be sure, these swaps might matter for China and Malaysia. But China does not yet have a convertible currency and therefore does not face large international capital flows that could undermine its efforts to maintain a fixed rate. Malaysia—which has only $3 billion available through the swap agreements (table 8-3)—is the only significant nation in the region for which these swaps might be relevant, but whether its fixed-rate policy will last many more years is doubtful.

The ASEAN+3 group's effort to create a set of swap agreements therefore appears to be more of a political move to prove to domestic constituencies and the international community that it has the resolve to make what appears to be a step toward regional cooperation. This image was important to various political leaders and governments that wanted to prove to their populations that they were standing up to unfair, heavy-handed pressure from the IMF and other sources, and the swap arrangements gave the Japanese government a chance to save face after the sharp rejection of its AMF idea in 1997. The swap agreements also enabled the rest of the region to demonstrate to the IMF and to Washington that they were capable of doing something independently. These arrangements represented a relatively innocent step that neither the U.S. government nor the IMF would oppose and a trivial one in terms of actual impact; they therefore served such political purposes perfectly. The Chinese government, meanwhile, both gained negotiating experience with its neighbors and demonstrated some flexing of its leadership muscle by offering to lend money to other central banks in the region, although Japan was first to negotiate such agreements.

In addition, the negotiations may have had another form of favorable political impact. The exercise enabled a group of finance ministry and central bank officials to build some negotiating experience among themselves. They had had no previous experience of close interaction except through APEC. Inasmuch as the gain in familiarity improved communication, it could be useful in any future regional financial crisis.

## Monetary Union

Various groups in East Asia endorse establishing a single currency as a long-term regional goal, as seen in the Japanese and Thai proposal for a Framework for Regional Monetary Stabilization, in the writings of C. H. Kwan, and in the Japanese study group report of 2000.

In addition, a somewhat similar proposal has recently emerged from Korean economists involved in a research project supported by the Korean central bank. They endorsed eventually establishing a monetary union and maintaining a common basket of currencies in the interim (participants would endeavor to observe the common currency policy, with some latitude for deviation within a certain band). However, the Koreans were somewhat skeptical of past Japanese proposals and Japanese leadership, noting that for any effort to achieve currency cooperation and unification to succeed, the Japanese must be more "responsible" and especially be more willing to act as a lender of last resort in the event of a currency crisis.[35]

Perhaps building on proposals such as these, the annual Asia-Europe government-level dialogue (ASEM) called for a cooperative research project on Asian currency issues. That led to formation of something called the Kobe Research Project, which involved researchers from around the region and Europe. Funding for the project came entirely from the Japanese Institute for International Monetary Affairs (IIMA), which is funded by the Japanese Ministry of Finance. This group produced a report, presented by Japanese finance minister Masajuro Shiokawa at the ASEM meeting in the summer of 2002. It, too, calls for eventual establishment of a single Asian currency buttressed by an Asian central bank by 2030.[36]

The concept of greater cooperation leading toward monetary union certainly appears to have received considerable support around the region. A poll conducted in early 2002 of executives in a number of East Asian countries showed that 43 percent of those polled favored eventual monetary union. The percentage varied from a low of about 15 percent in Australia to more than 50 percent in South Korea, Japan, and the Philippines. On the lesser step of forming an Asian monetary fund, 58 percent were in favor—including more than 80 percent of Malaysians and 75 percent of Japanese polled.[37]

The outpouring of talk, academic proposals, and poll data concerning regional monetary union certainly is interesting. The Australian central bank took the talk seriously enough to argue in 2001 that any regional monetary cooperation plan should include both Australia and New Zealand.[38] Ideas and analysis obviously are a necessary precursor to political decisions to move forward. But at the present, the emergence of a unified currency among East Asian nations remains unlikely, at least within the next two to three decades. The wariness with which the ASEAN+3 participants approached the central bank swap arrangements suggests that any further steps toward eventual currency union will emerge slowly if at all.

The data in this chapter suggest that the region is moving toward floating rates faster than toward any cooperative plans to reduce fluctuations. Look again at table 8-1. Thailand, Indonesia, and South Korea all abandoned pegged rates and moved to floating rates. That means that along with those that previously had floating rates, including Japan and Papua New Guinea, six of the fifteen countries in table 8-1 claimed to have floating rates.

Figure 8-6A and 8-6B confirm the information in table 8-1. Japan has had a floating rate since 1973, although it sometimes is manipulated by the government. Of the other eight in figure 8-7A, five show varying patterns of fluctuation against the dollar, and such variations are suggestive of floating rates. Only China, Hong Kong, and Malaysia maintained strict dollar pegs.

The smaller Asian economies show greater determination to maintain or return to rates pegged against the dollar. Macau, as earlier, followed the policy of China and Hong Kong in maintaining a strictly fixed rate. Vietnam, Cambodia, and Myanmar allowed a narrow band of 5 to 10 percent variations. Laos, whose currency had been battered so much in the earlier years of the 1990s, saw its currency fall another 50 percent and then reimposed a

Figure 8-6A. *Exchange Rates, 1999–2001*[a]

Index

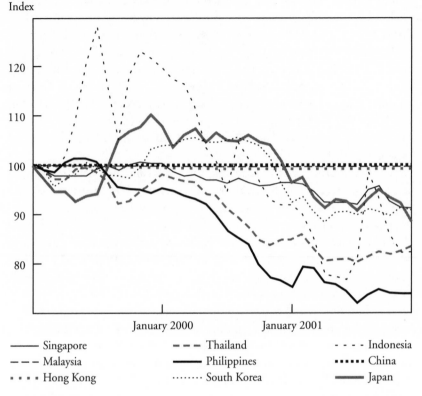

Source: International Monetary Fund, *International Financial Statistics,* various years, CD-ROM.
a. Index (January 1999 = 100).

dollar peg. Papua New Guinea, which had moved to a floating rate in 1997, stayed with it.

Rather than moving toward greater regional cooperation, which could lead toward limiting fluctuations among Asian currencies or toward establishing a common currency, the region is more likely over the next decade to move toward generalized floating. The big story of the next decade is likely to be the move of China (and Hong Kong and Macau) from its current pegged rate to a floating rate as it liberalizes its restrictions on exchange transactions and capital flows. Malaysia may well do the same after Prime Minister Mahathir leaves office. Those countries that move to floating rates will learn to live with the uncertainty involved, just as the developed

Figure 8-6B. *Monthly Exchange Rates, Other Asian Countries, 1999–2001*[a]

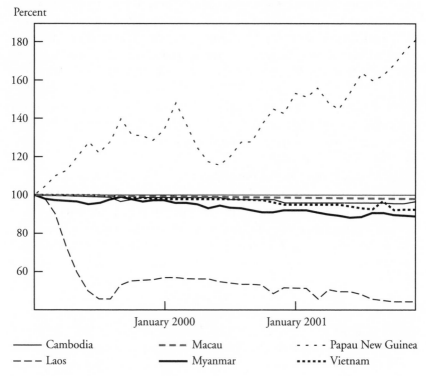

Source: International Monetary Fund, *International Financial Statistics,* various years, CD-ROM.
a. Index (January 1999 = 100).

nations adjusted back in the 1970s after the collapse of the Bretton Woods system. To be sure, governments across the region might be dissatisfied with floating rates a decade from now and put renewed energy into achieving eventual currency union. Nevertheless, the current discussion of currency union is likely to remain a matter of talk while practical governments continue to adopt floating rates.

## Conclusion

Over the course of the 1990s and particularly after the 1997 financial crisis, regional cooperation on currency matters became a hot topic in and among East Asian countries. The sudden and sharp depreciation of the currencies of Thailand, Indonesia, and then South Korea were deeply shocking events in the region, even though some of the smaller nations in the region with pegged rates had already had similar problems in the first half of the decade. Blaming the currency jolts and their negative impact on real economic activity on Western speculators and the IMF's mistaken policies, these countries found it useful to talk about regional cooperation as a means of protecting themselves from such pernicious international influences. By 2003, the outcome was a set of expanded swap arrangements among some of the central banks of the region, arrangements that would increase the foreign exchange resources available to a government attempting to defend its currency.

A popular theme around the region was to expand the swap arrangements into something more serious—from establishing a regional lending institution to help governments defend their currencies to using a basket approach for pegging regional currencies and even to working toward a unified currency similar to that in Europe. Nevertheless, the talk is unlikely to result in serious action, at least in the next decade, for the following five reasons.

First, there is little evidence that any of the countries in the region would be willing to sacrifice control over their domestic monetary policies for the sake of reducing or eliminating fluctuations among their currencies. Currency unification would require a single regional central bank—something that is inconceivable at the present. Even an agreement to adopt a basket approach to pegging currencies would require a strong commitment from all the governments to subordinate their domestic monetary policy to the agreed-on exchange rates. A few governments in the region, including China and Hong Kong, have appeared to have that commitment; others have not.

Second, a major problem faced by these nations is the unusually high volatility of the Japanese yen—not the volatility of the dollar. Any regional arrangement that ties currencies closer to the yen is likely to burden them with Japan's odd currency volatility.

Third, there has been no abatement in the various economic problems causing economic stagnation in Japan or in the poor policy choices made by the Japanese government. Japan must exhibit better economic performance and less idiosyncratic monetary and fiscal policies before others in the region might be willing to subordinate their monetary policies to Japan's. A better economic environment in Japan will eventually materialize, but in 2003 it was not yet in sight. The spectacle of stagnation, policy mistakes, and dithering over policy has seriously eroded the attractiveness of Japan as a nation to which others in the region would want to tie their own monetary policies.

Fourth, Japan's currency and financial policies in the past decade have been problematical for the rest of the region. The major depreciation of the yen in the 1995–97 period (from an unsustainably strong value) contributed to the Asian financial crisis, and a renewed effort to push the yen down in 2001–02 brought more complaints from around the region. Even the New Miyazawa Initiative provided less support than the Japanese government claimed, although it deserves credit as a positive step to help Japan's neighbors. The Japanese government's financial and currency policy thus was inimical to its attempt to create an image of Japan as a regional leader.

Fifth, the real issue facing the region was the flaw in pegged rates in general. If governments wanted to hedge the fluctuation in the currencies of their two major economic partners—Japan and the United States—the solution lay in floating rates, not in a mechanical basket approach. As countries in the region have chosen to integrate themselves into global capital markets, they have faced increased difficulty in maintaining an artificial exchange rate at odds with economic data available to global investors. One solution might be to impose capital controls in order to maintain a fixed rate policy, as in Malaysia, but the trend appeared to be in the opposite direction.

For all these reasons, the reality of the past decade has been an increase in the number of the countries in the region that have moved from fixed or managed rates to floating exchange rates. These countries have followed a logical and appropriate course of action. Over the next decade, others may follow their example, principally China, Hong Kong, and Macau and possibly Malaysia.

Policy action toward greater regional cooperation turned out to be less than advertised. The Japanese government made an initial show of challenging the United States and the West with its proposal for an ill-defined but apparently quasi-independent Asian monetary fund in 1997. But in reality the Japanese government was unwilling to seriously break with either the United States or the IMF over the issue of regionalism. That was evident with the swap arrangements as well. The Japanese government's insistence on IMF approval for activation of the bulk of the money committed to the arrangements indicated that, despite its occasionally feisty rhetoric, the government was unwilling to challenge the dominance of the IMF (of which Japan is a principal member) in dealing with regional financial crises.

This reality is reassuring since so much of the rhetoric about regional cooperation has had a strong anti-Western tinge to it. Establishment of an Asian monetary fund with the expressed goal of making the region less dependent on the IMF, for example, would be a disturbing development. If investors know that nations in the region can resist pressures for reform from the IMF (or individual creditor governments such as the United States) then they will be less willing to invest in the region. In addition, such an institutional development would enhance an unhealthy "us versus them" attitude in the region.

The presumption behind regional discussion of currency cooperation is that managed or fixed rates provide strong economic benefits. With currency unification, intraregional trade and capital flows would benefit from the zero risk of currency fluctuation. Managed rates, tied to some basket of other currencies, presumably ease the risk problem by reducing the amount of fluctuation that traders or investors face over any particular period of time. Nevertheless, the past three decades have produced a world in which the risks associated with floating exchange rates have been handled remarkably well. The Japanese government has never been satisfied with floating rates and has periodically intervened, primarily to suppress the exchange rate in order to help exports, a mistaken policy that probably has contributed to the high volatility of the yen. Despite Japan's approach, the probable outcome for the region over the next decade will be greater reliance on floating rates rather than any move toward regional cooperation on protecting or managing rates.

# 9

## Regional Leadership

Beyond the relatively straightforward matters of regional trade agreements and cooperation on currency
issues, regional economic integration entails questions of
leadership. For the East Asian countries considered in this
book to form any semblance of the European Union over
the next several decades would require substantial leadership, and only two countries in the region could supply it:
Japan and China. None of the others has the clout to assume such a role. Unlike in Europe, sharp disparities in size
of population, economic size, and affluence militate against
the possibility that a group of equals from three or four
East Asian nations might work closely together to realize a
shared vision for the region. Some countries, like Malaysia,
have had colorful national leaders who waved the banner of
East Asian regionalism, but Malaysia is too small to play
the role of regional unifier. Indonesia is larger in terms of
population but too mired in political instability to lead.
Similar problems apply to the rest of the smaller countries,
leaving only Japan and China as realistic possibilities. This
chapter, however, argues that neither Japan nor China is
likely to provide adequate leadership, underscoring the

problems previously identified concerning difficulties in forming trade or monetary agreements.

The implication of this conclusion is that economic regionalism will remain "soft," without evolving into the kind of tight integration represented by the European Union. Despite the lack of strong leadership, governments can meet to discuss issues of mutual interest, enhance familiarity and personal networks among government officials, and create some bilateral or subregional free trade areas. Talking and becoming familiar with one another represents a positive development and should not be dismissed as a trivial accomplishment. Nevertheless, regional discussions have frequently invoked the idea of the eventual creation of a European Union–style trade bloc. Over the next decade, however, neither China nor Japan is likely to provide the leadership necessary to move the region in that direction.

## Japan

Japan is the obvious candidate for regional leader and has aspired to fulfill that role informally for at least the past two decades. At market exchange rates, Japan has by far the largest and the most affluent economy; it also is the most technologically advanced Asian nation. It engages in direct investment throughout the region and provides large amounts of foreign aid to its less developed neighbors. Moreover, it is a member of the G-8 group of nations. As already discussed, the Japanese government has embarked on an effort to build its regional base through discussions of both free trade areas and cooperation on currency issues. All of this suggests the image of a major advanced nation acting in a determined fashion to create a regional economic bloc around itself. Despite that surface image, Japan's role as a regional leader is seriously hampered by four problems: its inability to abandon protectionism, even with its regional neighbors; its inability to deal with noneconomic aspects of its reputation, mainly the "history problem," the various diplomatic problems emanating from Japan's actions during the Second World War; its unwillingness to erode its primary relationship with the United States; and its underlying wariness about China.

### Continuing Protectionism

The Japanese government's unwillingness to harm inefficient domestic producers, especially in agriculture, has been a major constraint on its attempts to push cooperation with the rest of the region, and it undercuts the credibility of Japan's policy initiatives. This problem was embodied in the failure to include agricultural products in the Japan-Singapore free trade area, and it has appeared periodically when the government has reacted strongly to restrict imports from its Asian neighbors due to pressure from domestic groups—usually with the support of the ministries that have jurisdiction for the products involved. To be sure, Japan is hardly the only nation that irritates its trading partners and undercuts its negotiating position by such actions; witness the Bush administration's restrictions on steel imports and increased subsidies to farmers in 2002 just as the Doha round of WTO negotiations was getting under way. Nevertheless, it is important to recognize that the Japanese government has undermined its message of cooperation through such measures.

Consider, for example, a small but symbolically significant trade dispute with China that occupied most of 2001. Beginning early in the year, the government resorted to slowing down import inspections to reduce imports from China of leeks, shiitake mushrooms, and reeds for tatami mats. In April, the government formalized import restraints by invoking "safeguard" protections under the provisions of the WTO even though China had not yet been voted into the WTO and Japan therefore had no obligation to abide by WTO rules in its trade with China. The Chinese government quickly retaliated by restraining the import of automobile parts and other manufactured products from Japan, also by slowing down import inspections.[1] In June, China formalized its restrictions by imposing punitive tariffs on such things as automobiles, auto parts, air conditioners, and cellular phones.[2]

In this tit-for-tat exchange, the total import value of the Japanese products that the Chinese government succeeded in restricting was far higher than that of the Chinese products that the Japanese government had restricted. The agricultural products restricted by Japan had an annual import value of roughly $100 million, while the manufactured goods restricted by the Chinese government had an annual import value of $700 million.[3] Note also that the Chinese government picked high-value-added products to restrict, while the Japanese government restricted low-value-added agricultural products. The Japanese car industry itself estimated that the tariffs would cause it to lose a much higher ¥420 billion ($3.5 billion) in retail sales in China.[4] This appeared to have been a major miscalculation on the part of the Japanese government. The immediate and strong Chinese response must have been a surprise to the Japanese government, which was used to dealing with the United States, where the strong rule of law and whose membership in the WTO placed serious constraints on its ability to retaliate against Japanese trade barriers.

Over the course of the rest of the year, the Japanese government struggled to reach a compromise to prevent this issue from spiraling into further rounds of retaliation. Some progress occurred in October 2001, when Prime Minister Koizumi visited Beijing ahead of the APEC meeting in Shanghai. The primary purpose of his trip was to mend diplomatic relations frayed by Japan's approval of a nationalistic history textbook and by his visit to Yasukuni Shrine, a memorial to Japan's war dead. Nevertheless, he agreed with Premier Zhu Rongji that their trade officials should find an end to the dispute.[5] Takeo Hiranuma, the minister of economics, trade, and industry, followed up with a statement in October that Japan would resolve the issue through negotiation.[6]

In November, the Japanese government proposed a "private solution" in which Chinese farmers and Japanese importers would agree on upper limits for Chinese shipments to Japan, with Chinese farmers responsible for policing themselves.[7]

The solution moved forward on that basis. In December, some thirty-nine Chinese farmers representing 70 percent of the Japan-bound leek crop gathered "privately" in Shanghai with Japanese importers and agreed to limit their export of leeks to Japan to the previous year's level and establish a floor price. Similar private sector groups also worked out supposedly private, voluntary agreements to limit shipments to Japan of the other products involved in the dispute, shiitake mushrooms and rushes for tatami mats.[8]

Two aspects of this episode are important. First, the dispute proceeded at the same time that the Japanese government was negotiating its free trade area with Singapore and floating trial balloons about similar arrangements with other Asian nations. Japan's unwillingness to allow open trade to produce its natural consequences—the displacement of Japanese labor-intensive agricultural products by those from China—sent a strong signal concerning Japan's basic unwillingness to proceed very far in permitting open trade, at least in agriculture and other low-value-added goods.

This first conclusion should be tempered, however, by recognizing the reality of trade flows. In part, the Japanese attempted to curb the import of these three products because imports had increased dramatically. From 1996 through 2000, imports of leeks had increased twenty-four-fold (from a very low base), while imports of shiitake mushrooms were up 70 percent and imports of tatami rushes were up 80 percent (in physical volume).[9]

The 2001 restrictions and the "private" deal worked out put a limit on further expansion of these particular imports, but it did not seriously roll back the level of imports. Nevertheless, the episode still had strong symbolic importance, especially given the exposure it received in the press, as a negative signal around the region concerning the Japanese government's policy toward agricultural imports.

Second, the solution that was worked out set a particularly bad precedent. For decades, the Japanese government had decried the understanding in its relations with the United States that it would "voluntarily" restrain exports to the U.S. market in order to allow the United States to avoid the GATT prohibition on quotas imposed by the importing country. Although the Japanese government had been willing to be dragged into such negotiations with the U.S. government from the 1960s through the mid-1980s, its growing resistance led to cooperation with the Europeans during the Uruguay round of GATT negotiations to end the practice. Under the new WTO, voluntary export restrictions imposed by *exporting* governments would no longer be permitted. Having won that victory against American trade policy tools, the Japanese government proceeded to undermine the new WTO rule by creating a "private" agreement with the Chinese. It would be foolish to believe that Chinese farmers voluntarily agreed among themselves to limit exports to Japan. Chinese producers and Japanese importers may have met in a room in which no government officials were physically present, but the agreement was for all intents and purposes a government-to-government deal. This set an unfortunate precedent for the new WTO and sent a chilling message to Japan's Asian neighbors that any semblance of free trade with Japan would be subject to such dubious measures to undermine their access to Japanese markets. In theory, this agreement is a violation of the WTO, which enjoins its members to "not encourage or support" such private deals. However, no government filed a case against Japan and China, thereby establishing a precedent that might encourage others to engage in similar behavior on the presumption that it will not be challenged.

The Japanese government also engaged in a trade dispute with South Korea during 2001 over fishing rights in waters that Japan may not even control. Korea sought fishing rights near four small islands just north of Hokkaido that were seized by Russia at the end of World War II but claimed by Japan. Since the islands currently are part of Russia by virtue of almost sixty years of physical Russian occupation, it would seem logical that the Koreans would turn to Moscow to sign a fishing deal; however, the

Japanese government objected on the grounds that ownership of the islands and the waters around them was disputed. Amazingly, after some testy negotiations, the South Koreans backed down and promised to stop seeking rights from Russia in exchange for rights to harvest fish elsewhere in Japan's uncontested coastal waters.[10]

In this case, the Japanese government sent a strong-armed signal to its closest neighbor at the same time it was discussing the possibility of a free-trade agreement. In the process, the Japanese government forced the South Koreans to recognize the validity of its murky claims to the four islands by hitting them with the hard-ball tactic of withholding access to Japanese coastal fishing grounds. Again, the signal was hardly the one of openness and cooperation that Prime Minister Koizumi was preaching. It could have a chilling impact on the ability of the Japanese government to get others in the region to negotiate free trade areas, and it was a sobering clue to how incomplete the impact of such agreements would be in the face of actual policy actions by the Japanese government.

Occasional protectionist actions may not be insurmountable obstacles in the world of trade policy. Mexico and Canada have been willing parties to NAFTA despite U.S. behavior on issues such as Mexican truck drivers and Canadian lumber. The EU has similarly survived the sometimes aggressive protests of French farmers and other interest groups across the region. However, the situation with Japan appears to be more serious. Japan has a low level of imports and inward direct investment—the lowest in East Asia relative to the size of its economy. Many economists have argued for the past two decades that Japan's generally protectionist trade policy has been at least partly responsible for those statistics. Although measures of the impact of Japanese protectionism have declined in the past decade, events such as the 2001 disputes with China and South Korea indicate that the problem is by no means gone.

### Diplomatic Problems

The Japanese government also shoots itself in the foot with periodic statements and actions relating to World War II. Over the years these have included various justifications of Japan's actions (such as the claim that the Korean government had asked to become a colony of Japan), Japan's initial refusal to admit its officially organized forced prostitution of Asian women ("comfort women") for the benefit of its military, Japan's denial of Japanese atrocities (such as the "rape of Nanking"), and Japan's reluctance to issue official apologies for Japanese aggression during the war. At a time when the Japanese government was attempting to forge a new, closer economic relationship with the rest of the region, it would have been politically expedient to stifle such behavior; however, it continued unabated in the new century.

During 2001, the Japanese government went through yet another round of controversy over textbooks when the Ministry of Education approved a junior high school history textbook that portrayed events from the 1930s and 1940s in a highly nationalistic manner. This official approval created a storm of protest both at home and around the region. Partly because of the high visibility of the controversy, virtually no local school boards adopted the text. The ministry and the prime minister may have felt that this was the best of all outcomes: the political right wing was placated by having one of its nationalistic history texts officially approved for school use, while the public and foreign governments were placated by the lack of actual use of the book. Nevertheless, the issue, which appeared to be another in an endless series of similar actions, was damaging.

By allowing the whole textbook mess to proceed without intervening to stop it, Prime Minister Koizumi also damaged his personal position as a regional leader. Because of his rhetoric on economic reform, he had come into office with the image of being a relatively liberal member of the conservative Liberal Democratic Party. By not interfering with the bureaucracy in the textbook case—as he could have done easily—Koizumi sent a far less liberal message to the public and the region.

In the summer of 2001, Koizumi further damaged his regional reputation by becoming the first prime minister since Prime Minister Nakasone in the mid-1980s to make an official visit to Yasukuni Shrine. This Shinto shrine was established to honor Japan's war dead during the state sponsorship of Shintoism in the early twentieth century, much as other advanced nations honored their dead by dedicating national cemeteries and other such memorials. State sponsorship ended after the war, but controversy erupted when the shrine decided in the 1960s to honor a group of Class A war criminals—Japanese military leaders tried and executed after the war for conspiring to bring war to the world. As a result, visits by prime ministers to the shrine, especially on the politically significant August 15 anniversary of the nation's surrender, have been controversial at home and around the region. Prime Minister Nakasone made one visit to the shrine in the 1980s to please the right wing of the Liberal Democratic Party but then ceased, recognizing the negative political implications with the broader domestic public and neighboring nations.

Koizumi chose to repeat Nakasone's visit to the shrine in 2001. The visit, which was scheduled for August 15, was changed at the last minute to August 13, supposedly to reduce its political significance. While the gesture was appreciated, the visit still generated negative reactions around the region. Demonstrations occurred in Hong Kong, Beijing, Seoul, Taipei, and Kuala Lumpur.[11] Much of the strong vocal reaction to the "history problem" usually comes from China and South Korea, the two nations that suffered the most under Japanese colonialism and militarism, but after Koizumi's visit, even Singapore's *The Straits Times* commented that "Mr. Koizumi is bad news for Asia."[12]

Like Nakasone, Prime Minister Koizumi could have been expected to drop the shrine issue after an initial visit. Indeed, he appeared to be eager to put the issue behind him when he attempted in personal meetings prior to the APEC summit in Shanghai to placate both South Korea and China concerning the history issue and the trade dispute with China.[13] However, he chose to compound the damage by making a second official visit in the spring of 2002. That visit too was quickly denounced by both the Chinese and Koreans. The Chinese government even cancelled some upcoming bilateral meetings to indicate its displeasure, while in South Korea there were some protest marches and the governing and opposition parties joined one another in denouncing the visit.[14]

The "history problem" is difficult to assess in terms of its implications for Japanese leadership of the region. The victimized nations, especially China and South Korea, try actively to keep the issue alive and manipulate it to make demands on Japan. The memory of the war—and rubbing the Japanese government's face in every misstep it makes in dealing with war-related issues—is a "card" these governments can play to their own benefit. Therefore, one should be somewhat cautious in interpreting their reactions to such events. On the other hand, the failure of the Japanese government to cleanly and actively repudiate its wartime actions is both a moral blot on the national character and foolish behavior for a government attempting to forge a stronger economic relationship with the region. A government that makes improving regional relations a priority ought to be able to view its own behavior in that context and drop its periodic attempts to placate domestic right-wingers. The fact that the government is unwilling or unable to establish such policy priorities sends a negative signal to the rest of the region.

Behind the theatrics of political posturing lie real consequences. One of those is persistent anti-Japanese feeling in parts of Asia. A 2001 Japanese-sponsored opinion poll revealed that 73 percent of Chinese respondents and 62 percent of South Korean respondents disliked Japan.[15] While much of this general anti-Japanese sentiment is confined to China and South Korea, misgivings about the Japanese government and Japan in general crop up to a striking extent in conversations across the region, based on both the "history problem" and other aspects of Japanese diplomatic and economic behavior.

More important, such episodes may undermine the ability of the Japanese government to gain acceptance for its diplomatic initiatives. In the fall of 2001, the Japanese government acted quickly and firmly to ally itself with the United States in the war on terrorism. At the APEC summit meeting that year, President Bush elicited a general statement of support from all APEC members. The Japanese government attempted to repeat that performance by getting the members of the ASEAN+3 summit meeting held just two weeks after the APEC summit to issue their own declaration on antiterrorism. The effort failed, and it was described in the Japanese press as a "major blow for Prime Minister Junichiro Koizumi's efforts to show leadership in the absence of his U.S. and Russian counterparts."[16]

### American Primacy

A third problem regarding Japanese leadership in the region is the government's unwillingness to sacrifice its close economic and political relationship with the United States. That unwillingness has been obvious to other governments in a number of developments over the past decade.

As discussed, American pressure caused the Japanese government to shun Prime Minister Mahathir's EAEC proposal in the early 1990s. Criticism from the U.S. Treasury Department caused it to drop its AMF proposal in 1997 and led to its insistence on IMF approval before the bulk of the funds in the Chiang Mai swap arrangements could be released. In its leadership of the ADB, the Japanese government has been careful not to irritate the U.S. government too much.

Moreover, Japan is visibly linked to the United States through the nations' bilateral security treaty and the presence of American military bases in Japan. While these bases have occasionally been controversial with the Japanese people, the government values the security relationship. Recent government moves, such as the dispatching of Japanese navy vessels to the Indian Ocean to show support for the war on terrorism and the war against Iraq, only reinforce the image of Japan as an ally of the United States. If the government is eager to maintain this security relationship, obviously it is going to be very cautious in embracing any regional economic policies that exclude the United States.

The result is that often the government is willing to tweak the U.S. government by floating ideas such as the AMF but fundamentally unwilling to follow through with any policy that the U.S. government considers detrimental to its interests. If the other governments in the region want a regional leader willing and able to stand up to the United States or the IMF, they will not find it in Japan.

### Anxiety over China

Underlying much of Japan's regional approach has been a vague fear of China—both because of the presumption that China's economic prowess has caused a "hollowing out" of Japanese industry and because of China's rising military expenditures.[17] Japan's government, media, and academic establishment have long exhibited very ambiguous attitudes toward China. On one hand, China attracts Japan because it is the source of much of early Japanese culture and because it presented a trade opportunity for Japanese firms when its market began to open in the 1980s. On the other hand, China's vast pool of low-cost labor has fueled Japan's fears of the hollowing out of its industry and China's large, modernizing, nuclear-armed military raises Japan's anxieties about national security.

Japan's trade with China has grown quickly, as has that of other countries. Disputes over leeks and mushrooms have not prevented a rapid increase in Japanese imports from China. Meanwhile, Japanese firms have invested in China, often to produce products for export to Japan. Although the level of investment is not sufficient to justify fears of hollowing out, there has been enough to demonstrate that the fear of an economically dominant China has not prevented Japanese firms from expanding trade and investment just as firms from other countries have.

Nevertheless, the anxiety about China's economy persists and explains, in part, why the government is not interested in pursuing a free trade area. The existence of ASEAN+3 and the fact that the Japanese government agreed to the expanded central bank swap arrangements indicates that Japan is willing to work cooperatively with the Chinese government on some regional issues. However, the wariness of Japanese government officials and the media about China's economy remains strong.

A similar wariness characterizes Japanese attitudes regarding China's military power and its regional diplomatic stance. The presence of a nearby large, modernizing, nuclear-equipped military force is unsettling. Some of the Chinese government's behavior on diplomatic issues also has unsettled the Japanese; in the past several years, for example, the Japanese government has grown tired of Chinese efforts to play the history card.

More broadly, one senses Japanese anxiety over China's regional role. The ability of the Chinese government to engage ASEAN in free trade negotiations while the Japanese government has been unable so far to follow suit suggests that regional leadership is slipping from Japan to China. Whether concern over China's rising regional role will lead to tension and resistance from the Japanese government remains unclear, but Japanese uneasiness over aspects of Chinese behavior is palpable.

Such fears and anxieties are not a good foundation for building Japanese leadership in the region. Other nations in the region also have had concerns about China, and perhaps the Japanese government believes that its negative tone appeals to their concerns. But the reality is that ever since China began to reintegrate itself in the outside world, others have had to accommodate its presence—economically and politically. What the Japanese government would need to do as a regional leader would be to find a way to embrace China confidently as a beneficial economic partner—one that should be exporting more agricultural products and low-value-added manufactures to Japan, to the benefit of both economies—and as a force to be reckoned with in regional diplomacy. Periodic resurfacing of "history" issues, private arrangements to restrain Chinese exports to Japan, and other such actions hardly advance those goals.

## Summary

Japan's effort to lead the quest for Asian regionalism has not lived up to its rhetoric. Since the late 1970s, Japanese politicians, academics, and government officials have talked extensively about pressing for stronger Asian regionalism. They pumped up foreign aid in the wake of the Fukuda Doctrine in 1977. They toyed with participating in Prime Minister Mahathir Mohamad's East Asian Economic Caucus in the early 1990s. They proposed an Asian monetary fund during the 1997 financial crisis. They have indicated a strong desire to pursue bilateral or regional free trade areas. But the reality has fallen far short.

Even the single free trade area agreement, with Singapore, turned out to be very difficult to accomplish because of the Ministry of Agriculture's adamant opposition to including any significant agricultural products.

While that was acceptable to Singapore, it implied that creating a free trade area with Asian countries that have sizable and competitive agricultural sectors would be very difficult.

The rest of the region appeared to be willing to give lip service to Japan's being the regional leader as long as Japan was by far the dominant provider of foreign aid and an increasing source of direct investment and bank loans, as it was throughout the 1980s and early 1990s. But with the decline in Japan's foreign aid, investment, and loans, the rest of the region appears to see less reason to go along with Japan's ideas. Why bother if cooperation doesn't yield more cash?

Meanwhile, Japan periodically manages to offend its neighbors on other issues, such as the agricultural trade dispute with China, the textbook issue, and Prime Minister Koizumi's visits to Yasukuni Shrine. Other East Asian governments also are well aware of the Japanese government's unwilling-ness to seriously jeopardize its close economic and political relationship with the United States for the sake of regional initiatives. Finally, Japanese leadership is hampered by China. Close regional economic integration and cooperation necessarily involves cooperation between Japan and China. But the Japanese government, media, and public appear to be so wary of China that closer formal links are unlikely in the next decade.

For all these reasons, Japan does not appear to be a successful leader in the region. The government behaves cautiously rather than confidently with its neighbors, and its actions do not meet the expectations raised by its words. With all of these factors still in evidence and exacerbated by the overall economic malaise at home, it is difficult to see Japan's very timid approach changing soon.

## China

If Japan is incapable of leading an Asian regional bloc, what about China? With its rapid economic growth, huge population, historical legacy of influ-encing much of East Asia, and reintegration into global trade and invest-ment, China could become the de facto leader of Asian economic regional-ism. China's offer to form a regional free trade area with the ASEAN countries, its participation in the ASEAN+3 process, and other recent actions all point toward an emerging leadership role. In some respects, the Chinese government has successfully pursued actions that amount to exer-cising regional leadership, but the image outshines the reality.

The ASEAN-China free trade negotiation represents an interesting exercise of Chinese regional leadership. The economic benefits of the free trade area will be relatively small, but it was a move in which the ASEAN nations agreed to work cooperatively with China. Considering that ASEAN was originally formed in the 1960s in part as an anticommunist association, the new willingness of the ASEAN countries to negotiate with China is quite interesting. The deal also is interesting because it represents a snub of Japan. Since Japan has yet to put together a similar offer to form a free trade area with ASEAN, the contrast is quite obvious.

As a smaller but interesting example of success, consider the April 2002 Boao conference, convened by the Chinese government on Hainan Island. This meeting brought together business people, government officials, and academics in a close imitation of the well-known annual World Economic Forum gathering in Davos, Switzerland. The meeting itself appears to have been badly run, causing many complaints about accommodations and logistics. Technically, the Boao conference was a nongovernment affair, with initial input from the Philippines, Australia, and Japan. However, the Chinese government ended up with effective control of the event.[18] However badly it may have been run or how heavy-handed the Chinese government's de facto control, creating a new forum of this sort was a very simple exercise in regional leadership. The Japanese could have created a similar forum at any point in the past twenty years, but they failed to do so. Instead, they were put in the position of having their arm successfully twisted by the Chinese government to have Prime Minister Koizumi appear at the conference to make the keynote speech.[19]

Despite these examples of its regional leadership, China has three considerable problems in exercising this role: perceptions of its potential economic dominance, its incomplete transition to capitalism and democracy, and its continuing noneconomic disputes around the region—concerning, for example, the Spratly Islands, the island dispute with Japan, and the expansion of its navy.

## Economic Dominance

Concern about the possibility of China's economic dominance remains strong despite China's initiation of negotiations with ASEAN. Among more advanced nations, like Japan, a main concern has been the hollowing out of their manufacturing industries, although mainly through losing low-value-added jobs that should have migrated to low-wage nations years ago.

In Southeast Asia the main concern is the inability to compete with China for inward foreign direct investment because of China's large domestic market and low wages.

In both Japan and South Korea, however, the concern about China as a regional leader now extends beyond any fear of losing low-value-added jobs. In 2001, for example, several Korean organizations produced studies arguing that Chinese firms in a number of industrial sectors were more competitive than Korean firms in global markets (including those for more advanced goods such as machinery and information technology products) and that China's entry into the WTO would enhance their relative competitiveness.[20] Even in Japan some are concerned that the expertise of Chinese engineers is so high that China is quickly emerging as a leader in the manufacture of higher technology products, posing a direct threat to Japan's comparative advantage in international trade.

The reality is that the region does not face any "threat" from China. With the low wages in China, China's comparative advantage remains in manufacturing lower-value-added products that the advanced countries should be shedding anyway. And if WTO entry enhances China's position as the world's manufacturing base, that would help fuel its overall economic growth, making China a growing market for the exports of the rest of the world. What really matters is China's current account balance. If China's economic growth proceeds with a rough balance in its current account, then one cannot argue that its growth and entry into the WTO have hurt other nations in the region, since its imports in this case rise as fast as its exports. Furthermore, to the extent that China does become a more attractive location for global manufacturing investment, firms in other Asian countries have an equal opportunity to participate in that investment. To be sure, accommodating China implies making adjustments that often arouse political opposition from shrinking industries. The important point, however, is that *economically* the integration of China into the global trading system is a positive development. The economic benefits of China's economic emergence therefore stand in great contrast to the political unease it has aroused.

As discussed earlier, the ASEAN countries worry about competition with China for foreign investment. To be sure, China's emergence as a more open nation with an improving rule of law has made it more attractive to investors. However, because there is only so much cross-border investment by corporations in any given year, if China attracts more, other countries will receive less. But China's incorporation into the global economy also creates additional income and wealth in China itself, expanding the global economic pie and the investment accompanying that expansion. Furthermore, as argued previously, investment is motivated by many factors, of which low wages is only one. The ASEAN countries actually have little to fear as long as they fix their own domestic political problems and maintain an attractive setting for investment.

Regardless of the economic logic, the problem facing Chinese leadership in the region is to a large extent other countries' fear of economic denomination. This fear is common elsewhere. The inability to view economic ties as mutually beneficial has been characteristic of domestic politics in the United States, and concern over American economic dominance is a strong theme in many parts of the world. Nevertheless, such concerns have not prevented the United States from assuming a leadership role in global affairs—both economic and political. The question is whether such concerns will seriously hamper China in its regional setting. The entrance of ASEAN into free trade negotiations suggests that other countries will eventually adjust to the reality of China's emerging economic role in the region, but their adjustment may remain an uneasy one. For Japan, the uneasiness will remain strong.

### Incomplete Economic and Political Transition

China has undergone enormous change since undertaking reform in the late 1970s. However, China remains a socialist country and has not completed its transition to a market economy. This incomplete transition is a problem if China is to play a leadership role in a region where most members have had market-based economies for decades if not longer and some have moved toward democracy over the past several decades. To be sure, the transition away from nondemocratic authoritarianism is less far along and more fragile in Southeast Asia than Northeast Asia. Nevertheless, the attempt to maintain a communist form of government is at odds with the political evolution of much of the rest of the region. For all the flaws of the Japanese political system, for example, elections have been free and open for more than a half-century, and rights such as freedom of the press are deeply entrenched. South Korea and Taiwan also have moved toward democracy in the past two decades, abandoning what had been undemocratic, authoritarian governments.

On the economic side, China certainly has made progress toward institutionalizing capitalism. Nevertheless, huge state-owned enterprises (SOEs) continue to exist, along with government-run banks. Considerable progress has been made toward establishing a system of laws to govern private sector economic transactions, and WTO membership has aided that process, but serious problems in enforcing contracts and intellectual property rights remain. This situation poses problems for foreign firms investing in China and also creates a broader problem of regional leadership. With capitalism entrenched in most of the rest of the region—except for some of the recently emerging Southeast Asian nations, like Vietnam—having a country that is still in the throes of a long-term transition toward capitalism act as the de facto regional leader is problematic. As a regional leader, the government might decelerate reform efforts or feel freer to manipulate enforcement of its laws and regulations with respect to its East Asian neighbors so as to disadvantage their firms and benefit Chinese enterprises.

### Noneconomic Disputes

Like Japan, China raises concerns around the region because of its behavior regarding security and diplomatic issues. A main issue is China's treatment of Taiwan; the constant Chinese effort to diminish Taiwan's political legitimacy and participation in global and regional institutions is disturbing. Taiwan represents only 4 percent of the Asian economy, but that is enough to make it the fourth-largest economy in the region. In terms of per capita income, it is a mid-ranking country, again fourth in the region. Furthermore, with more than $120 billion in exports and almost $110 billion in imports in 2000, Taiwan is heavily engaged in global trade and investment.[21] It also is a major investor in China, and the institutional constraints on direct trade and investment between the two have gradually lessened.[22] If closer regional cooperation occurs, Taiwan would be a logical participant, and its exclusion is unfortunate. Its exclusion from narrow East Asian regional discussions also raises important security concerns, shifting the delicate political balance of the past quarter-century in an undesirable direction. If China succeeded in getting its neighbors to spurn Taiwan, the Chinese government might be emboldened to pursue a harsher diplomatic and military policy toward Taiwan. Such an outcome would be in the interest of no one, including the United States.

China has pursued other policies that also worry its neighbors. The dispute over ownership of the Spratly Islands, with their possible large oil and gas reserves, has simmered for years. China's increase in military spending and especially the signs that it is building a blue-water navy also raises concerns around the region. China has even pursued a dispute with

Japan over a small, rocky, uninhabited island for no good economic reason other than its implications for coastal fishing rights. The government also irritated Japan over its forcible removal of North Korean refugees who had successfully entered the Japanese consulate in Shenyang in the spring of 2002, although the Japanese Foreign Ministry officials involved in the incident also deserve some of the blame because they implicitly—and perhaps explicitly—accepted the Chinese actions. Finally, a 2001 incident with an American spy plane involving provocative (and fatal) behavior by a Chinese pilot is another example of aggressive Chinese action on China's borders.

Very much like Japan, China has been unwilling or unable to submerge these issues for the sake of carving out a stronger regional economic leadership position. China's neighbors can compartmentalize their relations to some extent, embracing rising trade and investment links for the sake of the economic benefits while continuing to maintain their wariness on security issues. Nevertheless, it is difficult to envision the emergence of China as the leader of a tighter form of economic regionalism in East Asia without some alteration of the government's behavior on such diplomatic and security issues.

The regional concerns over security and diplomatic issues are quite unlike those in North America or Europe. Like China, the United States is a nuclear power with small nonnuclear neighbors; however, neither Canada nor Mexico has had any reason to fear U.S. armed aggression since the mid-nineteenth century—even the armed incursion to pursue Pancho Villa in Mexico is now almost a century in the past. European concerns over German militarism and fascism were strong in 1945, but European economic regionalism included a militarily destroyed and democratized West Germany in its embrace in order to help maintain the new regime. Assisting economic reform and its supporters has been one rationale for extending WTO membership to China. That modest step, however, hardly amounts to tacit acceptance of China as a regional leader. Uneasiness over China's military stance still works against its assuming a role as de facto regional leader.

## Conclusion

Japan and China are the two logical potential leaders of the region. Of the two, Japan is the more obvious choice, given its economic size and affluence, technological sophistication, and regional engagement. But Japanese leadership is seriously hampered by a variety of factors. First is Japan's inability to abandon its protection of inefficient domestic industries, long a problem in Japan's economic engagement with the world. The government has been unable to carry out a truly liberal approach to trade, even with individual neighbors. Furthermore, the government's inability to more clearly repudiate the nation's ugly past has robbed it of moral leadership, thereby undercutting its regional economic agenda. Meanwhile, others in the region can easily discern Japan's unwillingness to disassociate itself from the primacy of its relationship with the United States. Japan's wariness toward China further hampers any effort to adopt a confident approach to the region. Japan, therefore, faces serious problems in performing successfully as a leader.

To a large extent, the past willingness of others in the region to acquiesce to Japanese policy initiatives appears to have been related to money—increasing foreign aid donations, commercial bank loans, and direct investment by Japanese firms. But as these aspects of Japan's engagement with the region stagnate, the issues of protectionism and nationalistic interpretations of history gain more influence in regional reactions to Japan, undermining Japan's ability to persuade others to follow its lead.

China might be an alternative to Japan, but it, too, faces serious problems as a leader. Principal among these is the fear, albeit somewhat irrational, of China drawing economic activity away from the rest of the region—a zero-sum game in which China becomes the manufacturing base of the world, at the expense of the rest of Asia. But in addition to these concerns there are important misgivings about a leader that has only halfway transformed itself from a socialist to a capitalist economy while maintaining its communist political system. And the Chinese government continues to irritate its neighbors with its diplomatic and military behavior, more seriously than Japan does with its history problem. A particularly troubling aspect of China's diplomatic behavior has been the exclusion of Taiwan from regional institutional arrangements except when American pressure has led to the inclusion of both China and Taiwan, as with APEC and the Asian Development Bank.

Of the two possibilities for de facto regional leader, however, China currently appears to be the more likely. China's rapid economic growth and engagement with the world over the past two decades has made it a rising trade and investment partner for all nations. It would be understandable if its neighbors accepted this shift in economic ties and embraced China and its regional policy initiatives. For example, the region, including Japan, has acquiesced in the exclusion of Taiwan from narrow regional groups such as ASEAN+3 and from consideration as a partner in bilateral free trade areas. Nonetheless, the region's wariness concerning China remains strong and hinders China's leadership role.

An alternative vision of regionalism might involve the joint leadership of Japan and China, much like Germany and France formed the core of the European move toward economic regionalism in the past half-century. This alternative also appears unlikely. Japan's "history" problem and other aspects of its economic and diplomatic policies toward China militate against establishing a new cooperative bond. China, too, shows few signs of putting aside policies that irritate or alarm Japan for the sake of forging bilateral cooperation on regional economic issues. The economic gains from the existing relationship appear strong enough to keep it from spinning out of control over economic or security disputes, but they do not appear to be viewed by either side as strong enough to drive them toward greater cooperation. Thus existing political will seems to be sufficient to resolve periodic irritations such as the 2001 dispute on leeks and mushrooms but not sufficient to produce a regionwide free trade area.

The central conclusion of this discussion is that the flaws in both Japanese and Chinese leadership would strongly limit any movement toward a stronger, narrow form of East Asian economic regionalism. The other nations of the region are simply unwilling to accept the exercise of political and economic leadership by either nation, and the relationship between the two is not evolving into joint leadership. Since this book takes a very dubious view of any narrow form of economic regionalism, this conclusion is comforting.

# 10

## *Conclusion and U.S. Policy Recommendations*

The East Asian countries considered in this book have undergone an amazing transformation over the past several decades. Many of them have experienced very high rates of economic growth, which has reduced poverty and brought growing affluence to their populations. Meanwhile, the political divisions of the cold war finally crumbled. Whereas thirty years ago the United States was stuck in a bitter war against communism in Vietnam, the 1980s saw the beginning of the reintegration of China, Vietnam, Cambodia, and Laos into the global economic system. The opening of China to trade and investment with the non-communist world over the past two decades has been a huge change for both the region and the rest of the world. In other parts of the region, entrenched ideologies and revolution gave way to economic development and, in some cases, democracy. There was a new willingness to foster efficiency in order to promote exports rather than rely on protectionism for the sake of import substitution, and governments abandoned fear of foreign domination to encourage inward foreign direct investment. There is much for East Asians to look back on with pride in their accomplishments.

With prolonged economic success in parts of the region and others becoming engaged in trade with the outside world, a major question has been how to foster regional cooperation. Since the 1960s, a plethora of overlapping forums has emerged, providing opportunities for academics, officials, and business people from across the region to talk about issues of mutual interest and concern. However, there are two big questions that must be addressed: What set of countries should be talking? What should they be talking about?

The first question was long determined by the cold war, with its sharp cleavage between communist and noncommunist countries; since then, other questions regarding participation have arisen. Should the focus be on the Asia-Pacific region, a broad area that includes North America, Australia, and New Zealand—and, in some definitions, the Central and South American nations facing the Pacific? Or should the East Asian nations converse only among themselves?

This book has argued forcefully for an expansive definition of the region based on its trade and investment links with the rest of the world. The concept of a narrow form of East Asian cooperation is undermined from the start by the region's characteristics. Along almost any dimension, the disparity or diversity of the region is very large relative to that of other areas where economic regionalism has had some success. The region includes the population giant China and tiny city-states like Singapore. It includes smaller economies like Singapore and Hong Kong that are open to and dependent on trade and investment, and it also includes Japan, an economic giant in terms of both absolute economic size and per capita income that turns out to be relatively closed to trade and investment. Furthermore, the region exhibits none of the historical, cultural, or religious commonalities that characterize Europe or North America. All of these disparities diminish the rationale for a primarily East Asian form of cooperation. Contrary to the claims of some political leaders in the region, there is no "Asian way" that draws these nations together, no common point of view that is intrinsically different from that of the West.

The simple notion that the East Asian region is experiencing a strong relative increase in intraregional trade flows is inaccurate. Intraregional trade flows have increased compared with trade links to the rest of the world but not at the expense of links to the United States or Europe. The East Asian countries remain closely tied to the United States through trade and to a somewhat lesser extent to Europe. Furthermore, much of the evidence of rising intraregional trade is due to the reintegration of China into the global economy—a phenomenon that has affected the whole world and not just the region.

Much the same is true for investment links. For a time in the late 1980s and early 1990s, the relative importance of Japanese investment around the region was rapidly growing. Since the mid-1990s and particularly after 1997, Japan's growing dominance was reversed. The Japanese were a major source of international bank lending to the region and to some countries in particular, like Thailand, but the outstanding total of Japanese loans has now dropped by almost 70 percent and the relative share of Japanese banks in total cross-border lending to East Asian countries has shrunk considerably. Japanese foreign aid continues to dominate, but the absolute amount of Japanese aid is now declining due to fiscal problems in Japan and to Japan's reassessment of the value of foreign aid, especially with respect to China. Direct investment from Japan was also growing in importance a decade ago, but the financial difficulties of many Japanese firms has reduced the size of Japanese investment absolutely and relative to that from other major investors.

To be sure, a broad Asia-Pacific dialogue and a narrower East Asian one are not mutually exclusive alternatives. East Asian governments have legitimate political reasons to engage in dialogue with their nearest neighbors—whether to prove their ability to manage their relations with neighbors or to reassure parochial domestic political constituencies that the government is not beholden to the United States or the International Monetary Fund.

Broadening the dialogue certainly brings in additional participants that do not have common historical or cultural backgrounds and that are at very different points along the continuum of economic development. Such diversity implies that broader Asia-Pacific groupings face as much or more difficulty finding common ground for cooperating on liberalizing their rules on trade and investment. Furthermore, the fact that the various regional discussion groups that have emerged in the past several decades have inconsistent national memberships or overlapping areas of discussion does not matter at the broadest level. As one analyst put it, "While it is probably right for policymakers to minimize duplication, some overlap in content and participation can be important to reaching consensus on an issue, to establishing familiarity and trust between policymakers, and to generating political commitment to change."[1] What would matter, however, would be for a narrow East Asian form of dialogue to flourish at the expense of a broader Asia-Pacific form.

This benign conclusion regarding a narrow East Asian form of dialogue hinges on the lack of substantial movement toward a tight economic bloc. If East Asia were moving toward something resembling the EU, with free internal trade and investment combined with a unified currency, then the United States should worry. The trade diversion effects and other economic and political consequences would be detrimental to American interests. But the existing dialogue is not leading in that direction, and there is no harm in talk. Nevertheless, this analysis concludes that APEC is a more appropriate institution for regional dialogue than ASEAN+3.

The second question, of what the participants should talk about, has elicited a variety of answers over the years. At the broadest level, one can take considerable satisfaction merely from the existence of dialogue. Business people, academics, and government officials from various countries connected by close economic ties ought to engage in personal communication. Whether new regional policies evolve or not, the decisionmaking process in each country is improved if the decisionmakers have a better personal understanding of the people in other countries and their motives. As trite as it may sound, furthering personal understanding appears to have been the main accomplishment of some of the early exercises in the Asia-Pacific region. The Pacific Basin Economic Council (PBEC) has never accomplished much in terms of making hard policy recommendations that affect the whole region, but, especially in the early years, it brought people into communication who might not have met otherwise, opening new business opportunities and increasing participants' understanding of attitudes, personalities, motives, and policies in other countries. The Pacific Trade and Development Conference (PAFTAD) has played a somewhat similar role in expanding the academic dialogue, exposing economists to research topics and results that they might not have thought about otherwise. The Pacific Economic Cooperation Council (PECC) has expanded the discussion to include government officials, even if only in a private capacity. APEC, finally, has brought together government officials in regular discussions that now cover a number of different economic policy areas.

Discussion for its own sake, however, is not permanently satisfying. APEC proposed an ambitious plan for the adoption of regional free trade and investment among its members, but "free trade" was left undefined, adoption of the proposal was voluntary, and the goal is proving unattainable. APEC has also tackled a variety of trade facilitation issues, hoping to forge regional reductions in the cost of doing business across national boundaries. The actual accomplishments of APEC are very modest, but they do begin to satisfy the need for something more substantial than personal networking to sustain regional dialogue.

The broad Asia-Pacific dialogue has not been sufficiently satisfying, however, to obviate the desire for a more geographically restricted East Asian forum. As discussed, the East Asian alternative has its roots in the anti-Western, anti-U.S. attitudes that blossomed in the past decade. While the countries of the region do not really share much in terms of history or culture, some have attempted to build a common image. More important, the 1997 Asian financial crisis gave nations around the region a common sense of irritation, frustration, and disagreement with the U.S. government and the IMF. In the early 1990s, those negative attitudes were insufficient to bring the EAEC into existence, but in the post-1997 atmosphere they have breathed life into ASEAN+3, which is a narrower, East Asian forum.

ASEAN+3 also needs something beyond personal networking to justify its existence, and that has involved trade and currency cooperation. The most startling development in the past few years has been the explosion among most East Asian nations of bilateral and regional proposals and negotiations regarding free trade areas. Some of these will certainly emerge. However, on theoretical grounds, this book has taken a skeptical view of the value of such arrangements in general. Some of the agreements now emerging, such as AFTA and the Japan-Singapore agreement, have not fully removed trade barriers as demanded by the rules of the WTO. Japan is likely to continue to experience difficulty in confronting its domestic protectionist forces, which will limit its ability to truly open up to its neighbors, and some ASEAN members may continue to experience the same difficulty. Meanwhile, the efforts of East Asian governments to negotiate bilateral free trade areas have by no means been limited to East Asian partners.

The 1997 Asian financial crisis provided a powerful motivation for discussions on the currency front. Deeply angered by the perception of uncaring Western speculators overpowering the ability of Thailand, Indonesia, South Korea, and to a lesser extent Malaysia to defend the fixed value of their currencies—and by initial mistakes in the IMF's policy advice—various governments have talked about regional cooperation to defend themselves from a repetition of such outside interference. Much of that analysis is wrong; the crisis was not due to speculators but to bankers who rightly perceived that large economic problems were emerging in these countries—including Japanese bankers who faced the additional need to reduce their lending due to problems back home. But as with trade, the good news is that the negative rhetoric has not led to institutions or policies that have advanced a regional approach at the expense of the IMF. The swap arrangements among central banks that emerged from the ASEAN+3 group are trivial in size and largely irrelevant in a region where nations are moving to floating exchange rates.

Hanging over the question of what topics regional discussion should include is the participation of the East Asian countries in broad multilateral institutions—the WTO and the IMF. All East Asian economies have benefited enormously from the global trade and capital markets that have been fostered by these institutions. Regional dialogue on trade and investment that supplements or feeds into the work of these broad institutions is useful; dialogue and policy actions that erode these institutions would be unfortunate. APEC has rather explicitly embraced the role of supplement, while ASEAN+3 was rooted in a desire to provide an alternative to existing institutions. Luckily, the political need to demonstrate to domestic constituencies that their governments were rallying to counter the IMF has not resulted in any policy decisions to undermine the IMF. Neither has talk of a regional trade bloc resulted in any pattern of bilateral or regional free trade area negotiations that would yield such an outcome. That outcome to date is encouraging, but it raises the question of how the U.S. government should respond.

## Implications for the United States

From the American perspective, the broad regional institutions—the ADB and APEC—have been flawed and somewhat disappointing. On the other hand, the more narrow regional alternatives on trade and finance could still move in a direction that would seriously harm American economic and security interests in the region.

On a general level, this harm could flow from several sources. First, narrow free trade areas always involve trade diversion effects. As major exporters to East Asian countries, American firms would find themselves at a disadvantage compared with parties to bilateral or regional agreements. That would be true especially with respect to Japanese firms, which often are major global competitors of American firms. A similar diversion could affect service sector firms if these agreements include a services component—as was the intent if not the result of the Japan-Singapore agreement. Even investment could be affected if trade agreements were to include an informal preference for direct investment by firms from group members.

The potential for harm would be particularly real if the Japanese government were to lead the region into adopting a more narrow form of regionalism, since some members of the Japanese government have long viewed an Asian bloc as an alternative to its close relationship with the United States. The Japanese government would likely use a tighter form of regionalism to achieve economic advantages for itself at the explicit expense of non-Asian developed countries.

A second source of potential harm is more diffuse, stemming from the anti-Western underpinnings of the narrow version of Asian economic regionalism. An East Asian region that chose to enhance its intraregional dealings on trade, investment, and economic policy could undermine the carefully crafted global economic system, possibly to the region's own detriment. If, for example, an Asian monetary fund was established and became a vehicle for Asian countries to avoid or minimize the economic reforms demanded by the IMF, the outcome could be a region that grew more slowly, attracted less foreign capital, and was more prone to economic crises. Such an outcome certainly is not in the interest of the United States.

Speaking even more broadly, a narrow form of economic regionalism could have a corrosive effect on the American security role in the region. Given that a strong motivation for Asian regionalism is dissatisfaction with and rejection of the United States and the West, a narrow form of regionalism would create obvious tension between the effort to exclude the United States from economic discussions and the strong role that the United States continues to play in regional security. It is only a small step from the anti-Western rhetoric promoting Asian economic regionalism to calls for getting the United States out of the region altogether. For example, Japan, buttressed by an Asian monetary fund, might someday reevaluate its security posture and decide that allowing American military bases in its territory is no longer in its interest. Or corrosive rhetoric could work on the United States itself, convincing Congress to withdraw American military personnel from Asian countries if they act to the detriment of U.S. trade and investment interests. To be sure, the contradiction in the case of Japan—a close military ally with large American bases that managed to keep its markets relatively closed for most of the past fifty years—never led to the withdrawal of American troops. Nevertheless, it certainly contributed to several decades of often acrimonious trade negotiations.

There is, however, a counterargument to this negative vision of the impact of a narrow form of regionalism on Asian security issues. If the Asian nations were to achieve real progress on economic cooperation and integration, it is reasonable to assume that such progress would lessen the probability of armed conflict among them. One aspect of the strong American role in ensuring security in Asia has been to act as the "cork in the bottle" in regard to Japan. That is, the U.S.-Japan alliance and the presence of American troops in Japan reduce anxiety about Japan among the other nations in the region. As discussed, one of the problems in the region has been the continuing argument over Japanese behavior during the 1930s ad 1940s, as well as expressions of concern, as unrealistic as it might be, over a resurgence of Japanese militarism in the future. If Japan truly embraces some of its neighbors through a free trade area and a strong ASEAN+3 dialogue, then that might have the same beneficial political outcome that occurred with Germany in postwar Europe. If the economic integration between Japan and South Korea deepens significantly as the result of a free trade area, for example, then the level of mutual political hostility would decline.

The fly in the ointment in this optimistic appraisal is that the real security threats in the region have nothing to do with Japan and probably would be unaffected by closer regional economic integration. The two truly serious security issues are those involving the Korean Peninsula and Taiwan. North Korea remains very much an outsider in all regional discussions and a source of serious tension over its nuclear weapons program. Closer economic integration between North Korea and South Korea might lessen the danger of conflict, but progress in that direction has been minimal over the past decade. Broader integration of North Korea into an Asian trade area appears even more remote.

Taiwan also is a problem. The ASEAN+3 dialogue is the principal forum for the narrow version of Asian regionalism, and this group excludes Taiwan. Deeper integration of Taiwan into the Chinese economy may deter China from taking an aggressive approach to unification, but there is no guarantee that it will. To the contrary, the Chinese government may feel emboldened by the fact that the rest of ASEAN+3 has acquiesced in excluding Taiwan as a member and refrained from considering it in bilateral free trade negotiations.

The situation regarding both North Korea and Taiwan implies, therefore, that the drive toward a stronger form of economic regionalism within East Asia would not necessarily reduce the security threats in the region. American involvement in ensuring regional security would therefore remain important, implying that the contradiction between East Asian economic regionalism and American involvement in Asian security may persist.

## U.S. Policy Options

The starting point for developing any U.S. policy is to recognize where American interests in East Asia lie. First, on the trade and direct investment front, American interests lie in furthering progress toward liberalizing trade throughout the world. American economic interests are global in scale, and they are best served by efforts to reduce barriers to trade and investment on the global level. At the regional level, American firms have economically important ties to Asian nations as a market for exports, a source of imports, and a location for direct investment. Those ties, and the economic benefits that flow from them, would be further enhanced if the Asian region becomes more open to trade and investment than it is now.

Second, on the financial front, American interests are best served by a region that continues to move forward on building a system of laws and regulations in each country that foster a more robust financial sector that exhibits greater openness to international capital flows and maintains flexible exchange rates. These elements are intertwined. As was painfully demonstrated in 1997, if a country is open to capital flows but does not maintain a robust financial system and pegs its exchange rates, the consequences can be disastrous. Ensuring that all of these goals are attained serves two important purposes. They make the process of economic growth and development in the region less likely to be undermined by serious misallocation of resources or by financial crises. A stable and growing region obviously benefits the United States, for both economic and security reasons. In addition, American and other developed-country financial institutions benefit from more stable and robust financial markets in these countries. The institutions obviously receive a direct benefit in the form of increased business and profits, but the host nations also benefit from access to the international capital that these institutions mediate.

The question is how, besides working at the global level, to achieve these regional goals or at least move in that general direction. The first part of the answer concerns discouraging or minimizing movement toward an East Asian economic bloc, which would retard or erode achievement of these goals. The essence of East Asian regionalism regarding trade and investment is to give preference to members of the region at the expense of those outside the region. This liability is something that many nations, including the United States, have been willing to accept in the general movement toward free trade areas. Nevertheless, it is a real loss for firms located outside the region. On the financial front, Asian regionalism could retard the creation of more robust financial sectors by deflecting pressures from the IMF or the governments of developed nations, leaving the region vulnerable to future problems of the sort that occurred in 1997. Any U.S. strategy therefore needs to consider how to discourage the region from sliding into a tighter form of regionalism.

The second part of the answer concerns encouraging a more economically open East Asia. What steps can the U.S. government take through APEC or on a bilateral basis to promote that goal? The U.S. government must consider what it should—and should not—do.

### *What Not to Do*

Since a narrow form of East Asian regionalism would not be in the U.S. interest, the government could work actively to discourage Asian nations from participating in exclusionary dialogue and institutions. This approach characterized the American response to Prime Minister Mahathir's proposal for an East Asian Economic Caucus in the early 1990s, as well as to Japan's proposal for an Asian monetary fund in 1997.

Applying pressure has been especially effective with Japan. As a close military ally of the United States and host to large American bases that are instrumental in the defense of Japan, the Japanese government has been reluctant to antagonize the U.S. government too much. That reluctance certainly did not prevent several decades of bitter bilateral trade negotiations, but there are limits to what the Japanese government is willing to do. The Japanese government has periodically worried that if the United States felt that the region was rejecting it as an economic partner, it would lose interest in maintaining its military presence in the region. Loath to lose its U.S. military protection, the Japanese government is usually reluctant to participate in antagonistic regional actions. American rejection of Japan's proposal for an AMF, for example, appears to have had an impact on the decision by the Japanese government to make activation of the ASEAN+3 group's central bank swap agreements contingent on IMF approval. Without the expressed opposition of the United States and the IMF in the 1997–98 period to more independent forms of regional monetary cooperation, it is quite possible that the IMF provision would not have been included in the swap arrangements. This suggests that at least on occasion, clear expressions of opposition do shape outcomes in a way that diminishes the probability of results detrimental to American or broader global interests.

However, as a general approach to the region, overt U.S. rejection of efforts to advance a narrow version of regionalism carries some danger—

that is, it can fan the urge to exclude the United States. Japan may be susceptible to American pressure, but other nations in the region may not. The anti-Western rhetoric of Prime Minister Mahathir Mohamad of Malaysia, for example, is so strong that any vocal American rejection of his proposals simply feeds his argument. He may be the most extreme example among the political leaders in the region, but the murmurings of discontent among Asian bureaucrats, academics, and journalists cannot be ignored.

Overt rejection presents the U.S. government with an additional problem. How can the U.S. government tell East Asian nations that they should not engage in a tighter form of economic regionalism when it has condoned the same behavior in Western Europe, created NAFTA, and is actively pursuing a free trade area of the Americas? Blanket rejection of Asian initiatives would expose a hypocrisy that the region would easily label—with some justification—as racist or imperialist. It appears best then to reserve rejection for specific East Asian proposals that clearly erode the function of the WTO or IMF or that are seriously at odds with American policy goals. Continued rejection of a regional monetary organization that would compete with the IMF, for example, is appropriate, whereas there is no point in discouraging regional or bilateral free trade areas.

### A Positive Agenda

Rather than oppose East Asian regionalism, the U.S. government should follow a positive policy that both diminishes the drive toward a narrow form of regionalism and encourages adoption of a broader form. This policy consists of two elements: emphasis on the World Trade Organization/International Monetary Fund system and reinvigoration of APEC.

WORLD TRADE ORGANIZATION/INTERNATIONAL MONETARY FUND. This book deals with regionalism, but the starting point for American policy must be the WTO and the IMF, not East Asia. To the extent that these broad multilateral institutions remain active and engaged in issues relevant to East Asia, the momentum for an East Asian regional alternative diminishes.

American leadership has been critical throughout the history of the WTO system, from the creation of the General Agreement on Tariffs and Trade (GATT) in the 1940s and the implementation of large trade negotiating rounds to the transformation of the GATT into the WTO. The Uruguay round, signed in 1994, was particularly important because it created the WTO and brought trade in services into the fold.

The global approach to trade remains the most consistent with economic theory, and it has diplomatic advantages as well. The common argument raised against relying on the WTO is that its process for achieving new agreements to reduce barriers is becoming slower and more uncertain. That may be true, but the movement toward a free-trade world is not a race. The past half-century brought considerable lowering of trade barriers, and continued slow progress in that direction is perfectly acceptable.

At the present time, the principal issue in the WTO is completing the Doha round, and that should be the key objective of the U.S. government as well. There are at least two issues being discussed in the Doha round that relate directly to East Asia. The first is the general issue of American protectionism. The Bush administration undermined its negotiating position by slapping dumping duties on steel manufacturers and increasing subsidies to farmers. If nothing else, the timing of these actions was unfortunate. More important, one of the drivers of talk of an East Asian trade bloc has been irritation over exactly this kind of unilateral American protectionism. Overall, access to American markets is very open; tariffs are low and nontariff barriers relatively few. That overall picture, however, is punctuated by exceptions—such as those for steel, agriculture (including sugar and beef), and textiles—which are highly visible and irritating to East Asian governments. Administration officials may have thought that they were using a "tough guy" approach to eventually bring others to an agreement on issues such as agricultural subsidies. But, as with other aspects of unilateralism in Bush administration policy, the main impact of that approach has been to antagonize trading partners and spur talk of bilateral and regional free trade areas as a means to strengthen alternatives to reliance on the American market.

The second issue has been American enforcement of antidumping regulations. Of all antidumping and countervailing duties in place, 41 percent are on products from East Asia, with China and Japan the leading sources. Few economists support the manner in which the U.S. antidumping laws are administered. The bar for proving dumping is so low that what would pass for legal competitive pricing by domestic firms becomes dumping when practiced by foreign firms shipping products to the United States. For observers in East Asia, manipulation of antidumping laws has long been a symbol of American hypocrisy regarding free trade. The Bush administration agreed to include antidumping rules in the Doha round, but how much flexibility the administration will show during negotiations remains to be seen. The use of antidumping laws in the 2002 restrictions on steel imports was not an encouraging opening shot.

American protectionism is arguably quite minor in its impact on overall trade and investment. As minor as it may be, it has strong symbolic value. Why should Japan reduce agricultural barriers, China improve enforcement of intellectual property rights, or Malaysia dismantle its national car project if they can see the U.S. government carving out its own exceptions to the principle of open access to markets? And if the U.S. government is so persistent in guarding its exceptions, why should the East Asian economies not band together to foster trade among themselves? This book's policy recommendation, therefore, is that the U.S. government stop undermining regional commitment to the WTO process through its protectionist actions and adopt a flexible negotiating stance on antidumping regulations. Successful completion of the Doha round will require achieving a broader set of objectives, but this is a starting point. Evidence of the determination of the U.S. government to make the Doha round an overall success—shown in a meaningful reduction in American protectionist behavior—would do much to undermine talk of an East Asian regional bloc.

However, the recommendation that the U.S. government stick to a primary emphasis on the WTO must contend with the reality of proliferating bilateral and regional free trade areas. This book has taken a strong stand against such arrangements, but they are obviously the flavor of the day. The U.S. government has already created free trade areas with Canada and Mexico (NAFTA), Singapore, Jordan, Israel, and Chile. As a corollary to emphasizing the WTO, the U.S. government also should abandon its own policy of eagerly forming free trade areas. It should be maximizing its efforts on the Doha round of the WTO rather than negotiating a free trade area of the Americas (FTAA), negotiating a free trade area with the Southern African Customs Union (SACU, which includes Botswana, Lesotho, Namibia, South Africa, and Swaziland), or forming free trade areas with Central America (CAFTA), Morocco, Australia, Thailand, or other individual ASEAN countries (as proposed in the U.S. government's October 2002 Enterprise for ASEAN Initiative).[2] The FTAA in particular reinforces attitudes among East Asian governments that they, too, should be pursuing their own free trade areas to protect themselves from trade diversion effects—or simply to jump on the bandwagon.

If East Asia moves more decisively toward forming its own regional trade bloc, then one must ask whether the U.S. government should retaliate or undermine the process by issuing a competitive offer to form free trade areas with individual nations in the region. Were the region obviously moving toward a regional trade bloc, a competitive offer would represent a reluctant second-best strategy. That is, having no free trade areas would be a better outcome, but given their inevitability, the United States could protect its own economic interests by imitating the behavior of others in the region. However, that situation does not currently exist; as already detailed, the regional move toward free trade areas is relatively weak and has not been leading to a regional bloc.

Unfortunately, with the U.S.-Singapore free trade area and the initiation of negotiations with Thailand, American policy already is proceeding toward forming free trade areas with East Asian nations. At present, these moves appear unnecessary; nothing is yet occurring within the region that justifies adopting the second-best strategy of making counterproposals. Without justification, all such U.S. action does is reinforce the unfortunate fad for forming free trade areas.

The IMF/World Bank system also remains the logical focus of U.S. policy on monetary issues. To the extent that these organizations are flawed, the solution lies in reform, not in a shift to other mechanisms. Even in a world of generally floating exchange rates, the IMF remains necessary because some countries will continue to face financial crises involving foreign currency–denominated debt. While a moral hazard does exist if international investors believe that any losses on loans to developing countries will be guaranteed by the IMF, affluent industrial nations have a moral interest, an economic interest, and a security interest in responding to such crises. Morally, these nations simply cannot let a crisis lead to excessive suffering of local populations. Economically, affluent nations have an interest in repairing problems so that growth resumes, to the benefit of their own firms doing business in crisis countries. In terms of security, the affluent nations cannot let financial crises develop into chronic serious problems for certain poor countries because the failure to help fosters anger among "have-nots" that may find expression in terrorism or military aggression. Similar arguments apply to the World Bank. Its role—and that of the regional development banks—may be limited in quantitative terms, but these institutions are a visible symbol that the developed world cares about what happens in poor countries. How to foster economic development remains a difficult and controversial subject, but the World Bank system remains the appropriate institutional setting in which to argue about appropriate approaches.

East Asian governments need to see the United States and others leading reform at the IMF and the World Bank. Some reform has incurred at
both institutions, but it needs to be an ongoing process. Having been badly
shocked by the IMF's behavior in the early phases of the 1997 Asian financial crisis, the East Asian nations need reassurance that the IMF has absorbed its lessons. If they are not reassured, the outcome will be a continuing impetus for dialogue within the region on how to diminish and
deflect the role of the IMF and the U.S. government in shaping regional
policies. That impetus has been blunted with the ASEAN+3 central bank
swap arrangements being explicitly designed to supplement the IMF. But
the message remains: East Asian governments are very restive concerning a
multilateral institution that they perceive to represent primarily rich Western nations that in 1997 took steps that were detrimental to the region.

APEC. The second element of the recommended American agenda is
the reinvigoration of APEC, which remains the logical institution for the
Asian region since it includes the broad set of countries that have close ties
with East Asia—the United States, Taiwan, Australia, and New Zealand.
This conclusion follows from the extensive evidence on trade and investment relationships presented in chapters 3 and 4 of this book, not just
from a desire to maintain American hegemony. The economic links
between East Asia and the United States have been so strong and enduring
that leaving the U.S. government out of a regional cooperation strategy
makes little sense. The same is true of Australia and New Zealand, two
small economies on the fringe of the region that also are closely linked to
East Asia. And the same is even more true of Taiwan—a centrally located
and important economy that is nevertheless the invisible orphan of the
region. Only APEC encompasses all of these economies.

An obvious problem is that the notion of APEC as a group of nations
that are mutually linked through trade and investment has been diluted; it
has added other members who have weaker relationships with East Asia.
Canada has only minor trade and investment links with Asia, and much
the same is true for the Latin American nations that are now members.
Russia also has only tenuous ties to the region. Since this broader membership is unlikely to be rolled back, however, there is no choice but to
accept the dilution of APEC's original sense of unity.

The more important problem for APEC is how to renew its centrality in
East Asian regional dialogue. As discussed previously, APEC is widely seen
as disappointing, though different participants have differing reasons for
being disappointed. The waning of interest in APEC has had important

consequences for the region, including increased interest in the ASEAN+3 process and in subregional and bilateral free trade area negotiations.

What can be done to reinvigorate APEC has been the subject of a series of annual reports by the APEC International Assessment Network (APIAN), a group of thirty-one participants from academic institutions. This group, like the eminent persons group in the mid-1990s, is playing the role of adviser to APEC governments on how to restructure the organization to make it more effective. A starting point, therefore, is to endorse the careful, thoughtful, and detailed recommendations of this group.[3]

The following list sticks to a handful of major ways in which APEC can continue to be a core participant in broad regional dialogue and policy actions. Some but not all of these recommendations parallel those of APIAN. Together these six recommendations form the basis of what would be a useful U.S. government policy stance toward APEC.

—*Modify the Bogor goals.* No one really believes that the vague Bogor commitment to free trade and investment throughout the APEC region will lead to the stated goal by the 2010/2020 dates established, and no real definition of that goal has emerged in the decade since the meeting. It would be far better to diminish expectations to a realistic level by restating the goal. One face-saving way to do that would be to endorse the general principle or sentiment embodied in the goal but to admit that defining it has been elusive. By accepting its vagueness, APEC could recast the goal as a strong commitment from all members (and especially the developing members with the highest trade barriers) to aggressively reduce their trade barriers through the Doha round and succeeding rounds of WTO negotiations. While the group might admit that the result will not be completely open access to all markets by 2020, that could remain the desired outcome. This "dumbing down" of APEC's central policy goal might seem an odd way to invigorate the APEC process. However, it would supply a dose of reality and recast the definition of fostering more open trade and investment in a global context, ending the ambiguity over the definition of regional free trade and investment.

—*Adopt the APIAN recommendation to put more emphasis on nontariff barriers.* The ways in which governments can impede trade in goods and services from abroad other than through tariffs are legion, and nontariff barriers are especially prevalent in the services sector. While nontariff barriers such as standards are covered by the WTO, the complexity and variety of these barriers opens the way for a useful supplemental dialogue within APEC.

—*Adopt the APIAN recommendation to put more emphasis on trade facilitation.* One of the problems in making progress on liberalizing trade and investment has been the reluctance of members to make politically difficult decisions on liberalization beyond the negotiated outcomes of the WTO. Generally, however, trade facilitation issues are not politically sensitive. Reducing the cost of and time spent in customs clearance through such measures as electronic filing of documents; facilitating the travel of business people across the region; making more information concerning tariffs and regulations available in English on the Internet; and other measures do have an impact on the ease of doing business. Each step may be minor in terms of its impact, but the trade facilitation agenda in total shows promise as an area in which APEC governments can make progress through the myriad working committees that now exist. However, the time has also come for APEC to move beyond voluntary codes and standards for trade facilitation. The process needs the firm commitment of members, or at least a substantial subset of members, to implement agreed-on trade facilitation measures.

—*Adopt the APIAN recommendation to involve APEC in negotiating members' bilateral and subregional free trade agreements.* These agreements are now a fact of life. However, the WTO has taken a rather weak stance in enforcing its own rule that free trade areas must cover substantially all products. APEC can establish its own trade agreement review panel. The goal here would be to monitor what APEC members are negotiating among themselves, discouraging aspects of agreements that counter the spirit of WTO and APEC principles. The peer pressure embodied in monitoring might prove insufficient to deter members from such deals, but publishing the outcomes of these reviews and forwarding them to the WTO to incorporate in its own trade agreement review process may strengthen scrutiny of trade agreements and influence the behavior of governments in negotiating bilateral deals.

—*Endorse more fully the "ecotech" agenda of APEC.* In the past decade, the U.S. government has been wary of this aspect of APEC because it has not wanted to be drawn into a north-south debate aimed at getting rich nations to make more of a financial contribution to developing countries. However, the wide disparity in members' economic development is a stark reality in APEC. Furthermore, the 9/11 terrorist attacks and the subsequent war on terrorism underscore the dangers of the failure of economic development. APEC provides a setting that enables its rich members to act collectively to strengthen the basis for continued economic growth and development of its developing members. The emphasis need not be on large expensive infrastructure projects; even the Japanese government has begun to move beyond using that model in offering foreign aid to the region. But "capacity building"—offering advice and assistance on institution building and training for those who run institutions—remains an important task. APIAN endorses the use of individual ecotech action plans similar to the annual plans that members produce concerning their individual actions on trade and investment barriers. This approach is inadequate. More important is taking collective action based on agreement among APEC members about what its developed members can do and on a list of what its developing members need most. In that regard, APIAN usefully recommends that the APEC agenda be linked to the ADB and the private sector, to which should be added the World Bank and academic institutions around APEC.

—*Engage in regional finance.* APEC should take the lead in establishing a modified Asian monetary fund that would include all APEC members in a regional financing facility that would supplement the IMF in times of crisis. Doing so would shift the impetus for such an organization away from the ASEAN+3 group to APEC, thereby including the United States and helping to ensure compatibility with the IMF.

This modest agenda should keep East Asia on a path of engagement with the world, avoiding the problems that may surface with a narrow form of regionalism. Unfortunately, neither the WTO nor APEC has much sex appeal in Washington, where regional and bilateral trade deals have captured the most attention. Nevertheless, the road to successful East Asian regional development lies in supporting global institutions and the broad, limited, regional approach of APEC.

# Notes

## Notes to Chapter One

1. See Gary Burtless, Robert Z. Lawrence, and Robert E. Litan, *Globaphobia: Confronting Fears about Open Trade* (Brookings, 1998).

2. Lester Thurow, *Head to Head: The Coming Economic Battle Among Japan, Europe, and America* (William Morrow, 1992).

3. C. Fred Bergsten, "America's Two-Front Economic Conflict," *Foreign Affairs*, vol. 80, no. 2 (March/April 2001), p. 19.

## Notes to Chapter Two

1. For a review of these arguments, see Richard Stubbs, "ASEAN Plus Three: Emerging East Asian Regionalism?" *Asian Survey*, vol. 42, no. 3 (May/June 2002), pp. 440–55.

2. Yoichi Funabashi, "The Asianization of Asia," *Foreign Affairs*, vol. 72, no. 5 (November/December 1993), pp. 75–85.

3. For an analysis of Japan's resistance to imports and a discussion of the academic debate concerning this issue, see Edward J. Lincoln, *Japan's Unequal Trade* (Brookings, 1989), or Lincoln, *Troubled Times: U.S.-Japan Economic Relations in the 1990s* (Brookings, 1999).

4. A. T. Kearney, The A. T. Kearney/*Foreign Policy* Magazine Globalization Index (Washington: A. T. Kearney Inc. and the Carnegie Endowment for International Peace, 2001).

5. Calculated from data in Council for Economic Planning and Development, Republic of China, *Taiwan Statistical Data Book 1985*, p. 205. Note that this drift away from Japan does not characterize Taiwan's

imports, with the share of imports from Japan rising from 30 percent to a peak of 45 percent in 1971 before dropping back below 30 percent by the early 1980s.

6. World Bank, *The East Asian Miracle: Economic Growth and Public Policy* (Washington: 1993).

## Notes to Chapter Three

1. Jeffrey A. Frankel, "Is a Yen Bloc Forming in Pacific Asia?" in Richard O'Brien, ed., *Finance and the International Economy*, vol. 5, *The AMEX Bank Review Prize Essays* (Oxford University Press, 1991), pp. 5–20, especially pages 6–9. In 1980, Asian nations generated 15 percent of global trade, and intraregional trade accounted for 33 percent of their total trade. This yields a regional trade bias factor for 1980 of 2.18 (0.33 divided by 0.15). Frankel then takes their share of global trade in 1989 (20 percent) and argues that intraregional trade should have risen to 44 percent (2.18 times 0.20 equals 0.436).

2. C. H. Kwan, *Yen Bloc: Toward Economic Integration in Asia* (Brookings, 2001), pp. 46–47.

3. Nicholas Lardy, *Integrating China into the Global Economy* (Brookings, 2002), p. 4.

4. Shinji Fukukawa, "Japan, Asia Need New Chapter," *Daily Yomiuri*, June 15, 2001 (www.yomiuri.co.jp/newse/20010615wo42.htm [June 15, 2001]).

## Notes to Chapter Four

1. Bank of Japan, table labeled "International Investment Position of Japan, End of 1995–2000" (www.boj.or.jp/en/siryo/siryo_f.htm [February 4, 2002]).

2. Ministry of Foreign Affairs, *Economic Cooperation Program for China*, October 2001 (www.mofa.go.jp/policy/oda/region/e_asia/china-2.html [September 22, 2003]).

3. Hisane Masaki, "Tokyo Set to Cut the Umbilical Cord," *Japan Times Online,* January 18, 2002 (www.japantimes.co.jp/cgi-bin/getarticle.p15?nb20020118a1.htm [March 19, 2002]), and "Has China Outgrown ODA?" *Daily Yomiuri Online,* April 16, 2002 (www.yomiuri.co.jp/newse/20020416wo81.htm [April 16, 2002]).

4. Hisane Masaki, "Japan and China to Tug Each Other over ODA," *Japan Times Online,* July 27, 2001 (www.japantimes.co.jp/cgi-bin/getarticle.p15?nn20010727a3.htm [July 27, 2001]).

5. Organisation for Economic Co-operation and Development, table: Net ODA from DAC Countries from 1950 to 2000 (www.oecd.org/xls/M00028000/M00028256.xls [May 3, 2002]).

6. Edward J. Lincoln, *Japan's New Global Role* (Brookings, 1993), p. 182.

7. Ministry of Foreign Affairs, "Zuhyō III-14, Nikokukan ODA no Chiikibetsu Haibun" [table III-14, "Regional Distribution of Bilateral ODA"], *ODA Hakusho 2002-Nenpan* [ODA White Paper 2002] (www.mofa.go.jp/mofaj/gaiko/oda/02_hakusho/ODA2002/html/zuhyo/zu03014.htm [October 6, 2003]).

8. Japan Bank for International Cooperation, *Annual Report 2001*, pp. 112–13 (www.jbic.go.jp/english/base/achieve/annual/2001/pdf/sta.pdf [September 10, 2003]).

9. Organisation for Economic Co-operation and Development, *Geographical Distribution of Financial Flows to Developing Countries, 1984–1987* (Paris: 1989), pp. 72, 88, 52, 164, 172, 222, 184, 228, 240, 266, 290; and *Geographical Distribution of Financial Flows*

*to Aid Recipients, 1995–1999* (Paris: 2001), pp. 115, 122, 160, 173, 178, 197, 182, 213, 216, 241, 258. Data assembled from individual country pages.

10. For an earlier analysis of the ways in which Japanese foreign aid served broader Japanese economic interests in the region, see Lincoln, *Japan's New Global Role*, pp. 111–33 and 181–83.

11. Ibid., p. 176.

12. Trish Saywell, "China: Powering Asia's Growth," *Far Eastern Economic Review,* August 2, 2001 (www.feer.com/2001/0108_02/p040money.html [July 30, 2001]).

13. Data in this paragraph on direct investment are from Ministry of Foreign Trade and Economic Cooperation, People's Republic of China (www.moftec.gov.cn/moftec_cn/tjsj/wztj/2000_9-22-13.html [January 30, 2002]), and from ASEAN Secretariat, *ASEAN Statistical Yearbook*, p. 135, table VI.2, "FDI in Asia by Source Country and Year during 1995–2000" (www.aseansec.org/macroeconomic/cataloguing.htm [August 2, 2002]).

14. Calculated from data from Ministry of Finance, Japan, "Inward Direct Investment: Country and Region"(www.mof.go.jp/english/e1c008.htm [June 28, 2001]); U.S. Department of Commerce, "U.S. Direct Investment Abroad: Balance of Payments and Direct Investment Position Data," individual pages for each year, 1994–2001 (www.bea.doc.gov/bea/di/di1usdbal.htm [July 16, 2002]), and tables from *Survey of Current Business*, August 1990, pp. 65–72; July 1993, pp. 101–04, and August 1995, pp. 99–100.

15. Walter Hatch and Kozo Yamamura, *Asia in Japan's Embrace: Building a Regional Production Alliance* (Cambridge University Press, 1996).

## Notes to Chapter Five

1. For a longer and more detailed analysis of the history and problems of the Asian Development Bank, see Edward J. Lincoln, "The Asian Development Bank: Time to Wind It Up?" in Mark Beeson, ed., *Reconfiguring East Asia: Regional Institutions and Organisations after the Crisis* (New York: Routledge Curzon, 2002), pp. 205–26.

2. Dick Wilson, *A Bank for Half the World: The Story of the Asian Development Bank 1966–1986* (Manila: Asian Development Bank, 1987), pp. 4–5.

3. Toyoo Gyohten, "Japan and the World Bank," in Devesh Kapur, John P. Lewis, and Richard Webb, eds., *The World Bank: Its First Half Century*, vol. 2, *Perspectives* (Brookings, 1997), p. 303–04.

4. Dennis T. Yasutomo, *The New Multilateralism in Japan's Foreign Policy* (New York: St. Martin's Press, 1995), p. 81.

5. Dennis T. Yasutomo, *Japan and the Asian Development Bank* (New York: Praeger, 1983), p. 5; Asian Development Bank, "Members" (www.adb.org/About/members.asp [September 15, 2003]).

6. Asian Development Bank, "ADB at a Glance" (www.adb.org/About/glance.asp [September 15, 2003]), and Asian Development Bank, *Annual Report 2001*, pp. 132 and 162 (www.adb.org/Documents/Reports/Annual_Report/2001/default.asp [November 10, 2003]).

7. "The 2002 Global 1000 Scorecard," *Businessweek Online* (http://bwnt.businessweek.com/global_1000/2002.index.html [April 11, 2003]).

8. For data on loans by country, see Asian Development Bank, *Annual Report 2001*, pp. 204–05. Of total loans made from 1983 through 2001, 61.6 percent of ODR loans and

33.1 percent of ADF loans went to East Asian countries. Applying these percentages to total OCR and ADF loan assets yields $33.1 billion.

9. Asian Development Bank, *Annual Report 2001*, p. 168.

10. Ibid., pp. 125, 176, and 184.

11. Asian Development Bank, *Annual Report 1999*, p. 245.

12. Edward J. Lincoln, *Japan's New Global Role* (Brookings, 1993), p. 138.

13. Asian Development Bank, *Annual Report 2001*, pp. 47, 207–08.

14. Pacific Basin Economic Council, "PBEC: Overview" (www.pbec.org/index.jsp? pageId=4770 [September 15, 2003]).

15. Ibid.

16. "PBEC United States Member Committee" (www.pbec.org/us/cor.htm [September 15, 2003]).

17. Pacific Basin Economic Council International Secretariat, "Implementing Transparency Principles in APEC" (Hawaii: 2002) (www.pbec.org/policy/2002/transparency.pdf [September 15, 2003]).

18. Hugh Patrick, *From PAFTAD to APEC: Economists Networks and Public Policymaking*, Discussion Paper 2 (Columbia University, APEC Study Center, January 1997), especially pp. 1–17.

19. Patrick, *From PAFTAD to APEC*, p. 18

20. PECC, "About PECC"(www.pecc.org/about_pecc.htm [September 15, 2003]).

21. Roberto Romulo, "PECC Statement to the APEC Ministers," Thirteenth APEC Ministerial Meeting, Shanghai, China, October 17–18, 2001 (www.pecc.org/statements/APEC/2001_China/AMM-Stmt.doc [November 10, 2003]).

22. PECC, *PECC Charter*, section 3.1.6 (www.pecc.org/charter.htm [November 10, 2003)].

23. *APEC Brochure 2000* (www.apecsec.org.sg/apec_organization/brochure2001.html [May 6, 2002]).

24. Ibid.

25. "Biographies of the APEC Business Advisory Council Members" (www.abaconline.org/aboutus [July 9, 2002]). There are two exceptions; in 2002, Papua New Guinea had only one representative on ABAC, and China had four.

26. For background information, see "International Consortium of APEC Study Centers: APIAN APEC International Assessment Network: Building the APEC International Assessment Network" (www.apecstudy.org/APIANBuild.htm [September 15, 2003]). See also "APEC Study Center: Columbia University in the City of New York" (www. columbia. edu/cu/business/apec/mission.htm [September 15, 2003]) and APIAN, *Learning from Experience: The First APIAN Policy Report* (Singapore: APEC Study Center, November 2000).

27. See *A Vision for APEC: Towards an Asia Pacific Economic Community—Report of the Eminent Persons Group to APEC Ministers* (Singapore: APEC, October 1993). The members of the eminent persons group were Narongchai Akransanee (chairman of Federal Finance and Securities Ltd., Thailand), C. Fred Bergsten (director of the Institute for International Economics, U.S.A.), Victor K. Fung (chairman of Prudential Asia Investments, Ltd., Hong Kong), Huang Wenjun (first vice president of the International Trade Association of China), Mahn Je Kim (various academic, government, and private sector positions, South Korea), Hank Lim (National University of Singapore), John S. MacDonald (chairman of MacDonald Dettwiler and Associates, Canada), Suhadi Mangkusuwondo (professor of eco-

nomics, University of Indonesia, and vice chairman of the Trade and Management Development Institute, Indonesia), Neville Wran (chairman of Turnbull and Partners Ltd., Australia), Rong-I Wu (president of the Taiwan Institute of Economic Research, Taiwan), Ippei Yamazawa (Hitotsubashi University, Japan), and Graeme Pirie (Ministry of Foreign Affairs and Trade, New Zealand).

28. For a highly detailed and critical assessment of APEC and its failures, see John Ravenhill, *APEC and the Construction of Pacific Rim Regionalism* (Cambridge University Press, 2001).

29. *APEC Brochure 2000* (www.apecsec.org.sg/apec_organization/brochure2001.html [May 6, 2002]), p. 2.

30. For example, see Kenneth Flamm and Edward J. Lincoln, *Time to Reinvent APEC*, Brookings Policy Brief 26 (November 1997).

31. *APEC Brochure 2000* (www.apecsec.org.sg/apec_organization/brochure2001.html [May 6, 2002]), p. 2.

32. "Asia-Pacific: APEC Adrift amid Doubts on Its Relevance," *Inter Press Service*, November 17, 2000 (www.abaconline.org/news/APECdoub.htm [February 21, 2002]).

33. See APEC, "Ministerial Statements" (www.apecsec.org.sg/apec/ministerial_statements.html [November 10, 2003]) and First APEC Finance Ministers' Meeting, "Joint Ministerial Statement," Honolulu, Hawaii, March 18–19, 1994, in "Selected APEC Documents: 1989–1994," pp. 148–50 (www.apecsec.org.sg/apec/publications/all_ publications/ apec_secretariat.html [November 10, 2003]).

34. Fifth APEC Finance Ministers' Meeting, "Joint Ministerial Statement," Kananakis, Alberta, Canada, May 23–24, 1998, pp. 29–37 (www.apecsec.org.sg/apec/publications/ all_publications/apec_secretariat.html [November 10, 2003]).

35. "Asia-Pacific: APEC Adrift amid Doubts on Its Relevance," *Inter Press Service*, November 17, 2000 (www.abaconline.org/news/APECdoub.htm [February 21, 2002]).

36. "Full Text of APEC Leaders' Declaration in Shanghai," *Japan Times Online*, October 22, 2001 (www.japantimes.co/jp/cgi-bin/getarticle.p15?nn20011022b2.htm [October 22, 2001]).

37. "APEC Economic Leaders' Declaration," Los Cabos, Mexico, October 27, 2002 , in "Key APEC Documents 2002," pp. 1–6 (www.apecsec.org.sg/apec/publications/all_ publications/apec_secretariat.html [November 10, 2003]).

38. Calculated from data in International Monetary Fund, *Direction of Trade Statistics* CD-ROM.

39. Ibid.

40. Mireya Solis, "Jumping on the FTA Bandwagon: Japan's New Preferential Trading Diplomacy," table 4. Paper presented at the annual meeting of the Association of Asian Studies, New York City, March 2003. The percentages are for foreign direct investment flows from 1994 through 1998.

41. APEC, "Achieving the APEC Vision: Free and Open Trade in the Asia Pacific—Eminent Persons Group Report," August 1994. Executive summary available at www.apecsec.org.sg/apec/publications/all_publications/eminent_persons_group.html.

42. C. Fred Bergsten, *Open Regionalism*, Working Paper Series 97-3 (Washington: Institute for International Economics, 1997), pp. 11–15.

43. Hisane Masaki, "APEC Nears Compromise," *Japan Times Online*, September 14, 2001 (www.japantimes.co.jp/cgi-bin/getarticle.p15?nb20010914a2.htm [September 14, 2001]).

44. APEC, "Joint Statement," Fourteenth APEC Ministerial Meeting, Los Cabos, Mexico, October 23–24, 2002, in "Key APEC Documents 2002," pp. 19–34 (www.apecsec.org. sg/apec/publications/all_publications/apec_secretariat.html [November 10, 2003]).

45. "APEC to Discuss 'Charter' for More Liberalization Efforts," *Japan Times Online*, June 4, 2001 (www.japantimes.com.jp/cgi-bin/getarticle.p15?nb20010604a2.htm).

46. APEC, "APEC Fora" (www.apecsec.org/sg/ [April 11, 2003]).

47. Ravenhill, *APEC and the Construction of Pacific Rim Regionalism*, p. 193.

48. Flamm and Lincoln, *Time to Reinvent APEC*, p. 6.

49. Patrick, *From PAFTAD to APEC*, p. 31.

## Notes to Chapter Six

1. Donald K. Emmerson, "Region and Recalcitrance: Rethinking Democracy through Southeast Asia," *Pacific Review* vol. 8, no. 2 (1995), p. 236; quote taken from Surain Subramaniam, "The Asian Values Debate: Implications for the Spread of Liberal Democracy," *Asian Affairs: An American Review*, vol. 27, no. 1 (Spring 2000).

2. For a discussion of the state of press censorship, see Gary Rodan, "The Implications of the Asian Crisis for Media Control in Asia," in Mark Beeson, ed., *Reconfiguring East Asia: Regional Institutions and Organizations after the Crisis* (New York: Routledge Curzon, 2002), pp. 61–82.

3. For a review of the concept of Asian values, see Nathan Glazer, "Two Cheers for 'Asian Values,'" *National Interest* (Fall 1999), pp. 27–34.

4. James Fallows, "What Is an Economy For?" *Atlantic Monthly* (January 1994), p. 76.

5. World Bank, *The East Asian Miracle: Economic Growth and Public Policy* (Washington: 1993).

6. Kozo Kato and others, *Policy-Based Finance: The Experience of Postwar Japan,* World Bank Discussion Paper 221 (Washington: World Bank, 1994), p. 235.

7. Author's notes from the World Bank Seminar on Policy-Based Finance, Tokyo, Japan, February 10, 1995. The comments are by Masashi Nagasu, of the OECF, and Masaki Shiratori, who served at the World Bank.

8. Shinji Fukukawa, "East Asia Needs a Free Business Zone," *Daily Yomiuri*, July 12, 2001, p. 16.

9. David E. Sanger, "Asia's Economic Tigers Growl at World Monetary Conference," *New York Times,* September 22, 1997, p. A1.

10. For example, Sangwon Suh, "Counter Strikes," *Asiaweek*, October 19, 2001 (www.asiaweek.com/asiaweek/magazine/dateline/0,8782,179091,00.html [October 3, 2003]).

11. Yoshikuni Sugiyama, "Japan Must Work toward Asian Trade Zone," *Daily Yomiuri On-Line,* May 21, 2002 (www.yomiuri.co.jp/newse/20020521wo11.htm [May 22, 2002]). Sugiyama is a deputy editor of *Yomiuri Shimbun*'s economic news department.

12. Department of Commerce, "Antidumping and Countervailing Duty Orders in Place as of April 7, 2003, by Country" (http://ia.ita.doc.gov/stats/iastats1.html [April 16, 2003]).

13. *The ASEAN Declaration (Bangkok Declaration),* Thailand, August 8, 1967 (www.aseansec.org/1629.htm [November 11, 2003]).

14. Calculated from data from World Bank, *2001 World Development Indicators*, CD-ROM; "The Economy: Macroeconomic Indicators" (www.gio.gov.tw/taiwan-website/5-

gp/yearbook/chpt10-1.htm [July 12, 2002]); and Ministry of Foreign Affairs, Government of Taiwan, "Economic Indicators," table A-1, "GNP and Expenditures on GDP" (www. moea.gov.tw/~meco/stat/four/english/a1.htm [August 16, 2002]).

15. The preamble of the Bangkok Declaration, for example, speaks specifically about foreign bases being temporary and would "remain only with the expressed concurrence of the countries concerned and are not intended to be used directly or indirectly to subvert the national independence and freedom of States in the region." *The ASEAN Declaration (Bangkok Declaration).*

16. Thanat Khoman, "ASEAN Conception and Evolution," in *The ASEAN Reader* (Singapore: Institute of Southeast Asian Studies, 1992) (www.aseansec.org/view.asp?file=/history/asn_his2.htm [August 9, 2002]). He had been an advocate of forming ASEAN and was foreign minister of Thailand when the agreement was negotiated in 1967.

17. "Association of Southeast Asian Nations: An Overview" (www.aseansec.org/64.htm [October 30, 2003]).

18. ASEAN Secretariat, "History and Evolution of ASEAN" (www.aseansec.org/history/asn_his2htm [February 6, 2002]).

19. Bilson Kurus, "Understanding ASEAN: Benefits and Raison d'Etre," *Asian Survey*, vol. 33, no. 8 (August 1993), pp. 828–29, makes this point about regional security stability contributing to economic development.

20. "Association of Southeast Asian Nations: An Overview" (www.aseansec.org/64.htm [August 9, 2002]).

21. For a more detailed review of these developments, see Edward J. Lincoln, *Japan's New Global Role* (Brookings, 1993), pp. 160–200, or Walter Hatch and Kozo Yamamura, *Asia in Japan's Embrace* (Cambridge University Press, 1996).

22. Keisuke Sasaki, *Japanese Oil Policy in the 21st Century*, USJP Occasional Paper 01-7 (Harvard University Program on U.S.-Japan Relations, 2001), pp. 24–26.

23. Asia Pacific Energy Research Centre (www.ieej.or.jp/aperc/ [April 16, 2002]).

24. Richard Stubbs, "ASEAN Plus Three," *Asian Survey*, vol. 42, no. 3 (May/June 2002), p. 441.

25. Ibid., p. 442, plus personal recollection of events at the 1994 and 1995 annual APEC meetings.

26. Ibid., pp. 442–43.

27. ASEAN Secretariat, "External Relations: ASEAN+3 Process" (www.aseansec. org/asc/r9899/ar98995 [July 22, 2002]); ASEAN, "Press Release: East Asian Foreign Ministers to Meet" (www.aseansec.org/politics/amm_33.htm [July 22, 2002]); ASEAN, "The First Meeting of the ASEAN Economic Ministers and the Ministers of People's Republic of China, Japan and Republic of Korea: 2 May 2000, Yangon, Myanmar, Joint Press Statement" (www.aseansec.org/603.htm [October 30, 2003]); ASEAN, "Press Statement: The First Meeting of ASEAN and China, Japan and Korea Tourism Ministers, 25 January 2002, Yogyakarta, Indonesia" (www.aseansec.org/10248.htm [October 30, 2003]).

## Notes to Chapter Seven

1. E. Denis Hew and Mely C. Anthony, "ASEAN and ASEAN+3 in Postcrisis Asia," *NIRA Review*, vol. 7, no. 4 (Autumn 2000), p. 25. The authors are at the Institute of Strategic and International Studies in Malaysia.

2. This section relies heavily on Arvind Panagariya, "Preferential Trade Liberalization: The Traditional Theory and New Developments," *Journal of Economic Literature,* vol. 38 (June 2000), pp. 287–331.

3. J. Bhagwati, D. Greenaway, and A. Panagariya, "Trading Preferentially: Theory and Policy," *Economic Journal,* vol. 108, no. 449 (1998), pp. 1128–48.

4. These requirements are contained in Article 24, sections 5 and 8. For an easily accessible source for Article 24, see World Trade Organization, "Regionalism: the Basic Rules for Goods" (www.wto.org/wto/english/tratop_e/region_e/regatt_e.htm [July 12, 2002]).

5. World Trade Organization, "Regionalism: The Service Rules" (www.wto.org/wto/english/tratop_e/region_e/regatt_e.htm [July 12, 2002]).

6. World Trade Organization, "Regionalism" (www.wto.org/wto/english/tratop_e/region_e/region_e.htm and www.wto.org/wto/english/tratop_e/region_e/regfac_e.htm [October 8, 2003]); World Trade Organization, *Annual Report 2002,* p. 40.

7. For an ambitious effort to estimate the overall impact on economic welfare of a number of different possible East Asian bilateral, subregional, and even APEC-wide combinations, see Robert Scollay and John P. Gilbert, *New Regional Trading Arrangements in the Asia Pacific?* (Washington: Institute for International Economics, 2001), including p. 115 for discussion of Japan-Singapore and p. 119 for Japan-Korea.

8. Joseph Grunwald and Kenneth Flamm, *The Global Factory* (Brookings, 1985), p. 138.

9. International Trade and Industry Division, United Nations Economic and Social Commission for Asia and the Pacific, *The Bangkok Agreement* (www.unescap.org/itid/BKKAGR.HTM [October 8, 2003]), and "Trade Policy Section" (www.unescap.org/itid/TPS.htm [July 12, 2002]).

10. ASEAN, "Trade" (www.aseansec.org/view.asp?file=/economic/ov_trd.htm [August 2, 2002]).

11. Lee Kuan Yew, "ASEAN Must Balance China in Asia," *New Perspectives Quarterly,* vol. 18, no. 3 (Summer 2001), p. 21.

12. Colin James, "Trade: Tariff Terminator," *Far Eastern Economic Review,* August 17, 2000 (www.feer.com/ [October 8, 2003]).

13. Trish Saywell, "Trade: Going It Alone," *Far Eastern Economic Review,* December 7, 2000 (www.feer.com/ [October 8, 2003]).

14. ASEAN, "Trade" (www.aseansec.org/view.asp?file=/economic/ov_trd.htm [February 6, 2002]); "Thirteenth Meeting of the ASEAN Free Trade Area (AFTA) Council," September 29, 1999 (www.aseansec.org/1620.htm [October 30, 2003]); and "Frequently Asked Questions on Non-Tariff Issues (NTIs)" (www.aseansec.org/view.asp?file=/economic/afta/ntis.htm [February 6, 2002]).

15. ASEAN, "Trade" (www.aseansec.org/view.asp?file=/economic/ov_trd.htm [February 6, 2002]), p. 3.

16. "Joint Press Statement: the Eleventh AFTA Council Meeting," October 15, 1997 (www.aseansec.org/1891.htm [October 30, 2003]).

17. "Press Statement: The Third AFTA Council Meeting," December 11, 1992 (www.aseansec.org/1184.htm [October 30, 2003]).

18. "Frequently Asked Questions on Non-Tariff Issues (NTIs)" (www.aseansec.org/view.asp?file=/economic/afta/ntis.htm [February 6, 2002]).

19. Ben Dolven and others, "Southeast Asia: Hidden Hitches," *Far Eastern Economic Review,* July 20, 2000 (www.feer.com [October 8, 2003]).

20. Lorien Holland, "Car Making: Moment of Truth," *Far Eastern Economic Review,* November 23, 2000 (www.feer.com [October 8, 2003]).

21. "The Thirteenth Meeting of the ASEAN Free Trade Area (AFTA) Council," September 29, 1999 (www.aseansec.org/1620.htm [October 30, 2003]).

22. G. Pierre Goad, "Investment: Anemic ASEAN," *Far Eastern Economic Review*, September 7, 2000 (www.feer.com [October 8, 2003]).

23. "Joint Press Statement, the Fifth AFTA Council Meeting," September 21, 1994 (www.aseansec.org/2144.htm [October 30, 2003]).

24. ASEAN, "Trade" (www.aseansec.org/view.asp?file=/economic/ov_trd.htm [February 6, 2002]), p.1.

25. Association of Southeast Asian Nations, "The Sixteenth Meeting of the ASEAN Free Trade Area (AFTA) Council, 11 September 2002, Bandar Seri Begawan Brunei Darussalam: Joint Press Statement," September 11, 2002 (www.aseansec.org/12412.htm [October 8, 2003]).

26. Daniel Gay, "Singapore: The Neighborhood's on Fire," *Asiaweek*, May 4, 2001, p. 2; ASEAN, "The Sixteenth Meeting of the ASEAN Free Trade Area (AFTA) Council, 11 September 2002: Joint Press Statement."

27. See, for example, Amy Kazmin, "ASEAN Hampered by Political Problems of Members," *Financial Times,* July 23, 2001, p. 4.

28. Such views are expressed in Frank Ching, "Eye on Asia: ASEAN Needs to Revitalize Itself," *Far Eastern Economic Review,* August 17, 2000 (www.feer.com [October 8, 2003]).

29. "Fact Sheet: Enterprise for ASEAN Initiative" (www.whitehouse.gov/news/releases/2002/10/20021026-7.html [June 11, 2003]).

30. Shuhei Kishimoto, "Regional Challenge in IT Era," speech delivered at "Japan: Year in Review," a conference of the Japan Society of Northern California, January 25, 2001.

31. "Agreement Between Japan and the Republic of Singapore for a New-Age Economic Partnership" (www.mti.gov.sg/public/FTA/frm_FTA_Default.asp?sid=28 [October 8, 2003]). Media information kit available at website.

32. Author's interview with Naoko Munakata, spring 2002.

33. "Jiyu Boeki Kyōtei: Singapōru to Goi" [Free Trade Agreement Settled with Singapore], *Asahi Shimbun*, October 13, 2001, p. 1; and Atsushi Yamada, " Sectionalism Mars Free Trade Talks," *Asahi.com*, October 16, 2001 (www.asahi.com/english/business/K2001101600437.html [October 16, 2001]).

34. "China Daily Slams Japan-S'pore Pact," *The Straits Times Interactive*, January 17, 2002 (http://straitstimes.asia1.com.sg/money/story/0,1870,97151,00.html [January 17, 2002]).

35. "Think-Tank Chief Slams Agreement," *The Straits Times*, November 16, 2000 (www.abaconline.org/news/TTCS.htm [February 21, 2001]).

36. Tatsushi Ogita, *An Approach towards Japan's FTA Policy*, APEC Study Center, Institute of Developing Economies, Working Paper Series 01/ 02–4, pp. 12–13.

37. "Koizumi Signs Japan's First Free Trade Pact with Singapore," *Japan Digest,* January 14, 2002, p. 4.

38. *Agreement between Japan and the Republic of Singapore for a New-Age Economic Partnership,* pp. 57–72 (www.mti.gov.sg/public/FTA/frm_FTA_Default.asp?sid=28 [October 8, 2003]).

39. Ibid., pp. 22–23.

40. C. Fred Bergsten, *Open Regionalism*, Working Paper Series 97-3 (Washington: Institute for International Economics, 1997), p. 17.

41. "Trade and Investment Facilitation and Business Links in APEC," pp. 6–7, updated April 20, 2000 (www.apecsec.org.sg/business_center/service_business/trade_biz_links.html [June 3, 2002]).

42. *APEC Economic Leaders' Declaration*, Shanghai, China, October 21, 2002, APEC Secretariat (www.apecsec.org.sg/ [June 3, 2002]).

43. "Japan, Mexico Launch Joint Panel on Exploring FTA," *Japan Times Online*, September 27, 2001 (www.japantimes.co.jp/cgi-bin/getarticle.p15?nb20010927a6.htm [September 26, 2001]).

44. Author's interviews with Ministry of Foreign Affairs and Ministry of Economics, Trade, and Industry officials, January 2001.

45. Japan-Mexico Joint Study Group on the Strengthening of Bilateral Economic Relations, "Final Report," July 2002; and Ministry of Foreign Affairs of Japan, "Japan-Mexico Summit Meeting: Overview and Evaluation" (www.mofa.go.jp/policy/economy/apec/2002/mexico.html [April 17, 2003]).

46. Ministry of Foreign Affairs of Japan, "Nichi-Mekishiko Keizai Renke: Kyōka no tame no Kyōtei Dai-2-kai Shuseki Daihyō Reberu Kaigō," [The Second Working Level Meeting for the Japan-Mexico Closer Economic Relationship Agreement] (www.mofa.go.jp/mofaj/area/mexico/keizai_renkei.html [April 17, 2003]).

47. Japan-Mexico Joint Study Group, "Final Report," p. 10.

48. For excellent background on the origin of the Mexico-Japan negotiation, see Mireya Solis, "Jumping on the FTA Bandwagon: Japan's New Preferential Trading Diplomacy," paper presented at the annual meeting of the Association for Asian Studies, New York City, March 29, 2003.

49. "Japan, Thailand Agree to Start Talks on Free Trade Agreement," *Japan Digest*, April 15, 2002, p. 4

50. "Thailand's Thaksin Offers to Set Aside Agriculture in Free Trade Talks," *Japan Digest*, March 11, 2003, p. 3.

51. The Ministry of Foreign Affairs of Japan, "Joint Announcement of the Japanese and the Thai Prime Ministers on the Initiation of Negotiations for Establishing the Japan-Thailand Economic Partnership Agreement," December 11, 2003 (www.mofa.go.jp/region/asia-paci/thailand/joint0312.html [January 8, 2004]).

52. David Ibison, "Tokyo and Seoul Explore Free-Trade Pact," *Financial Times*, March 18, 2002, p. 4.

53. "Japan, Malaysia Agree to Study FTA," *Japan Times Online*, December 13, 2002 (www.japantimes.co.jp/cgi-bin/getarticle.p15?nb20021213a5.htm [April 9, 2003]).

54. "Premiers Talk of Reform at Sino-Japanese Summit," *Nikkei Weekly*, April 15, 2002, p. 2.

55. Ministry of Foreign Affairs of Japan, "Japan's FTA strategy: Summary," October 2002 (www.mofa.go.jp/policy/economy/fta/strategy0210.html [April 29, 2003]).

56. "Australia Rejects Koizumi's Appeal to Sign Kyoto Protocol," *Mainichi Interactive*, May 1, 2002 (http://mdn.mainichi.co.jp/news/20020501p2a00m0fp013000c.html [May 1, 2002]).

57. "Australia Seeking to Boost Economic Ties with Japan," *Japan Times Online*, April 16, 2002 (www.japantimes.co.jp/cgi-bin/getarticle.p15?nb20020416a2.htm [April 16, 2002]).

58. "Japan and ASEAN Mull Free Trade Pact," *Japan Times Online,* April 29, 2001 (www.japantimes.co.jp/cgi-bin/getarticle.p15?nn20010429a3.htm [April 30, 2001]); and "Nihon-ASEAN: Jiyu Boeki Kyōtei Shiya ni Kyōgi" [Japan-ASEAN: Conference Accepts Vision of a Free Trade Agreement], *Nihon Keizai Shimbun,* September 7, 2001, p. 1. Both articles announce the start of the study group; why the second meeting, five months after the first, was necessary to bring about final establishment of the study group is unclear.

59. Adianto P. Simamora, "Government Told to Broach FTA with Japan," *Jakarta Post,* January 13, 2002 (www.thejakartapost.com/yesterdaydetail.asp?fileid=20020113.A01 [October 8, 2003]).

60. "Closer Trade Ties Top Thai Agenda," *Bangkok Post,* January 11, 2002 (www.bangkokpost.com/110102_News/11Jan2002_news27.html [January 18, 2002]).

61. "Tokyo, Bested by China, Will Scramble for Free Trade Pact with ASEAN," *Japan Digest,* January 8, 2002, p. 1.

62. "Japan and ASEAN in East Asia—a Sincere and Open Partnership," speech by Prime Minister Junichiro Koizumi, January 14, 2002, Singapore (www.mofa.go.jp/region/asia-paci/pmv0201/speech.html [October 8, 2003]).

63. "Asia in a New Century—Challenge and Opportunity," speech by Prime Minister Junichiro Koizumi at the Boao Forum for Asia, April 12, 2002 (Ministry of Foreign Affairs press release) (www.mofa.go.jp/region/asia-paci/china/boao0204/speech.html [October 8, 2003]).

64. Annastashya Emmanuelle, "RI, Japan for Regional Integration," *Jakarta Post,* January 13, 2002 (www.thejarkatapost.com/detailweekly.asp?fileid=20020113.@01 [January 24, 2002]).

65. "Opinion and Editorial: Koizumi's Speech," *Jakarta Post,* January 16, 2002 (www.thejakartapost.com/yesterdaydetail.asp?fileid=20020116.C01 [October 9, 2003]).

66. Saritdet Marukatat and Bhanravee Tansubhapol, "Two-Way Trade Deal Spurned, but Broad Alliance with ASEAN on Cards," *Bangkok Post,* January 12, 2002 (www.bangkokpost.com/120102_News/12Jan2002_news02.html [January 18, 2002]).

67. Lim Hua Sing, "Point of View: Advancing Regional Economic Integration Is Key," *Asahi.com,* January 11, 2001 (www.asahi.com/english/op-ed/K2002011100284.html [January 14, 2002]).

68. "Editorial: Worthwhile Cooperation Plan Emerges from Koizumi's Trip," *Asahi.com,* January 16, 2002 (www.asahi.com/english/op-ed/K2002011600447.html [January 16, 2002]).

69. "ASEAN, Japan Discuss Possible FTA," *Japan Times Online,* March 11, 2003 (www.japantimes.co.jp/cgi-bin/getarticle.p15?nb20030311a8.htm [March 11, 2003]).

70. "METI Eyes East Asian FTA," *Daily Yomiuri On-Line,* May 9, 2002 (www.yomiuri.co.jp/newse/20020509wo13.htm [May 9, 2002]).

71. "Japan Considering Creation of East Asia Free-Trade Area Before 2010," *Japan Times Online,* April 14, 2002 (www.japantimes.co.jp/cgi-bin/getarticle.p15?nn20020414a1.htm [April 15, 2002]).

72. Comments by Yutaka Kawashima at a Center for Northeast Policy Studies (CNAPS) luncheon at the Brookings Institution, January 23, 2002.

73. For an analysis of that process and its implications for the increased openness of China's markets, see Nicholas R. Lardy, *Integrating China into the Global Economy* (Brookings, 2002).

74. These data are from the ASEAN-China Expert Group on Economic Cooperation, *Forging Closer ASEAN-China Economic Relations in the Twenty-First Century*, October 2001, pp. 8, 13, 22–3, 45, 60, 71, 150, 152.

75. Ibid, p. 152.

76. Ibid, p. 29, for a complete list of trade facilitation items.

77. Ibid., pp. 22-23.

78. Ibid., p. 13.

79. Yoichi Funabashi, "Point of View, Yoichi Funabashi: New Geopolitics Rages Over Various Parts of Asia," *Asahi.com*, January 15, 2002 (www.asahi.com/english/op-ed/K2002011500444.html [January 16, 2002]).

80. "Taiwan Eager to Sign Free Trade Pacts: ROC WTO Representative," *Taiwan News*, March 28, 2002 (http://th.gio.gov.tw/show.cfm?news_id=13729 [October 9, 2003]).

81. "Taiwan's WTO Name May Help in Agreements: Officials," (http://th.gio.gov.tw/show.cfm?news_id=12082 [January 29, 2002]).

82. "Government Establishes Free Trade Agreement Task Force," *Taiwan Economic News*, November 14, 2001, available on *Taiwan Headlines* (http://th.gio.gov.tw/show.cfm?news_id=12144 [January 29, 2002]).

83. "President Inks Documents for Taiwan's WTO Entry," *Central News Agency*, November 23, 2001, available on *Taiwan Headlines*, (http://th.gio.gov.tw/show.cfm?news_id=12324 [January 29, 2002)).

84. For one such expression of concern, or at least the economic side of it, by the Mainland Affairs Council of the government, see "Taiwan to Seek Free Trade Agreements," *Taiwan Economic News*, February 20, 2002 (http://th.gio.gov.tw/show.cfm?news_id=13402 [October 9, 2003]).

85. United States International Trade Commission, *U.S.-Taiwan FTA: Likely Economic Impact of a Free Trade Agreement between the United States and Taiwan*, USITC Publication 3548, October 2002.

86. "Taiwan, Japan May Sign Free Trade Pact within Two Years: JETRO Head," *Taiwan Economic News*, June 13, 2002 (http://th.gio.gov.tw/show.cfm?news_id=14429 [October 9, 2003]).

87. "Lin Yi-fu Welcomes Japan's Proposed Asia Free Trade Zone," *Taiwan News*, April 16, 2002 (http://th.gio.gov.tw/show.cfm?news_id=13878 [October 9, 2003]).

## Notes to Chapter Eight

1. On this topic and the broader economic dilemmas it has created for Japan, see Akio Mikuni and R. Taggart Murphy, *Japan's Policy Trap: Dollars, Deflation, and the Crisis of Japanese Finance* (Brookings, 2002).

2. Eisuke Sakakibara, "Mr. Yen Looking Back/The Makings of an Economic Crisis," *Daily Yomiuri Online* (www.yomiuri.co.jp/newse/113ec18.htm [November 13, 2000]).

3. Martin N. Baily, Diana Farrell, and Susan Lund, "The Color of Hot Money," *Foreign Affairs*, vol. 79, no. 2 (March/April 2000), pp. 99–109, especially p. 105.

4. C. H. Kwan, *Yen Bloc: Toward Economic Integration in Asia* (Brookings, 2001), pp. 183–84.

5. Ibid., p. 72.

6. Ibid., p. 128.

7. Ibid., pp. 2–4. Much of the analysis in Kwan's book is seriously flawed. He engages in very selective use of data (especially in using 1985 as a starting point for much of his analysis of trade flows, a year in which flows were skewed temporarily by an unusually high value of the dollar). He also often draws conclusions not justified by his own data and draws other conclusions without producing any data at all to justify them. Nevertheless, this book and his writings in Japanese represent a serious line of analysis that is quite popular in Japan and around the region.

8. International Monetary Fund, *International Financial Statistics Yearbook 1993* (Washington: IMF, 1993), p. x.

9. For a somewhat similar analysis, see Michael Mussa and others, *Occasional Paper 193: Exchange Rate Regimes in an Increasingly Integrated World Economy* (Washington: International Monetary Fund, 2000), p. 39.

10. For an excellent study of the government's broad set of policies to suppress the value of the yen, see Mikuni and Murphy, *Japan's Policy Trap*.

11. Mussa and others, *Occasional Paper 193*, p. 33.

12. For an analysis of such problems, see Gordon de Brouwer, "Financial Markets and Policies in East Asia: Does a Formal Common-Basket Peg in East Asia Make Economic Sense?" paper prepared for "Financial Markets and Policies in East Asia," a conference at Australia National University, September 2000, p. 8.

13. Kwan, *Yen Bloc*, pp. 138–44.

14. Cornelis Keijzer, "Japan and Asian Regional Economic Integration," Institute for International Monetary Affairs Research Report 1, 2001 (September 30, 2001), p. 25.

15. Stephen Leong, "How to Achieve Domestic and International Economic Stability: A Malaysian Perspective" (www.mof.go.jp/singikai/gaitame/siryou/h120207b.htm [October 10, 2003]), p. 8.

16. Eisuke Sakakibara, "Thai Crisis Played Part in IMF Idea,"*Daily Yomiuri*, November 26, 1999 (www.yomiuri.co.jp/newse/1126in18.htm. [November 29, 1999]).

17. Kwan, *Yen Bloc*, pp. 34–35. Kwan, of course, is highly sympathetic to this attempt to escape the clutches of the "Washington consensus."

18. Eisuke Sakakibara, "Mahathir Determined to Do Things 'His Way,'" *Daily Yomiuri,* January 14, 2000 (www.yomiuri.co.jp/newse/0114ec02.htm [January 14, 2000]). With his typical lack of humility, Sakakibara further claims that he "calmed down the United States" when the Clinton administration objected to Malaysian controls.

19. See, for example, the strong criticisms voiced by Nobel Prize winner Joseph E. Stiglitz (former chief economist of the World Bank) in *Globalization and Its Discontents* (New York: W.W. Norton, 2002), as well as the stinging rebuttals from the International Monetary Fund in Kenneth Rogoff, "An Open Letter," at IMF, Views and Commentaries for 2002 (www.imf.org/external/np/vc/2002/070202.htm [October 10, 2003]) and Thomas C. Dawson, "Stiglitz, the IMF, and Globalization: A Speech to the MIT Club of Washington," IMF, Speeches for 2002 (www.imf.org/external/np/speeches/2002/061302.htm [October 10, 2003]).

20. Chalongphob Sussangkarn, "A Framework for Regional Monetary Stabilization," *NIRA Review*, vol. 7, no. 4 (Autumn 2000), pp. 17–20; and Kiyoshi Miura, "Framework for Regional Monetary Stabilization in East Asia," *IIMA Newsletter*, no. 6 (September 29, 2000) (www.iima.or.jp/pdf/NEWSLETTER2000NO6.pdf [November 12, 2003]).

21. Policy Council of the Japan Forum on International Relations, *Economic Globalization and Options for Asia* (Tokyo: Japan Forum on International Relations, May 2000), p. 17 The council included mainstream economists and public figures, including Hisao Kanamori (long-term head of the Japan Center for Economic Research), Diet member Kazuo Aichi, Yasuo Hattori (head of Seiko Epson), Kuniko Inoguchi (a senior political scientist at Sophia University), Kazumasa Iwata (an economics professor at the University of Tokyo who later served in the Koizumi government), Koji Kakizawa (a former foreign minister), Takeshi Kondo (a former managing director of Itochu Corporation, now a Liberal Democratic Party member of the Diet), Makoto Kuroda (a former vice minister for international affairs at the Ministry of International Trade and Industry), Ryohei Murata (former ambassador to the United States), and Toshiaki Ogasawara (publisher of the *Japan Times*).

22. Ibid., p. 17.

23. East Asia Study Group, *Final Report of the East Asia Study Group*, November 4, 2002, Phnom Penh, Cambodia (www.mofa.go.jp/region/asia-paci/asean/pmv0211/report.pdf [November 12, 2003]).

24. Sandra Sugawara, "Japan to Unveil Plan to Aid Asian Nations; $30 Billion Package to Face G-7 Scrutiny," *Washington Post,* September 30, 1998, p. C3.

25. Mikei Kiyoi, "On-the-Record Briefing, 14 November 1998, Ministry of Foreign Affairs" (www.mofa.go.jp/policy/economy/apec/1998/brief14.html [October 10, 2003]).

26. Ministry of Foreign Affairs of Japan, "ODA Loan to Indonesia—Assistance under the New Miyazawa Initiative for the Socially Vulnerable," March 12, 1999 (www.mofa.go.jp/announce/announce/1999/3/312-3.html [May 17, 2002]).

27. "Japan Will Give ¥100 Million to Fund 'Chiang Mai Initiative' Office," *Japan Digest,* September 26, 2001, pp. 2–3.

28. C. Randall Henning, *East Asian Financial Cooperation* (Washington: Institute for International Economics, September 2002), p. 20, table 3.1.

29. Ministry of Finance, "International Reserves/Foreign Currency Liquidity (as of March 31, 2003)" (www.mof.go.jp/english/e1c006.htm [April 30, 2003]).

30. Tadahiro Asami, "After the Chiang Mai Initiative," *IIMA Newsletter*, no. 5 (August 5, 2001), pp. 1–3.

31. "Asian Economic Integration Drive Hits Speed Bump," Reuters, May 13, 2002 (www.nytimes.com/reuters/business/business-economy-asia-cooperation.html [May 13, 2002]). This meeting was held in conjunction with the annual ADB meeting held in Shanghai in May 2002.

32. Neil Saker, "Shroff: Asian Currency Markets: The Foundations of Stability," *Far Eastern Economic Review*, May 24, 2001(www.feer.com [October 10, 2003]).

33. Asami, "After the Chiang Mai Initiative," pp. 4–5.

34. For an interpretation along these lines, see Heibert Dieter, "The 5th Column: East Asia's Puzzling Regionalism," *Far Eastern Economic Review*, July 12, 2001 (www.feer.com [October 10, 2003]). Dieter, an advocate of increased Asian independence on currency matters, was deeply disappointed with the 10 percent limitation.

35. Woosik Moon, Yeongseop Rhee, and Deok Ryong Yoon, "Asian Monetary Cooperation: A Search for Regional Monetary Stability in the Post-Euro and the Post-Asian Crisis Era," *Bank of Korea Economic Papers*, vol. 3, no. 1 (May 2000), pp. 159–93 and especially pp. 188–89.

36. "Shiokawa Proposal to ASEM Would Create Asian Monetary Union by 2030," *Japan Digest*, vol. 13, no. 120 (July 9, 2002), p. 1; see also Natsuko Waki, "Asia Embarks on Single Currency Voyage a la Europe," Reuters, July 6, 2002.

37. "Asian Executives Poll," *Far Eastern Economic Review*, December 30, 2001 (www.feer.com [October 10, 2003]).

38. "Australia 'Should Be Part of Asian Monetary Union,'" *The Straits Times Interactive*, July 25, 2001 (http://straitstimes.asia1.com.sg/money/story/0,1870,59469,00.html [July 25, 2001]).

## Notes to Chapter Nine

1. For details on the early phases of this dispute, see "Imports to be Curbed via Quarantine Crackdown," *Japan Times Online*, March 23, 2001 (www.japantimes.co.jp/cgi-bin/getarticle.p15?nb20010323a4..htm [July 12, 2002]); "Cabinet Approves Import Curbs on China Leeks, Shiitake, Straw," *Japan Times Online*, April 11, 2001 (www.japantimes.co.jp/cgi-bin/getarticle.p15?nn20010411a2.htm [July 12, 2002]); and "Japan and China Prepare to Discuss Emergency Import Curbs," *Japan Times Online*, June 2, 2001 (www.japantimes.co.jp/cgi-bin/getarticle.p15?nb?20010602a5.htm [June 4, 2001]).

2. "Japan-China Trade Panel to Hold First Talks Next Week," *Japan Times Online*, January 30, 2002 (www.japantimes.co.jp/cgi-bin/getarticle.pl5?nb20020130a7.htm [July 12, 2002]).

3. Ken Hijino, "Chinese Trade Talks with Japan Stall," *Financial Times*, November 2, 2001, p. 5.

4. "Chinese Tariffs to Cost Japan's Car Firms 420 Billion Yen," *Japan Times Online*, October 13, 2001 (www.japantimes.co.jp/cgi-bin/getarticle.p15?nb20011013at.htm [July 12, 2002]).

5. Charles Hutzler, "China, Japanese Leaders to Set Aside Tensions to Negotiate Trade Solution," *Wall Street Journal*, October 9, 2001 (http://interactive.wsj.com/archive/retrieve.cgi?id=SB1002569617434107040.djm [October 9, 2001]).

6. Akihiko Suzuki, "Japan Out to Defuse Safeguard Trade Flap," *Asahi.com*, October 20, 2001 (www.asahi.com/english/international/k2001102000424.html [October 23, 2001]).

7. "Japan to Seek 'Private' Solution to Dispute with China," *Japan Digest*, November 5, 2001, pp. 3–4.

8. "As Expected, China Moves to Settle Trade Dispute by Indirection," *Japan Digest*, December 17, 2001, p. 2.

9. "Cabinet Approves Import Curbs on China Leeks, Shiitake, Straw," *Japan Times Online*, April 11, 2001 (www.japantimes.co.jp/cgi-bin/getarticle.p15?nn20010411a2.htm [July 12, 2002]).

10. "Japan, South Korea Resolve Dispute over Fishing around Northern Islands," *Japan Digest*, January 8, 2002, p. 2.

11. "Anti-Japan Anger Spreads across Asia," *The Straits Times*, August 8, 2001 (http://straitstimes.asia1.com.sg/home [August 16, 2001]).

12. Kwan Weng Kin, "Koizumi's Uncompromising Stance Is Bad News for Asia," *The Straits Times Interactive*, July 30, 2001 (http://straitstimes.asia1.com.sg/analysis/story/0,1870,60602,00.html [July 31, 2001]).

13. "Tokyo Moves to Strengthen Ties with Beijing, Seoul," *Mainichi Interactive*, November 5, 2001 (http://mdn.mainichi.co.jp/news/20011105p2a00m0dm009002c.html [November 6, 2001]).

14. "Jiang Zemin Personally Denounces Koizumi's Latest Yasukuni Visit," *Japan Digest*, April 30, 2002, p. 2; "Koizumi's Yasukuni Foray Causes China to Scrap Visits, Koreans to Off a Pig," *Japan Digest*, April 24, 2002, p. 1; Howard W. French, "Koizumi's Visit to War Shrine Angers Japan's Neighbors," *New York Times*, April 22, 2002 (www.nytimes.com/2002/04/22/international/asia/22JAPA.html [April 22, 2002]).

15. Shinji Fukukawa, "Japan, Asia Need New Chapter," *Daily Yomiuri*, June 15, 2001 (www.yomiuri.co.jp/newse/20010615wo42.htm [June 15, 2001]). The same poll found the percentages much lower in Thailand and Singapore, in the range of 20 to 25 percent.

16. "Japan Fails to Get ASEAN Nations to Adopt Antiterrorism Accord," *Daily Yomiuri Online*, November 7, 2001 (www.yomiuri.co.jp/newse/20011107wo41.htm [November 7, 2001]).

17. For a discussion of these fears in Japan, see James Brooke, "Tokyo Fears China May Put an End to 'Made in Japan,'"*New York Times*, November 20, 2001 (www.nytimes.com/2001/11/20/business/worldbusiness/20JAPA.html [May 1, 2002]).

18. Tom Mitchell, "One Forum, Four Agendas at Boao," *South China Morning Post*, April 14, 2002.

19. China's Asia Forum Limps to Apologetic Close," *Financial Times*, April 15, 2002, p. 5.

20. Caroline Cooper, "Does China Pose an Economic Threat to Korea?" *Korea Insight*, vol. 4, no. 1 (January 2002), p. 1.

21. Government Information Office, Republic of China (Taiwan), "Statistical Data on the Republic of China" (www.gio.gov.tw/taiwan-website/5-gp/stats/ [July 12, 2002]).

22. For a detailed study of these issues, see Nicholas R. Lardy, *Strategic Implications of China-Taiwan Economic Relations* (Brookings, forthcoming).

## Notes to Chapter Ten

1. Gordon de Brouwer, "Research Focus: Strengthening the Policy Dialogue in East Asia," *APEC Economies Newsletter*, vol. 6, no. 1 (January 2002). This is the newsletter of the Asia Pacific School of Economics and Management at Australia National University.

2. For a current listing of free trade negotiations being pursued by the U.S. government, see USTR Resources, "Free Trade Agreement Negotiations" (www.ustr.gov/new/fta/index.htm [October 15, 2003]).

3. See for example, APEC International Assessment Network, *APIAN Update: Shanghai, Los Cabos, and Beyond: the Second APIAN Policy Report*, October 2001, and *Remaking APEC as an Institution: The Third APIAN Report*, August 2002. Both can be found at http://203.127.220.67/apec/publications/all_publications/apec_study_centre.html [November 12, 2003].

# Index

ABAC (APEC Business Advisory Council), 128
ADB. *See* Asian Development Bank
AFTA. *See* ASEAN Free Trade Area
Agricultural products in Japanese trade negotiations: with China, 233; with Mexico, 180; as roadblock to trade agreements, 184–85, 233; with Singapore, 177, 178, 192, 241; with Thailand, 181
AMF. *See* Asian monetary fund (AMF) proposal
Antidumping regulations, 149, 261–62
APEC. *See* Asia-Pacific Economic Cooperation
APEC Business Advisory Council (ABAC), 128
APEC International Assessment Network (APIAN), 128, 265–66
ASEAN (Association of Southeast Asian Nations), 10; foreign direct investment in member countries, 104–07, 169, 188; preferential trading arrangement (PTA), 152, 182; trade among members, 33, 150–53, 183; trade talks with China, 11, 185–86, 241, 243
ASEAN Free Trade Area (AFTA), 4, 10, 11, 152, 167, 168–75, 191; disregard of WTO requirements, 254; reasons for forming, 20–21; smaller countries' fear of China, 19, 40, 188, 244–45
ASEAN+3, 10, 155, 156–57, 192, 257; swap agreements, 11, 213, 220–24, 240, 255, 264
ASEAN+5 proposal, 184, 190
Asia-Europe Meeting (ASEM), 156, 224–25
Asian Currency Crisis Support Facility, 119
Asian Development Bank (ADB), 9, 115, 116–22, 130, 138, 189
Asian Development Bank Institute (ADBI), 120, 121
Asian financial crisis of *1997*, 3, 4, 11, 202–03; and APEC role, 130–31; exchange rates as factor in, 197–98, 202; as factor in creating regionalism, 16, 254; Japan's assistance proposals,

214–20. *See also* International Monetary Fund (IMF)

Asian monetary fund (AMF) proposal, 12, 213–16, 239, 259, 267

Asian values, concept of, 16, 38, 40, 142–43, 251

Asia-Pacific Economic Cooperation (APEC), 6, 9, 127–37, 146, 253; accomplishments of, 135–37, 254; and Asian financial crisis of 1997, 130–31; assessment of effectiveness of, 6, 115, 130, 133–37, 138–39, 175–76, 193, 264–65; Bogor Declaration, 10, 128–29, 133, 134, 265; early voluntary sectoral liberalization (EVSL) agreement, 130, 134, 138; ecotech trade agenda, 129, 134, 136–37, 266–67; individual action plans (IAPs) of members, 129, 134–35, 139; information technology agreement (ITA), 129–30, 134; leaders' meetings, 127–28, 131; Los Cabos meeting *(2002)*, 131; membership, 132–33, 189; Osaka Action Agenda, 129, 134, 138; recommended reinvigoration of, 264–67; Shanghai Accord and meeting, 131, 135; U.S. focus on, 7, 13, 70, 264–67

Association of Southeast Asian Nations. *See* ASEAN

Australia: APEC role of, 13, 127, 138, 155, 264; opposition to EAEC, 155; trade with, 13, 66–68, 168, 169, 181–82; on unitary regional currency, 225; U.S. direct investment in, 109–10

Bangkok Agreement, 167, 168
Bangkok Declaration, 150–51
Bank for International Settlements (BIS), 81
Bank lending, 9, 80–85, 112, 252
Bergsten, C. Fred, 4, 128, 134, 177, 178
Boao conference, 243
Bogor Declaration, 10, 128–29, 133, 134, 265
Bretton Woods system, 195, 196

Brunei, 25, 151, 173
Buddhism, 36
Bush administration. *See* U.S. East Asia relations

Cambodia: ASEAN membership, 151; economic position of, 25, 27; exchange rate of, 199, 203, 225; pre-crisis finances in, 74; and free trade agreements, 172

Canada, 37, 107–08, 264. *See also* North American Free Trade Agreement (NAFTA)

Capitalism in East Asian countries, 143, 145, 246

Characteristics of East Asia, 15–41, 251; diversity, 7, 36–38, 40; economic disparities, 20–30, 39; openness to investment, 34–36, 39; openness to trade, 30–34, 39, 174, 234; population disparities, 7, 17–20, 38; social and economic differences/commonalities of, 7–8, 16, 38, 141–45

Chiang Mai Initiative, 131, 157, 220, 222, 239

Chile, 132, 192

China: APEC membership, 132, 185; and ASEAN relations, 11, 185–88, 241, 243; communist form of government, as obstacle to leadership role, 245; diplomatic issues of, 246–47; economic comparison with Japan, 20; economic dominance of, in view of other countries, 22, 243–45; economic transition of, 245–46; EU trade with, 61; exchange rate of, 198–99, 213, 225, 226; fear of job losses to, 18, 25–27, 39, 188; finances pre-crisis finances in, 74; foreign aid to, 88, 89, 90; foreign direct investment in, 40, 101, 105–06, 188; income level of, 25; Japan, relations with, 18, 25–26, 154, 181, 188, 233–35, 238, 240–41; PECC membership, 126; population of, 17–19; purchasing power of, 22–23; regional leadership role of, 12, 19, 242–49;

regional trade negotiations of, 4, 11, 181, 185–89; South Korea, relations with, 244; and swap agreements, 223, 224; Taiwan, treatment of, 246, 257; trade data on, 44–45; trade evolution of, 8, 30, 32, 43, 53, 55, 59–62, 69–70; WTO accession, effect of, 27, 70, 105–06, 187–88, 244. *See also* U.S.-China relations

Chino, Tadao, 121

Christianity, 36

Cold war, relations during, 3–4, 150, 250–51

Common Effective Preferential Tariff Scheme (AFTA), 171

Confucian teachings, 142

Corruption and foreign aid, 90

Crawford, John, 125–26

Currency issues, 5, 195–97, 254; alternative strategies for pegging, 210–12; floating vs. fixed exchange rates, 198–202, 209, 210, 212–13, 225–27, 229, 230; historical background, 197–213; nominal effective exchange rate, 207–08; single currency for region, proposal of, 5, 12, 154, 224–27. *See also* Swap agreements; Yen, currencies pegged to

Diversity, 7, 36–38, 40, 141–45, 251, 252

Dollar vs. yen. *See* Yen, currencies pegged to

Drysdale, Peter, 125–26

East Asian Economic Caucus (EAEC), 155–56, 159, 175, 239, 259

*The East Asian Miracle* (World Bank study), 41, 121, 144

East Asia Study Group, 216

E-commerce. *See* Technology

Economics: affluence comparison, 25–30; China, in transition, 245–46; disparities among countries, 7, 20–30, 39; NAFTA and Europe comparison, 23–25; and principles of trade, 160–66; purchasing power parity comparison, 21–23. *See also* Investment links; *specific organizations to foster economic relations*

Economies of scale, 2, 162

Emmerson, Donald K., 142

Employment and labor issues: fear of job losses to China, 25–27, 39, 188; Japanese direct investment in U.S. and Europe, effect of, 98; Japan's shrinking workforce, 18

Energy supply, 154–55, 246

Enterprise for ASEAN Initiative, 175, 262

ESCAP (United Nations Economic and Social Commission for Asia and the Pacific), 167

European Union (EU): bank loans from, 82; direct investment in ASEAN countries, 104–05; direct investment in East Asian countries, 99–101, 103–04; East Asian bloc formation to counter, 146–47; economic comparison with East Asia, 23–24, 27–28, 29–30; euro as unified currency of, 195; Japanese direct investment in, 94–95, 98; trade with East Asian countries, 49, 53, 54, 57, 58, 61, 69; trade with Mexico, 166; trade with U.S., 64; U.S. direct investment in, 108, 110

Exchange rates. *See* Currency issues

Exports. *See* Trade; *specific countries*

Fallows, James, 143

Fishing rights, 235–36, 247

Floating exchange rates. *See* Currency issues

Foreign aid, 9, 87–90, 112, 154; to China, 88, 89, 90; and corruption, 90; countries not qualifying for, 87; from U.S., 89, 90

Foreign direct investment, 9, 27, 34, 90–111, 113, 154; ASEAN, 40, 104–07, 169, 188; liberal capital markets to foster, 196. *See also specific countries*

Framework for Regional Monetary Stabilization (FRMS) proposal, 215–16, 224

Frankel, Jeffrey, 46–48
Free trade agreements, 4, 11, 164, 167–91,
    262; agricultural products as roadblock
    to, 177, 178, 180, 181, 184–85, 192,
    233, 241; APEC recommended role in,
    266; background and number of, 165.
    *See also specific agreements or countries*
Fukuda Doctrine, 182
Fukukawa, Shinji, 147
Funabashi, Yoichi, 16, 188

GATS. *See* General Agreement on Trade in
    Services
GATT. *See* General Agreement on Tariffs
    and Trade
GDP comparisons, 20–30; trade as share
    of, 30–34
General Agreement on Tariffs and Trade
    (GATT), 4, 160, 164, 165, 235, 260
General Agreement on Trade in Services
    (GATS), 164–65, 260
Geographical scope of East Asia, 7, 16,
    251
Globalism, effect of, 2–3
Gross capital flows, 79–87, 113

Hatakeyama, Noboru, 190
Hatch, Walter, 112
Hew, E. D., and Anthony, M. C., 159
Hiranuma, Takeo, 234
History discrepancies among East Asian
    countries, 37–38
Hong Kong: affluence of, 25; bank loans
    from, 82; exchange rate of, 198, 225;
    foreign direct investment from, 101;
    foreign direct investment in, 34; money
    center versus regional loan recipient
    status, 81; openness to trade, 30;
    portfolio investments in, 85; possible
    inclusion in ASEAN+3, 184; trans-
    shipment of goods through, 44, 59

IIMA. *See* Institute for International
    Monetary Affairs
IMF. *See* International Monetary Fund
Imports. *See* Trade; *specific countries*

Income disparities, 25–30
Indonesia: AFTA participation, 173; in
    Asian financial crisis of *1997*, 202–03;
    currency exchange rate of, 198, 225;
    and EAEC, 155; economic status of, 27,
    74; foreign aid to, 90; foreign direct
    investment in, 34, 91–92, 106;
    population of, 17
Institute for International Monetary
    Affairs (IIMA), 215, 224
International Monetary Fund (IMF):
    continued viability of, 255; and
    exchange rates, 198, 207, 210; Japanese
    aid packages tied to approval of,
    215–16, 222–23, 229–30, 239, 259;
    pressure for reforms from, 3, 147–48;
    role in Asian financial crisis of *1997*, 3,
    130, 147–48, 157, 194, 203, 213, 215,
    219, 254, 264; trade data from, 44;
    U.S. focus on, 6–7, 12–13, 260–64
International Trade Commission (ITC) on
    U.S. trade with Taiwan, 190, 191
Investment: links, 8–9, 72–113, 145, 252;
    Asian Development Bank loans,
    117–18; bank lending, 9, 80–85, 112,
    252; foreign aid, 9, 87–90, 112; foreign
    direct investment, 9, 90–111, 113; gross
    capital flows, 79–87, 113; net financial
    resource flow, 73–79; openness to
    investment, 34–36, 39; portfolio
    investments, 85–87; strength of, 41

Japan: affluence of, 25, 39; and APEC
    early voluntary sectoral liberalization
    (EVSL) agreement, 130; and
    ASEAN+3, 156–57; and Asian
    Development Bank, 116–17, 118–22;
    Asian monetary fund (AMF) proposal
    by, 213–16; bank lending from, 80–82,
    84–85; China, relations with, 18,
    25–26, 188, 233–35, 238, 240–41;
    currencies pegged to yen, 195, 197,
    203–10, 228; and EAEC participation,
    155, 156; economic model of, adoption
    by other countries, 40–41, 144–45,
    154; economic size of, 20–23; EU trade

with, 49, 53; exchange rate of, 198; pre-crisis finances in, 74; floating exchange rate of, 225; foreign aid to other East Asian countries, 72, 75, 87–90, 111, 112, 154, 215–20, 222, 252; foreign direct investment in, 9, 34–36, 92, 98–101, 113; foreign direct investment in Canada, 108; foreign direct investment in other East Asian countries, 93–101, 103–04, 113, 154, 252; foreign direct investment in U.S., 93–95, 98, 112; and free trade agreements, 25, 147, 175–85, 191; historical relations with other East Asian countries, 37, 236–38; manufacturing relocated around region, 60, 71, 78, 97–98, 101; Mexico, relations with, 11, 166–67, 180, 184, 191; Middle East trade with, 50, 53, 76, 155; NAFTA, views on, 166–67, 180; New Miyazawa Initiative to bail out Asian financial crisis, 213, 216–20; population of, 17, 18; portfolio investments of, 85–87; private financial sector's volatility, 210; protectionism of, 232–36, 254; regional balance of payments of, 75–79; regional strategy of, 153–55; regional trade initiatives of, 146, 181–84; Singapore, agreement with, 11, 165–66, 176–79, 191, 241–42, 254; South Korea, relations with, 37, 166, 168, 191, 235–36, 257; swap agreements with, 221–23; Taiwan, trade talks with, 182, 190; trade evolution of, 4, 8, 30–34, 39, 43, 49–53, 57–58, 69, 70, 234; and World Bank, 143–44; World War II, policy on, 37, 236–38. *See also* Japan's leadership; U.S.-Japan relations
Japan Bank for International Cooperation (JBIC), 89, 120, 218–19
Japan Development Bank, 144
Japan Economic Research Institute, 144
Japan Leasing, 101
Japan's leadership, 12, 146, 153–55, 197, 247–49; advocating narrow form of regionalism, 256; anti-Japanese

sentiment of other East Asian countries, 238–39; in Asian Development Bank, 117, 121; currency problems as disincentive for, 229; diplomatic problems of, 236–39, 242; economic problems as disincentive for, 228–29; economic status as giving power to, 20, 32–33; and foreign aid, 87, 112; in lending to other nations, 84–85; protectionism as obstacle to, 232–36; and U.S.-Japan relationship, 137, 239–40

Kearney, A. T., 32, 34
Kobe Research Project, 224
Koizumi, Junichiro, 180, 181, 182–83, 184, 234, 236, 237–38, 239, 243
Kojima, Kiyoshi, 125
Korea. *See* South Korea
Kwan, C. H., 53, 204–05, 211–12, 214, 216, 224

Labor. *See* Employment and labor issues
Laos: ASEAN membership, 151; economic position of, 25, 27, 74; exchange rate of, 199, 203, 213, 225; and free trade agreements, 172
Lardy, Nicholas, 59
Latin American countries as APEC members, 132, 264. *See also specific countries*
Leadership. *See* Japan's leadership; Regional leadership
Lee Kuan Yew, 142, 169
Lending. *See* Bank lending; Investment links

Macau, 44, 59, 199, 203, 225
Mahathir Mohamad: anti-Western stance of, 142, 147, 260; and EAEC, 155, 156, 158, 175, 259; Japan's support of, 214; political troubles of, 174; as proponent of Asian Way, 40; in trade talks with Japan, 181
Malaysia: in Asian financial crisis of *1997*, 203, 214, 215; EAEC formation on initiative of, 155; exchange rate of, 198,

225, 226; pre-crisis finances in, 74;
foreign direct investment in, 106; and
free trade agreements, 171, 172, 191;
GDP rates comparison, 27; openness to
trade, 30; pro–regional bloc stance of,
142; and swap agreements, 223
Meade, James, 160
Mexico: APEC membership, 132; EU
relations with, 166; Japanese relations
with, 11, 166–67, 180, 182, 184, 191;
South Korea relations with, 192; U.S.
relations with, 37. *See also* North
American Free Trade Agreement
(NAFTA)
Middle East trade, 50, 53, 69, 76, 155
Miyazawa, Keiichi, 217
Monetary cooperation, 11–12, 194–230;
AMF proposal, 213–16; ASEAN+3 swap
agreement, 220–24; forces against,
228–29; historical background,
197–213; New Miyazawa Initiative, 213,
216–20; single currency proposal, 5, 12,
154, 224–27. *See also* Currency issues
Most-favored-nation (MFN) status, 10,
134, 173
Muslim, 36, 148
Myanmar, 34, 151, 172, 199, 203, 225

NAFTA. *See* North American Free Trade
Agreement
Net financial resource flow, 73–79
New Miyazawa Initiative to bail out Asian
financial crisis, 213, 216–20
New Zealand: APEC role of, 13, 264;
South Korea relations with, 192; Taiwan
trade initiative with, 189; trade agree-
ment with Singapore, 168, 169, 177,
192; trade relations with East Asian
countries, 66–68; and unitary regional
currency, 225; U.S. direct investment
in, 109–10
Nissan Motor Company, 101
Nominal effective exchange rate, 207–08
North American Free Trade Agreement
(NAFTA): East Asian bloc formation to
counter, 146–47; economic comparison

with East Asia, 23–25, 27–28, 39–40;
Japan's trade relations with, 50, 52;
population comparison with East Asia,
18–20; trade comparison with, 70; U.S.
direct investment in partners of,
110–11, 132; U.S. trade patterns with,
effect of, 62–63, 65, 70, 166
North Korea, 257

Official development assistance (ODA).
*See* Foreign aid
Oil and gas. *See* Energy supply
Okita, Saburo, 125–26
Organisation for Economic Co-operation
and Development (OECD) on foreign
aid given by members, 89
Osaka Action Agenda, 129, 134, 138

Pacific Basin Economic Council (PBEC),
9, 115, 122–24, 138, 253
Pacific Economic Cooperation Council
(PECC), 9, 115, 126–27, 138, 253
Pacific Trade and Development Confer-
ence (PAFTAD), 9, 115, 125–26, 138,
253
Papua New Guinea: APEC membership,
132; exchange rate of, 199, 203, 225,
226; pre-crisis finances in, 74
Patrick, Hugh, 125, 139
PBEC. *See* Pacific Basin Economic
Council
PECC. *See* Pacific Economic Cooperation
Council
People's Republic of China. *See* China
Philippines: AFTA participation, 173;
Asian Development Bank's headquarters
in, 117; in Asian financial crisis of 1997,
203; currency exchange rate of, 198;
pre-crisis finances in, 74; foreign direct
investment in, 106; and free trade
agreements, 191; GDP rates
comparison, 27
Population disparities among East Asian
countries, 7, 17–20, 38; comparison
with NAFTA, 18–20
Portfolio investments, 85–87

Ravenhill, John, 136

Regional bloc: in anger toward West, 2, 3, 147–48, 155, 230, 254; emergence of trade bloc, 45–48; narrow form of regionalism as possibility, 6, 253, 256; in reaction to exclusion from Western blocs, 146–47; reasons for forming, 2, 13, 16, 141–49; in recognition of Japan's ascendancy, 146; in response to U.S. unilateralism and protectionism, 3, 148–49, 262; social and economic commonalities of, 141–45; talk of forming, 1–2, 13–14, 149–53; U.S. need to discourage formation of, 258–67

Regional institutions, 9, 114–39. *See also specific institutions by name (for example, Asia-Pacific Development Bank)*

Regional leadership, 12, 231–49; by China, 12, 19, 242–49; joint leadership of Japan and China, 249. *See also* Japan's leadership

Religion, 36. *See also specific religion*

Russia as APEC member, 132

Sakakibara, Eisuke, 202, 213, 214, 215

Security issues, 239, 256, 257

Shanghai Accord and APEC meeting, 131, 135

Shinawatra, Thaksin, 181

Shinsei Bank, 101

Shintoism, 36, 237

Shiratori, Masaki, 144

Singapore: affluence of, 25; in ASEAN Free Trade Area, 169–70, 171; in Asian financial crisis of 1997, 203; bank loans from, 82; currency exchange rate of, 198; economic policy of, 27; foreign direct investment in, 106; free trade agreements with, 11, 168, 169, 171, 173, 177, 191, 192, 263; Japan-Singapore trade agreement, 11, 165–66, 176–79, 191, 241–42, 254; money center vs. regional loan recipient status, 81; portfolio investments in, 85; pro–regional bloc stance of, 142; trade activity of, 30

Soros, George, 147

Southeast Asian Treaty Organization, 150

South Korea: in Asian financial crisis of 1997, 203; China's relations with, 244; currency exchange rate of, 198, 225; foreign direct investment in, 34, 102–04, 106; Japan's relations with, 37, 166, 168, 182, 191, 235–36, 257; portfolio investments in, 85; security issues of, 257

Spratly Islands, 246

Steel trade, 149, 261

Strategic trade, 162

Sutton, Jim, 177

Swap agreements, 5, 228; ASEAN+3 swap agreements, 11, 213, 220–24, 240, 255, 264; as part of New Miyazawa Initiative, 217

Taiwan: APEC membership of, 13, 127, 132, 264; China's treatment of, 246, 257; exclusion from ASEAN+3 and possible inclusion in ASEAN+5, 157, 184, 190, 257; free trade initiatives of, 13, 189–91; PECC membership of, 126; portfolio investments in, 85; trade data on, 44; trade talks with Japan, 182, 190; WTO accession of, 189

Technology: APEC ecotech trade agenda, 129, 134, 136–37, 266–67; APEC information technology agreement (ITA), 129–30, 134; and paperless trading, 178–79

Terrorism. *See* War on terrorism

Textiles trade, 149, 151

Thailand: in Asian financial crisis of 1997, 202; currency exchange rate of, 198, 202, 225; economic position of, 27; pre-crisis finances in, 74; foreign direct investment in, 106, 202; free trade initiatives, 181, 182, 263

Thailand Development Research Institute (TRDI), 215

Thurow, Lester, 4

Trade, 8, 42–71, 145, 251; agriculture in, 177-78, 180–81, 184–85, 192, 233,

241; antidumping regulations, 149, 261–62; diplomacy and trade blocs, 166–67; and economic regionalism, 160–66; and economies of scale, 162; and emerging East Asian bloc, 45–48; evolution by region, 44, 48–68; openness to, 30–34, 39, 174, 234; steel, 149; strategic trade, 162; strength of interregional trade, 41, 42–45; textiles, 149, 151. *See also* Regional bloc; *specific countries or organizations intended to foster trade*
TRDI (Thailand Development Research Institute), 215

United Nations Economic and Social Commission for Asia and the Pacific (ESCAP), 167
U.S.-China relations: trade relations, 59, 61, 64; U.S. direct investment in China, 101
U.S.-East Asia relations: in Asian financial crisis of *1997*, 3, 147, 157, 219, 254; Bush administration's current policy, 6, 175, 239, 261; direct investment in ASEAN countries, 104–05; foreign direct investment from U.S., 108–11; lending from U.S. banks, 83–84; opposition to EAEC, 155–56, 239; policy recommendations for, 6–7, 13, 258–67; security issues, 239, 256, 257; trade, 8, 54, 55, 56–57, 58, 62–66, 69, 70, 251; trade agreements with specific countries, 168, 190, 263; unilateralism and protectionism of U.S., effect of, 3, 148–49, 262; U.S. membership in ADB, 117, 121; U.S. participation in APEC, 127, 131, 136, 138, 139; U.S. participation in PBEC, 123–24; war on terrorism, effect of, 148. *See also* U.S.-China relations; U.S.-Japan relations; *specific East Asian countries and organizations*

U.S.-Japan relations: direct investment in Japan, 99–101, 108–09; and EAEC, 155, 156, 239; and independence of Japan in East Asian policy, 121–22; Japanese direct investment in U.S., 93–95, 98, 112; as obstacle to Japan taking regional leadership role, 239–40; trade relations, 49, 51, 62, 63, 65, 69, 235

Vietnam: APEC membership, 132; ASEAN membership, 151; economic position of, 27, 74; exchange rate of, 199, 203, 225
Viner, Jacob, 160

War on terrorism, 148, 239, 266
World Bank: in Asian financial crisis of *1997*, 130; *The East Asian Miracle* (research study), 41, 121, 144; economic development role of, 263; and Japan, 143–44; pressure for reforms from, 147. *See also* Asian Development Bank (ADB); International Monetary Fund (IMF)
World Trade Organization (WTO): APEC as source of policy proposals for, 129–30; China's accession to, effect of, 27, 70, 105–06, 187–88, 244; Doha round and interests of East Asia, 131, 261–62, 265; Japan's loss of focus on, 4; reduction of trade barriers by, 160, 164, 165; Taiwan's accession to, effect of, 189; trading agreements in disregard of, 235, 254; U.S. focus on, 6, 12–13, 260–64
World War II, Japanese policy on, 37, 236–38

Yamamura, Kozo, 112
Yen, currencies pegged to, 195, 197, 203–10, 228
Yeo, George Yong-Boon, 177